Clymer Motorcycle Repair Series

HONDA

CX & GL500/650 TWINS · 1978-1983
SERVICE · REPAIR · MAINTENANCE

By
ED SCOTT

CLYMER PUBLICATIONS

The world's finest publisher of mechanical how-to manuals

INTERTEC PUBLISHING CORPORATION
P.O. Box 12901, Overland Park, Kansas 66212

Copyright ©1983 Intertec Publishing Corporation

FIRST EDITION
First Printing February, 1979
Second Printing May, 1979
Third Printing July, 1979
Fourth Printing April, 1980

SECOND EDITION
Updated by Ed Scott to include 1980-1982 models
First Printing October, 1980

THIRD EDITION
Updated by Ed Scott to include 1983 models
First Printing December, 1983
Second Printing November, 1984
Third Printing September, 1985
Fourth Printing May, 1987
Fifth Printing January, 1988
Sixth Printing May, 1989
Seventh Printing December, 1989
Eighth Printing October, 1990
Ninth Printing October, 1991

Printed in U.S.A.
ISBN: 0-89287-295-0

MOTORCYCLE INDUSTRY COUNCIL

Technical assistance by Brian Slark, Costa Mesa, California. Technical illustrations by Errol McCarthy.

COVER: Photographed by Michael Brown Photographic Productions, Los Angeles, California. Assisted by Tim Lunde. Helmet courtesy of Simpson Sports, Torrance, California. Motorcycle courtesy of Bill Krause Sportcycles, Inglewood, California.

CONTENTS

HONDA

CX & GL500/650 TWINS · 1978-1983
SERVICE • REPAIR • MAINTENANCE

QUICK REFERENCE DATA

FLUID CAPACITIES

Fuel capacity (total)	
CX500	
1980-1981 Deluxe	17.0 liters (4.5 U.S. gal., 3.7 Imp. gal.)
1980-1982 Custom	11.0 liters (2.9 U.S. gal., 2.4 Imp. gal.)
GL models	17.6 liters (4.6 U.S. gal., 3.9 Imp. gal.)
CX650C	12.4 liters (3.28 U.S. gal., 2.73 Imp. gal.)
Oil capacity	
Oil and filter change	2.5 liters (2.6 U.S. qt., 2.2 Imp. qt.)
At overhaul	3.0 liters (3.2 U.S. qt., 2.6 Imp. qt.)
Fork oil type	DEXRON automatic transmission fluid
Front fork oil capacity (each fork leg)	
CX500	
1980	135 cc (4.7 oz.)
1981 Deluxe	185 cc (6.3 oz.)
1981-1982 Custom	220 cc (7.5 oz.)
GL500 & Interstate	210 cc (7.1 oz.)
GL650 & Interstate	275 cc (9.3 oz.)*
CX650C	480 cc (16.2 oz.)*
Final drive oil type	
Above 41° F (5° C)	Hypoid gear oil SAE 90
Below 41° F (5° C)	Hypoid gear oil SAE 80
Final drive oil capacity	5.8 oz. (170 cc)
Coolant	Ethelene glycol for aluminum engines
Radiator and engine quantity	1.9 U.S. qt. (1.8 liters)
Coolant recovery tank	0.21 U.S. qt. (0.20 liters)
Coolant/water ratio	
Above -25° F (-32° C)	45/55 coolant/water
Above -34° F (-37° C)	50/50 coolant/water
Above -48° F (-44° C)	55/45 coolant/water

* Capacity after disassembly. Honda does not provide information for draining procedure.

ENGINE TORQUE SPECIFICATIONS

Item	Foot-pounds	Newton meters
Cylinder head bolts		
6mm	6-9	8-12
12mm	33-40	45-54
Camshaft locknut	58-72	79-98
Camshaft sprocket bolts	12-14	16-19
Crankshaft end cap bolts	14-17	19-23
Rod bearing cap nuts	20-23	27-31
Cooling fan bolt	14-18	19-24
Oil filter bolt	14-18	19-24
Alternator rotor bolt	58-72	79-97
Clutch center nut	58-72	79-97
Radiator drain bolt	1-2	1.4-2.7

TUNE-UP SPECIFICATIONS

Cylinder head bolts	
12 mm	33-40 ft.-lb. (45-54 N•m)
6 mm	6-9 ft.-lb. (8-12 N•m)
Valve clearance (cold)	
1978-1982	
Intake	0.003 in. (0.08 mm)
Exhaust	0.004 in. (0.10 mm)
1983	
Intake	0.004 in. (0.10 mm)
Exhaust	0.005 in. (0.12 mm)
Compression pressure	
(at sea level)	184 ±28 psi
	(13.0 ±2.0 kg/cm^2)
Spark plug type (1981)	
Standard heat range	
U.S.	ND X24ES-U or NGK D8EA
Canadian	ND X24ESR-U or NGK DR8ES-L
Cold weather*	
U.S.	ND X22ES-U or NGK D7EA
Canadian	ND X22ESR-U or NGK DR7ES
Extended high-speed riding	
U.S.	ND X27ES-U or NGK D9EA
Canadian	ND X27ESR-U or NGK DR9ES
Spark plug type (1982)	
Standard heat range	
U.S. and Canadian	ND X24ESR-U or NGK DR8ES-L
Cold weather*	
U.S. and Canadian	ND X22ESR-U or NGK DR7ES
Extended high-speed riding	
U.S. and Canadian	ND X27ESR-U or NGK DR8EA
Spark plug type (1983)	
Standard heat range	
U.S.**	ND X24EPR-U9 or NGK DPR8EA-9
Extended high-speed riding	
U.S.**	ND X27EPR-U9 or NGK DPR9EA-9
Spark plug gap	
1980-1982	0.6-0.7 mm (0.024-0.028 in.)
1983	0.8-0.9 mm (0.031-0.035 in.)
Ignition timing @ idle	Non-adjustable
All models	F1/TR (right-hand cylinder)
	F1/TL (left-hand cylinder)
Timing speed	1,100 ±100 rpm
Idle speed	1,100 ±100 rpm

* Cold weather climate—below 41° F (5° C).
** Honda does not provide Canadian specifications for 1983.

ADJUSTMENTS

Item	Inch	mm
Clutch lever free play	3/8-3/4	10-20
Rear brake pedal free play	3/4-1 1/4	20-30
Throttle grip free play	0.08-0.24	2-6 (grip rotation)
Rear brake light switch (pedal travel)	3/4	20

NOTE: If you own a 1980 or later model, first check the Supplement at the back of the book for any new service information.

CHAPTER ONE

GENERAL INFORMATION

This book provides maintenance and repair information for the Honda CX500, GL500, CX650 and GL650.

Read the following service hints to make the work as easy and pleasant as possible. Performing your own work can be an enjoyable and rewarding experience.

MANUAL ORGANIZATION

This manual provides service information and procedures for the Honda CX500, GL500, CX650 and GL650.

All dimensions and capacities are expressed in English units familiar to U.S. mechanics as well as in metric units.

Chapters One through Twelve contain general information on all models and specific information on 1978-1979 models. The Supplement at the end of the book contains specific information on 1980 and later models.

This chapter provides general information and specifications. See **Table 1** at the end of this chapter. It also discusses equipment and tools useful both for preventive maintenance and troubleshooting.

Chapter Two provides methods and suggestions for quick and accurate diagnosis and repair of problems. Troubleshooting procedures discuss typical symptoms and logical methods to pinpoint the trouble.

Chapter Three explains all periodic lubrication and routine maintenance necessary to keep your bike running well. Chapter Three also includes recommended tune-up procedures, eliminating the need to constantly consult chapters on the various assemblies.

Subsequent chapters describe specific systems such as the engine, transmission, and electrical system. Each chapter provides disassembly, repair, and assembly procedures in simple step-by-step form. If a repair is impractical for a home mechanic, it is so indicated. It is usually faster and less expensive to take such repairs to a dealer or competent repair shop. Specifications concerning a particular system are included at the end of the appropriate chapter.

Some of the procedures in this manual specify special tools. In all cases, the tool is illustrated either in actual use or alone. A well-equipped mechanic may find that he can substitute similar tools already on hand or he can fabricate his own.

The terms NOTE, CAUTION, and WARNING have specific meanings in this manual. A NOTE provides additional information to make a step or procedure easier or clearer. Disregarding a NOTE could cause inconvenience, but would not cause damage or personal injury.

A CAUTION emphasizes areas where equipment damage could result. Disregarding a CAUTION could cause permanent mechanical damage; however, personal injury is unlikely.

A WARNING emphasizes areas where personal injury or even death could result from negligence. Mechanical damage may also occur. WARNINGS *are to be taken seriously*. In some cases, serious injury or death has resulted from disregarding similar warnings.

Throughout this manual keep in mind two conventions. "Front" refers to the front of the bike. The front of any component such as the engine is the end which faces toward the front of the bike. The "left" and "right" side refer to positions from the perspective of a person sitting on the bike facing forward. For example, the shift lever is on the left side. These rules are simple, but even experienced mechanics occasionally become disoriented.

SERVICE HINTS

Most of the service procedures covered are straightforward and can be performed by anyone reasonably handy with tools. It is suggested, however, that you consider your own capabilities carefully before attempting any operation involving major disassembly of the engine.

Some operations, for example, require the use of a press. It would be wiser to have these performed by a shop equipped for such work than to try to do the job yourself with makeshift equipment. Other procedures require precision measurements. Unless you have the skills and equipment required, it would be better to have a qualified repair shop make the measurements for you.

Repairs go much faster and easier if your machine is clean before you begin work. There are special cleaners, like Gunk Cycle Degreaser, for washing the engine and related parts. Just brush or spray on the cleaning solution, let it stand, then rinse it away with a garden hose. Clean all oily or greasy parts with cleaning solvent as you remove them.

WARNING
Never use gasoline as a cleaning agent. It presents an extreme fire hazard. Be sure to work in a well-ventilated area when using cleaning solvent. Keep a fire extinguisher, rated for gasoline fires, handy in any case.

Special tools are required for some repair procedures. These may be purchased at a dealer, rented from a tool rental dealer, or may be fabricated by a mechanic or machinst, often at a considerable savings.

Much of the labor charge for repairs made by dealers is for the removal and disassembly of other parts to reach the defective unit. It is frequently possible to perform the preliminary operations yourself and then take the defective unit in to the dealer for repair at considerable savings.

Once you have decided to tackle the job yourself, read the entire section in this manual which pertains to it, making sure you have identified the proper one. Study the illustrations and text until you have a good idea of what is involved in completing the job satisfactorily. If special tools are required, make arrangements to get them before you start. It is frustrating and time-consuming to get partly into a job and then be unable to complete it.

Simple wiring checks can be easily made at home; but knowledge of electronics is almost a necessity for performing tests with complicated electronic testing gear.

During disassembly of parts, keep a few general cautions in mind. Force is rarely needed to get things apart. If parts are a tight fit, like a bearing in a case, there is usually a tool designed to separate them. Never use a screwdriver to pry apart parts with machined surfaces such as crankcase halves and valve covers. You will mar the surfaces and end up with leaks.

Make diagrams wherever similar-appearing parts are found. For instance, case cover bolts are often not the same length. You may think you can remember where everything came from — but mistakes are costly. There is also the possibility that you may be sidetracked and not return to work for days or even weeks — in which interval carefully laid out parts may have become disturbed.

Tag all similar internal parts for location and mark all mating parts for position. Record number and thickness of any shims as they are removed. Small parts such as bolts can be identified by placing them in plastic sandwich bags. Seal and label the bags with masking tape.

Wiring should be tagged with masking tape and marked as each wire is removed. Again, do not rely on memory alone.

Disconnect battery ground (negative) cable before working near electrical connections and before disconnecting wires. Never run the engine with the battery disconnected; the alternator could be seriously damaged.

Protect finished surfaces from physical damage or corrosion. Keep gasoline and brake fluid off painted surfaces.

Frozen or very tight bolts and screws can often be loosened by soaking with penetrating oil, like WD-40 or Liquid Wrench, then sharply striking the bolt head a few times with a hammer and punch (or screwdriver for screws). Avoid heat unless absolutely necessary, since it may melt, warp, or remove the temper from many parts.

Avoid flames or sparks when working near a charging battery or flammable liquids such as brake fluid or gasoline.

No parts, except those assembled with a press fit, require unusual force during assembly. If a part is hard to remove or install, find out why before proceeding.

Cover all openings after removing parts to keep dirt, small tools, etc., from falling in.

When assembling two parts, start all fasteners, then tighten evenly.

Clutch plates, wiring connections, and brake pads and discs should be kept clean and free of grease and oil.

When assembling parts, be sure all shims and washers are replaced exactly as they came out.

Whenever a rotating part butts against a stationary part, look for a shim or washer. Use new gaskets if there is any doubt about the condition of old ones. Generally you should apply gasket cement to one mating surface only so the parts may be easily disassembled in the future. A thin coat of oil on gaskets helps them seal effectively.

Heavy grease can be used to hold small parts in place if they tend to fall out during assembly. However, keep grease and oil away from electrical components or brake pads and discs.

High spots may be sanded off a piston with sandpaper, but emery cloth and oil do a much more professional job.

Carburetors are best cleaned by disassembling them and soaking the parts in a commercial carburetor cleaner. Never soak gaskets and rubber parts in these cleaners. Never use wire to clean out jets and air passages; they are easily damaged. Use compressed air to blow out the carburetor only if the float has been removed first.

A baby bottle makes a good measuring device for adding oil to forks and transmissions. Get one that is graduated in ounces and cubic centimeters.

Take your time and do the job right. Do not forget that a newly rebuilt motorcycle engine must be broken in the same as a new one. Keep rpm's within the limits given in your owner's manual when you get back on the road.

SAFETY FIRST

Professional motorcycle mechanics can work for years and never sustain a serious injury. If you observe a few rules of common sense and safety, you can enjoy many hours servicing your own machine. You could hurt yourself or damage the bike if you ignore these rules.

1. Never use gasoline as a cleaning solvent.

2. Never smoke or use a torch in the vicinity of flammable liquids, such as cleaning solvent in open containers.

3. Never smoke or use a torch in an area where batteries are being charged. Highly explosive hydrogen gas is formed during the charging process.

4. If welding or brazing is required on the machine, remove the fuel tank to a safe distance, at least 50 feet away. Welding on gas tanks requires special safety procedures and must be performed by someone skilled in the process.

5. Use the proper sized wrenches to avoid damage to nuts and injury to yourself.

6. When loosening a tight or stuck nut, be guided by what would happen if the wrench should slip. Protect yourself accordingly.

7. Keep your work area clean and uncluttered.

8. Wear safety goggles during all operations involving drilling, grinding, or use of a cold chisel.

9. Never use worn tools.

10. Keep a fire extinguisher handy and be sure it is rated for gasoline and electrical fires.

PARTS REPLACEMENT

Honda makes frequent changes during a model year — some minor, some relatively major. When you order parts from the dealer or other parts distributor, always order by engine and chassis number. Write the numbers down and carry them with you. Compare new parts to old before purchasing them. If they are not alike, have the parts manager explain the difference to you.

EXPENDABLE SUPPLIES

Certain expendable supplies are also required. These include grease, oil, gasket cement, wiping rags, cleaning solvent, and distilled water. Ask your dealer for the special locking compounds, silicone lubricants, and other products which make motorcycle maintenance simpler and easier. Solvent is available at most service stations and distilled water for the battery is available at most supermarkets.

TOOLS

To properly service your motorcycle, you will need an assortment of ordinary hand tools. As a minimum, these include:

a. Combination wrench
b. Socket wrenches
c. Plastic mallet
d. Small hammer
e. Snap ring pliers
f. Phillips screwdrivers
g. Slot screwdrivers
h. Impact driver
i. Pliers
j. Feeler gauges
k. Spark plug gauge
l. Spark plug wrench
m. Drift

An original equipment tool kit, like the one shown in **Figure 1**, is available through most

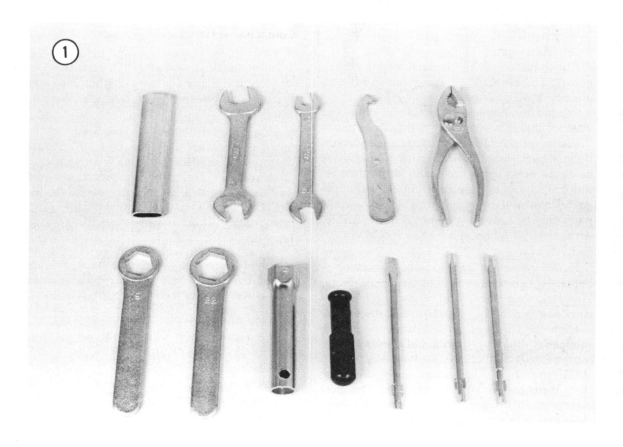

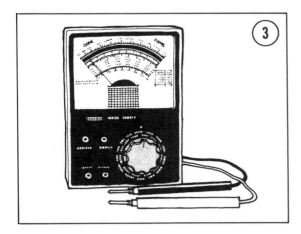

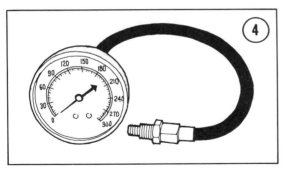

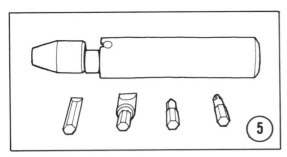

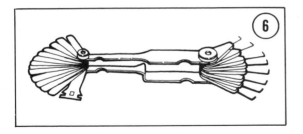

Honda dealers and is suitable for most minor servicing.

Engine tune-up and troubleshooting procedures require a few more tools, described in the following sections.

Hydrometer

This instrument measures state of charge of the battery, and tells much about battery condition. Such an instrument is available at any auto parts store and through most larger mail order outlets. See **Figure 2**.

Multimeter or VOM

This instrument (**Figure 3**) is invaluable for electrical system troubleshooting and service. A few of its functions may be duplicated by locally fabricated substitutes, but for the serious hobbyist, it is a must. Its uses are described in the applicable sections of this book. Multimeters are available at electronics hobbyist stores and mail order outlets.

Compression Gauge

An engine with low compression cannot be properly tuned and will not develop full power. A compression gauge measures engine compression (**Figure 4**). They are available at auto accessory stores or by mail order from large catalog order firms.

Impact Driver

This tool makes removal of engine components easy and eliminates damage to bolt heads. Good ones are available at larger hardware stores. See **Figure 5**.

Ignition Gauge

This tool has round wire gauges for measuring spark plug gap. See **Figure 6**.

Strobe Timing Light

This instrument is necessary for tuning. By flashing a light at the precise instant the cylinder fires, the position of the flywheel at that instant can be seen. Marks on the flywheel are lined up with the crankcase mark while the engine is running.

Suitable lights range from inexpensive neon bulb types to powerful xenon strobe lights. See **Figure 7**. Neon timing lights are difficult to see and must be used in dimly lit areas. Xenon strobe timing lights can be used outside in bright sunlight. Both types work on this motorcycle; use according to manufacturer's instructions.

Other Special Tools

A few other special tools may be required for major service. These are described in the appropriate chapters and are available from Honda dealers.

SERIAL NUMBERS

You must know the model serial number for registration purposes and when ordering special parts.

The frame serial number is stamped on the right side of the steering head **(Figure 8)** and on the VIN plate on the left side of the steering head. The engine number is stamped on the lower left-hand side of the crankcase **(Figure 9)**.

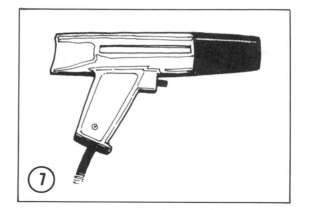

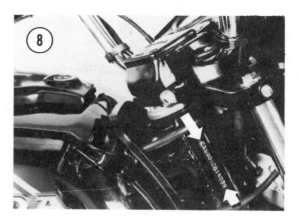

Table 1   GENERAL SPECIFICATIONS

Engine type	Liquid cooled, 4-stroke, OHV, 80° V-twin
Bore and stroke	3.071 × 2.047 in. (78 × 52mm)
Displacement	30.3 cu. in. (497cc)
Compression ratio	10:1
Carburetion	2 Keihin 35mm constant velocity
Ignition	Capacitor discharge ignition (CDI)
Lubrication	Wet sump, filter oil pump
Clutch	Wet, multi-plate (7)
Transmission	5-speed, constant mesh
Transmission ratios	
1st	2.733
2nd	1.850
3rd	1.416
4th	1.148
5th	0.931
Final reduction ratio	3.091
Starting system	Electric starter
Wheelbase	57.3 in. (1,455mm)
Steering head angle	26°5′ from vertical
Trail	3.9 in. (100mm)
Front suspension	Telescopic forks, 5.5 in. (13.9mm) travel
Rear suspension	Swing arm, 5-way adjustable shock absorbers 3.3 in. (85mm) travel
Front tire	3.25 S19—4PR
Rear tire	3.75 S18—4PR
Ground clearance	15.9 in. (150mm)
Seat height	31.9 in. (810mm)
Overall height	46.3 in. (1,176mm)
Overall width (handlebar)	34.1 in. (865mm)
Overall length	86.0 in. (2,185mm)
Fuel capacity	
Main	3.6 U.S. gal. (13.6 liter)
Reserve	0.9 U.S. gal. (3.5 liter)
Engine oil capacity	3.2 U.S. qt. (3.0 liter)
Cooling system capacity	1.0 U.S. qt. (1.8 liter)
Front fork oil capacity	
Dry	4.7 oz. (135cc)
Refill	4.4 oz. (125cc)

CHAPTER TWO

TROUBLESHOOTING

Diagnosing mechanical problems is relatively simple if you use orderly procedures and keep a few basic principles in mind.

The troubleshooting procedures in this chapter analyze typical symptoms, and show logical methods of isolating causes. These are not the only methods. There may be several ways to solve a problem, but only a systematic, methodical approach can guarantee success.

Never assume anything. Do not overlook the obvious. If you are riding along and the bike suddenly quits, check the easiest, most accessible problem spots first. Is there gasoline in the tank? Is the shutoff valve in the ON or RESERVE position? Has a spark plug wire fallen off? Check ignition switch. Sometimes the weight of keys on a key ring may turn the ignition off suddenly.

If nothing obvious turns up in a cursory check, look a little further. Learning to recognize and describe symptoms will make repairs easier for you or a mechanic at the shop. Describe problems accurately and fully. Saying that "it won't run" isn't the same as saying "it quit on the highway at high speed and wouldn't start," or that "it sat in my garage for three months and then wouldn't start."

Gather as many symptoms together as possible to aid in diagnosis. Note whether the engine lost power gradually or all at once, what color smoke (if any) came from the exhaust, and so on. Remember that the more complicated a machine is, the easier it is to troubleshoot because symptoms point to specific problems.

After the symptoms are defined, areas which could cause the problems are tested and analyzed. Guessing at the cause of a problem may provide the solution, but it can easily lead to frustration, wasted time, and a series of expensive, unnecessary parts replacement.

You do not need fancy equipment or complicated test gear to determine whether repairs can be attempted at home. A few simple checks could save a large repair bill and time lost while the bike sits in a dealer's service department. On the other hand, be realistic and do not attempt repairs beyond your abilities. Service departments tend to charge heavily for putting together a disassembled engine that may have been abused. Some won't even take on such a job — so use common sense, don't get in over your head.

OPERATING REQUIREMENTS

An engine needs three basics to run properly: correct gas/air mixture, compression, and a spark at the right time. If one or more are missing, the engine won't run. The electrical system is the weakest link of the three basics. More problems result from electrical breakdowns than from any other source. Keep that in mind before you begin tampering with carburetor adjustments and the like.

If a bike has been sitting for any length of time and refuses to start, check the battery for a charged condition first, and then look to the gasoline delivery system. This includes the tank, fuel shutoff valve, lines, and the carburetors. Rust may have formed in the tank, obstructing fuel flow. Gasoline deposits may have gummed up carburetor jets and air passages. Gasoline tends to lose its potency after standing for long periods. Condensation may contaminate it with water. Drain old gas and try starting with a fresh tankful.

TROUBLESHOOTING INSTRUMENTS

Chapter One lists many instruments needed along with detailed instructions on their use.

EMERGENCY TROUBLESHOOTING

When the bike is difficult to start or won't start at all, it does not help to grind away at the starter or kick the tires. Check for obvious problems even before getting out your tools. Go down the following list step-by-step. Do each one; you may be embarrassed to find your kill switch off, but that is better than wearing out your leg or wearing your battery down with the starter. If the bike still will not start, refer to the appropriate troubleshooting procedures which follow in this chapter.

1. Is there fuel in the tank? Do not trust the fuel gauge. Remove the filler cap and rock the bike; listen for fuel sloshing around.

WARNING
Do not use an open flame to check in the tank. A serious explosion is certain to result.

2. Is the fuel shutoff valve on? Turn it to RESERVE (**Figure 1**) to be sure that you get the last remaining gas.

3. Is the kill switch on? (**Figure 2**).

4. Are spark plug wires on tight? (**Figure 3**).

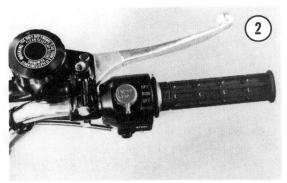

5. Is the choke in the right position? It should be pulled out for a cold engine and pushed in for a warm engine (**Figure 4**).

6. Is the battery dead? Check it with a hydrometer.

7. Has the main fuse (**Figure 5**) blown? Replace it with a good one.

8. Is the transmission in NEUTRAL or the clutch lever pulled in? The starter will not operate with the bike in gear without pulling in the clutch lever or having the transmission in the NEUTRAL position.

9. Is the vent hole in the fuel cap clogged (**Figure 6**)? If so, clean it out.

STARTER

Starter system troubles are relatively easy to isolate. The following are common symptoms and cures.

1. *Engine cranks very slowly or not at all* — If the headlight is very dim or not lighting at all, most likely the battery or its connecting wires are at fault. Check the battery condition using the procedures described in Chapter Eight. Check the wiring for breaks, shorts, and dirty connections.

If the battery and connecting wires check good, the trouble may be in the starter, starter solenoid, or wiring. To isolate the trouble, short the 2 large starter solenoid terminals together (not to ground); if the starter cranks

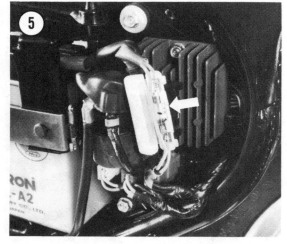

normally, check the starter solenoid wiring as described under symptoms 2 and 3. If the starter still fails to crank properly, remove the starter and test it. Refer to Chapter Seven.

2. *Starter only operates when clutch lever is pulled in, even in neutral* — If neutral light comes on normally, the diode is shorted; a shorted diode will not prevent the starter from operating.

If neutral light does not come on in NEUTRAL, but engine starts when clutch lever is pulled in, the neutral switch is defective or the connecting wire is open.

3. *Starter operates while transmission is in gear without pulling in the clutch lever* — The neutral switch or connecting wire is shorted to ground.

4. *Starter will not operate while transmission is in gear with the clutch lever pulled in* — The clutch lever switch or connecting wire is shorted to ground.

5. *Starter engages, but will not disengage when ignition switch is released* — This trouble is usually caused by a sticking starter solenoid.

CHARGING SYSTEM

Troubleshooting an alternator system is somewhat different from troubleshooting a generator. For example, *never* short any terminals to ground on the alternator or the voltage regulator/rectifier. The following symptoms are typical of alternator charging system troubles.

1. *Battery requires frequent charging* — The charging system is not functioning or is undercharging the battery. Test the alternator and voltage regulator/rectifier as described in Chapter Seven.

2. *Battery requires frequent additions of water or lamps require frequent replacement* — The alternator is probably overcharging the battery. Check voltage regulator/rectifier as described in Chapter Seven.

ENGINE

These procedures assume that the starter cranks the engine over normally. If not, refer to *Starter* section in this chapter.

Poor Performance

1. *Engine misses erratically at all speeds* — A cause for intermittent trouble like this can be difficult to find. The fault could be in the ignition system, exhaust system (exhaust restriction), or fuel system. Follow troubleshooting procedures for these systems carefully to isolate the trouble.

2. *Engine misses at idle only* — Trouble could exist anywhere in ignition system. Refer to *Ignition System* in Chapter Seven. Trouble could exist in the carburetor idle circuits.

3. *Engine misses at high speed only* — Trouble could exist in the fuel system or ignition system. Check the fuel lines, etc., as described under *Fuel System* troubleshooting. Also check spark plugs and wires. Refer to *Ignition System* in Chapter Seven.

4. *Poor performance at all speeds, lack of acceleration* — Trouble usually exists in ignition or fuel system. Check each with the appropriate troubleshooting procedure.

5. *Excessive fuel consumption* — This can be caused by a wide variety of seemingly unrelated factors. Check for clutch slippage, brake drag, and defective wheel bearings. On models with *automatic transmission*, check engine oil level. The engine oil is used in the torque converter also and it may be low. Check ignition and fuel system as described later.

ENGINE NOISES

1. *Valve clatter* — This is a light to heavy tapping sound from under the valve covers. Usually caused by excessive valve clearance. Adjust clearance as described under *Valve Clearance Adjustment* in Chapter Three. If noise persists, disassemble the rocker arm mechanism as described under *Rocker Assemblies* in Chapter Four. Look for broken springs, worn rocker arms, and shafts.

2. *Knocking or pinging during acceleration* — Caused by using a lower octane fuel than recommended. May also be caused by poor fuel available at some "discount" gasoline stations. Pinging can also be caused by spark plugs of the wrong heat range. Refer to *Correct Spark Plug Heat Range* in Chapter Three.

3. *Slapping or rattling noises at low speed or during acceleration* — May be caused by piston slap, i.e., excessive piston-cylinder wall clearance.

4. *Knocking or rapping while decelerating* — This noise is usually caused by excessive rod bearing clearance.

5. *Persistent knocking and vibration* — This is usually caused by excessive main bearing clearance.

6. *Rapid on-off squeal* — Could be caused by a compression leak around cylinder head gaskets or spark plugs.

EXCESSIVE VIBRATION

This can be difficult to find without disassembling the engine. Usually this is caused by loose engine mounting hardware or worn engine or transmission bearings.

LUBRICATION TROUBLES

1. *Excessive oil consumption* — May be caused by worn rings and bores. Overhaul is necessary to correct this; see Chapter Four. May also be caused by worn valve guides or defective valve guide seals. Also check for exterior leaks.

2. *Oil pressure lamp does not light when ignition switch is on* — The oil pressure sending switch is located on the engine front cover above the clutch housing (**Figure 7**). To gain access to it, remove the radiator as described under *Radiator Removal/Installation* in Chapter Eight. Check that the wire is connected to the sender and makes good contact. Pull off wire and ground it. If the lamp lights, replace the sender. If the lamp does not light, replace the lamps.

3. *Oil pressure lamp lights or flickers when engine is running* — This indicates low or complete loss of oil pressure. *Stop the engine immediately*; coast to a stop with the clutch disengaged. This may simply be caused by a low oil level, or an overheating engine. Check the oil level. Check for a shorted oil pressure sender with an ohmmeter or other continuity tester. Listen for unusual noises indicating bad bearings, etc. Do not restart the engine until you know why the light went on and the problem has been corrected.

FUEL SYSTEM

Fuel system troubles must be isolated to the carburetor, fuel tank, fuel shutoff valve or fuel lines. These procedures assume that the ignition system has been checked and properly adjusted.

1. *Engine will not start* — First determine that the fuel is being delivered to the carburetor. Turn the fuel shutoff valve to the OFF position, remove the flexible fuel line to the carburetor. Place the loose end onto a small container, turn the shutoff valve to the ON or RESERVE position. Fuel should run out of the tube. If it does not, remove the shutoff valve and check for restrictions within it or the fuel tank. Refer to Chapter Six.

2. *Rough idle or engine miss with frequent stalling* — Check carburetor adjustment. See Chapter Three.

3. *Stumbling when accelerating from idle* — Check idle speed adjustment. See Chapter Three.

4. *Engine misses at high speed or lacks power* — This indicates possible fuel starvation. Clean main jets and float needle valves.

5. *Black exhaust smoke* — Black exhaust smoke means a badly overrich mixture. Check

that manual choke disengages. Check idle speed. Check for leaky floats or worn float needle valves. Also check that jets are proper size.

CLUTCH

1. *Slippage* — This is most noticeable when accelerating in a high gear at relatively low speed. To check slippage, shift to 2nd gear and release the clutch as if riding off. If the clutch is good, the engine will slow and stall. If the clutch slips, continued engine speed will give it away.

Slippage results from insufficient clutch lever free play, worn discs or pressure plate, or weak springs.

2. *Drag or failure to release* — This trouble usually causes difficult shifting and gear clash, especially when downshifting. The cause may be excessive clutch lever free play, warped or bent pressure plate or clutch disc, or broken or loose linings.

3. *Chatter or grabbing* — A number of things can cause this trouble. Check tightness of engine mounting bolts. Also check lever free play.

TRANSMISSION

Transmission problems are usually indicated by one or more of the following symptoms:

    a. Difficulty shifting gears

    b. Gear clash when downshifting or when shifting from high to low

    c. Slipping out of gear

    d. Excessive noise in NEUTRAL

    e. Excessive noise in gear

Transmission symptoms are sometimes hard to distinguish from clutch symptoms. Be sure that the clutch is not causing the trouble before working on the transmission. Refer to Chapter Five.

BRAKES

1. *Brake lever or pedal goes all the way to its stop* — There are numerous causes for this including excessively worn linings or pads, air in the hydraulic system, leaky brake lines, leaky calipers, or leaky or worn master cylinder. Check for leaks and thin brake linings or pads. Bleed the brakes. If this does not cure the trou-

ble, rebuild the calipers and/or master cylinder. Also improper rod adjustment may be a cause.

2. *Spongy lever* — Normally caused by air in the system; bleed the brakes.

3. *Dragging brakes* — Check for swollen rubber parts, due to improper brake fluid or contamination, and obstructed master cylinder bypass port. Clean or replace defective parts. Check for broken or weak return springs.

4. *Hard lever or pedal* — Check brake linings or pads for contamination. Also check for a restricted brake line and hose and a brake pedal that might need lubrication.

5. *High speed fade* — Check for glazed or contaminated brake linings or pads. Ensure that recommended brake fluid is installed. Drain entire system and refill if in doubt.

6. *Pulsating lever or pedal* — Check for out-of-round drum or excessive brake disc runout. Undetected accident damage is also a frequent cause of this.

LIGHTING SYSTEM

Bulbs which continuously burn out may be caused by excessive vibration, loose connections that permit sudden current surges, poor battery connections, or installation of the wrong type bulb.

A majority of light and horn or other electrical accessory problems are caused by loose or corroded ground connections. Check those first, and then substitute known good units for easier troubleshooting.

FRONT SUSPENSION AND STEERING

1. *Too stiff or too soft* — Make sure forks have not been leaking and oil is correct. If in doubt, drain and refill as described under *Front Forks* in Chapter Nine.

2. *Leakage around seals* — There should be a light film of oil on fork tubes. However, large amounts of oil on tubes means the seals are leaking. Replace seals as described under *Front Fork Seal Replacement* in Chapter Nine.

3. *Fork action is rough* — Check for bent tube.

4. *Steering wobbles* — Check for correct steering head bearing tightness as described under *Steering Head Adjustment* in Chapter Nine.

NOTE: If you own a 1980 or later model, first check the Supplement at the back of the book for any new service information.

CHAPTER THREE

PERIODIC MAINTENANCE
AND LUBRICATION

Regular maintenance is the best guarantee of a trouble-free, long lasting motorcycle. An afternoon spent now, cleaning and adjusting, can prevent costly mechanical problems in the future and unexpected breakdowns on the road.

The procedures presented in this chapter can be easily carried out by anyone with average mechanical skills. The operations are presented step-by-step; if they are followed, it is difficult to go wrong.

ROUTINE CHECKS

The following simple checks should be performed at each stop at a service station for gas.

Engine Oil Level

Refer to *Checking Engine Oil Level* under *Periodic Lubrication* in this chapter.

Coolant Level

Check the coolant level when the engine has warmed up to normal operating temperature.

Check level in the recovery tank (**Figure 1**). Top it up if the level is below the FULL mark.

WARNING
Do not remove the radiator pressure cap when the engine is hot. The coolant is

Table 1   TIRE PRESSURES

Load	Front	Rear
Rider only Up to 200 lb. (90 kg)	24 psi (1.75 kg/sq.cm)	28 psi (2.00 kg/sq.cm)
Rider and passenger and/or luggage Up to 330 lb. (150 kg)*	24 psi (1.75 kg/sq.cm)	36 psi (2.50 kg/sq.cm)
*Vehicle maximum load limit		

extremely hot and under pressure and can scald you.

General Inspection

1. Quickly examine the engine for signs of oil, fuel, or coolant leakage.

2. Check the tires for imbedded stones. Pry them out with your ignition key.

3. Make sure all lights work.

NOTE
At least check the brake light. It can burn out anytime. Motorists cannot stop as quickly as you and need all the warning you can give.

Tire Pressure

Tire pressure must be checked with the tires cold. Correct tire pressure depends a lot on the load you are carrying. See **Table 1**.

Battery

Remove the left-hand side cover and check battery electrolyte level. The level must be between the upper and lower level marks on the case (**Figure 2**). For complete details see *Battery — Checking Electrolyte Level* in this chapter.

Check the level more frequently in hot weather.

SERVICE INTERVALS

The services and intervals shown in **Table 2** are recommended by the factory. Strict adherence to these recommendations will go a long way toward insuring long service from your Honda.

For convenience of maintaining your motorcycle, most of the services shown in the table are described in this chapter. However, some procedures which require more than minor disassembly or adjustment are covered elsewhere in the appropriate chapter.

TIRES

Pressure

Tire pressure should be checked and adjusted to accommodate rider and luggage weight. A simple, accurate gauge **(Figure 3)** can be purchased for a few dollars and should be carried in the motorcycle tool kit. The appropriate tire pressures are shown in **Table 1**.

Inspection

Check tread for excessive wear, deep cuts, imbedded objects such as stones, nails, etc. If you find a nail in a tire, mark its location with a light crayon before pulling it out. This will help locate the hole in the inner tube. Refer to *Tire Changing* in Chapter Nine.

Check local traffic regulations concerning minimum tread depth. Measure with a tread depth gauge **(Figure 4)** or small ruler. Honda recommends replacement when the front tread depth is $\frac{1}{16}$ in. (1.5mm) or less and rear tread depth is $\frac{3}{32}$ in. (2mm) or less. Tread wear indicators appear across the tire when tread reaches minimum safe depth. Replace the tire at this point.

BATTERY

Checking Electrolyte Level

The battery is the heart of the electrical system. It should be checked and serviced as indicated. The majority of electrical system troubles can be attributed to neglect of this vital component.

The electrolyte level may be checked with the battery installed. However, it is necessary to remove the left-hand side panel **(Figure 5)**. The electrolyte level should be maintained between the two marks on the battery case **(Figure 2)**. If the electrolyte level is low, it is a good idea to remove the battery so that it can be thoroughly serviced and checked.

1. Remove the left-hand side panel **(Figure 5)**.

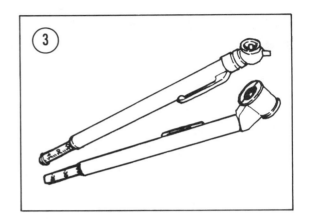

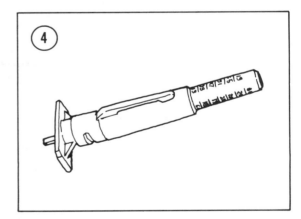

Table 2   SERVICE INTERVALS

Every Month	• Check tire pressure and condition. • Check battery electrolyte level.
Every 250 Miles	• Check engine oil level. • Check coolant level in recovery tank.
Every 1,800 Miles	• Check brake fluid in master cylinder. • Lubricate all control cables with oil. • Adjust brake (disc brake is non-adjustable).
Every 3,600 Miles	• Tune-up engine. • Check crankcase breather tubes. • Clean air cleaner element. • Inspect spark plugs; regap if necessary. • Check carburetor idle speed. • Adjust camshaft chain tensioner. • Check clutch free play adjustment. • Check rear brake pedal free play adjustment. • Examine disc brake pads for wear. • Check valve clearance. • Inspect throttle operation. • Check engine mounts for side play. • Check all suspension components. • Lubricate rear brake pedal pivot. • Inspect wheels. • Inspect fuel lines for chafed, cracked, or swollen ends.
Every 7,200 Miles	• Change engine oil. • Replace oil filter. • Replace spark plugs. • Inspect cooling system and hoses. • Inspect steering head and bearings. • Replace air cleaner element. • Check oil level in final drive unit. • Change fluid in front forks. • Check stoplight switch operation. • Inspect brake system. • Inspect throttle operation. • Lubricate final drive joint. • Check all nuts, bolts, and fasteners.
Every 10,800 Miles	• Repack wheel bearings with grease. • Dismantle and clean both carburetors.
Every 21,000 Miles	• Drain and replace coolant. • Drain and replace final drive lubricant. • Drain and replace disc brake fluid.

3

2. Remove negative electrical cable (ground) from the battery **(Figure 6)**.

3. Remove the nut **(Figure 7)** securing the retaining strap and pivot the strap out of the way.

4. Remove the positive electrical cable (A, **Figure 8**) and the breather tube (B, **Figure 8**).

5. Pull the battery out and remove it.

CAUTION
Be careful not to spill battery electrolyte on painted or polished surfaces. The liquid is highly corrosive and will damage the finish. If it is spilled, wash it off immediately with soapy water and thoroughly rinse with clean water.

6. Remove the caps from the battery cells and add distilled water to correct the level. *Never add electrolyte (acid) to correct the level.*

7. After the level has been corrected and the battery allowed to stand for a few minutes, check the specific gravity of the electrolyte in each cell with a hydrometer **(Figure 9)**. Follow the manufacturer's instructions for reading the instrument.

Testing

Hydrometer testing is the best way to check battery condition. Use a hydrometer with numbered graduations from 1.100 to 1.300 rather than one with color-coded bands. To use the hydrometer, squeeze the rubber ball, insert the tip in the cell and release the ball. Draw enough electrolyte to float the weighted float inside the hydrometer. Note the number in line with surface of the electrolyte; this is the specific gravity for this cell. Return the electrolyte to the cell from which it came.

The specific gravity of the electrolyte in each battery cell is an excellent indication of that cell's condition. A fully charged cell will read 1.275-1.280, while a cell in good condition may read from 1.250-1.280. A cell in fair condition reads from 1.225-1.250 and anything below 1.225 is practically dead.

Specific gravity varies with temperature. For each 10° that electrolyte temperature exceeds 80°F, add 0.004 to reading indicated on hydrometer. Subtract 0.004 for each 10° below 80°F.

If the cells test in the poor range, the battery requires recharging. The hydrometer is useful for checking the progress of the charging operation. **Table 3** shows approximate state of charge.

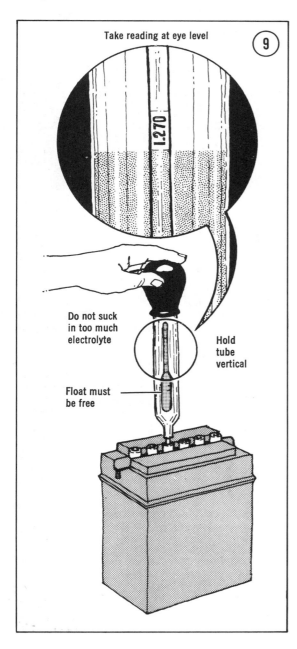

Take reading at eye level

9

1.270

Do not suck in too much electrolyte

Hold tube vertical

Float must be free

Charging

CAUTION
Always remove the battery from the motorcycle before connecting charging equipment.

WARNING
During charging, highly explosive hydrogen gas is released from the battery. The battery should be charged only in a well-ventilated area, and open flames and cigarettes should be kept away. Never check the charge of the battery by arcing across the terminals; the resulting spark can ignite the hydrogen gas.

1. Connect the positive (+) charger lead to the positive battery terminal and the negative (−) charger lead to the negative battery terminal.

2. *Remove all vent caps from the battery*, set the charger at 12 volts, and switch it on. If the output of the charger is variable, it's best to select a low setting — 1½ to 2 amps.

3. After battery has been charged for about 8 hours, turn off the charger, disconnect the leads and check the specific gravity. It should be within the limits specified in **Table 3**. If it is, and remains stable after one hour, the battery is charged.

4. Clean the battery terminals, case, and tray and reinstall them in the motorcycle, reversing the removal steps. Coat the terminals with Vaseline or silicone spray to retard decomposition of the terminal material. *Install the breather tube without any kinks or sharp bends.* It must be clear in order to dissipate the gas normally given off by the battery.

Table 3   STATE OF CHARGE

Specific Gravity	State of Charge
1.110 - 1.130	Discharged
1.140 - 1.160	Almost discharged
1.170 - 1.190	One-quarter charged
1.200 - 1.220	One-half charged
1.230 - 1.250	Three-quarters charged
1.260 - 1.280	Fully charged

PERIODIC LUBRICATION

Checking Engine Oil

Engine oil level is checked with the dipstick located on the left-hand side of the crankcase (**Figure 10**).

1. Start the engine and allow it to run for a couple of minutes.

2. Shut off the engine and allow the oil to settle. Remove the dipstick, wipe it clean, reinsert it, *do not screw it in*. Remove it and check level. The motorcycle must be level for a correct reading.

3. The level should be between the 2 lines (**Figure 11**) but above the lower one. If necessary, add the recommended weight of oil (**Figure 12**) to correct the level. Install the dipstick, and tighten it securely.

Changing Engine Oil and Filter

The factory recommends oil change intervals every 7,200 miles. The filter should be changed with every other oil change. This assumes that the motorcycle is operated in moderate climates. In extreme cold climates, oil should be changed every 30 days. The time interval is more important than the mileage interval because acids formed by gasoline and water vapor from combustion will contaminate the oil even if the motorcycle is not run for several months. Also, if the motorcycle is operated under dusty conditions the oil will get dirty more quickly and should be changed more frequently than recommended.

Use only a detergent oil with an API rating of SE or better. The quality rating is stamped on top of the can. Try always to use same brand of oil. Oil additives are not recommended.

CAUTION
Do not use any friction reducing additives as they will cause clutch slippage. Also, do not use an

engine oil with graphite added. The use of graphite oil will void any applicable Honda warranty. It is not established at this time if graphite will build up on the clutch friction plates and cause clutch problems. Until further testing is done by the oil and motorcycle industry, do not use this type of oil.

Refer to **Figure 12** for the correct weight of oil to use under different temperatures.

1. Place the motorcycle on the centerstand.

2. Start the engine and run it until it reaches normal operating temperature, then turn it off.

3. Place a drip pan under the crankcase and remove the drain plug (A, **Figure 13**) with a 17 mm wrench. Remove dipstick (**Figure 10**); this will speed up the flow of oil.

4. Let it drain for at least 15-20 minutes.

NOTE
Before removing the filter cover, thoroughly clean off all road dirt and oil around it.

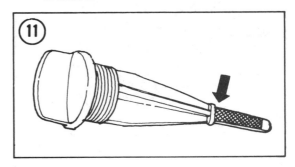

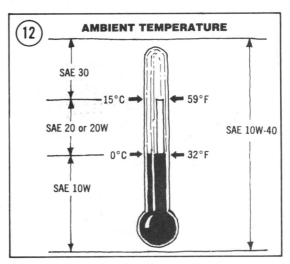

AMBIENT TEMPERATURE

5. To remove the oil filter, unscrew the bolt securing the filter cover (B, **Figure 13**) to the crankcase.

6. Remove the cover and the filter, discard the old filter and clean out the cover and the bolt with cleaning solvent and dry thoroughly. Remove all solvent residue.

7. Inspect the O-ring (A, **Figure 14**) on the bolt and the seal (B, **Figure 14**) on the cover. Replace any if damaged or deteriorated.

NOTE: *Prior to installing the cover, clean off the mating surface of the*

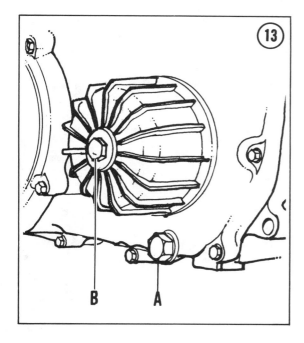

crankcase — do not allow any road dirt to enter into the oil system.

8. Insert the bolt into the cover and install the spring and washer (**Figure 15**). Insert the filter and reinstall into the crankcase.

9. Tighten the filter cover bolt to 14-18 ft.-lb. (19-24 N•m) and install the drain plug.

10. Fill the crankcase with the correct weight (**Figure 12**) and quantity of oil.

NOTE: *The capacity is approximately 3.2 qt. (3.0 liters).*

11. Screw in the dipstick and start the engine, let it idle at moderate speed and check for leaks.

12. Turn off the engine and check for correct oil level.

13. Remove the dipstick and wipe it clean. Reinsert it, but *do not screw it in*. Remove it and check level. Maintain the level between the upper and lower marks (**Figure 11**).

Front Forks

The damping oil in the front fork should be changed every 7,200 miles or at any time excessive bouncing of the front end indicates a low oil level. There is no practical way of checking and correcting the level; each fork leg should contain 4.5-4.7 oz. (135-140 cc) of damping oil for the front suspension to operate correctly.

It is necessary to completely disassemble the forks to change the oil. Refer to *Front Fork Disassembly/Assembly* in Chapter Nine.

Final Drive

Every 7,200 miles, check the oil level in the final drive. Rest the bike on the centerstand on level ground. Remove the cap (**Figure 16A**). The level should just reach the bottom of the hole. Top up if necessary with the lubricant recommended in **Table 4**.

At the same interval, inject a small amount of multipurpose grease into the Zerk fitting (**Figure 16B**). Use a small hand-held grease gun. See **Table 4**.

Control Cables

Every 4,000 miles (6,400 km) the control cables should be lubricated. They should also be inspected at this time for fraying and the cable sheath should be checked for chafing. The cables are relatively inexpensive and should be replaced when found to be faulty.

The control cables can be lubricated either with oil or with any of the popular cable lubricants and a cable lubricator. The first method requires more time and the complete lubrication of the entire cable is less certain.

Examine the exposed end of the inner cable. If it is dirty or the cable feels gritty when moved up and down in its housing, spray it with a lubricant/solvent such as LPS-25 or WD-40. Let this solvent drain out, then proceed with the following steps.

Oil method

1. Disconnect the cables from the clutch lever and the throttle grip assembly.

> *NOTE*
> *It is necessary to remove the screws that clamp the throttle housing together to gain access to the throttle cable ends.*

2. Make a cone of stiff paper and tape it to the end of the cable sheath (**Figure 17**).
3. Hold the cable upright and pour a small amount of light oil (SAE 10W/30) into the cone. Work the cable in and out of the sheath for several minutes to help the oil work its way down to the end of the cable.

> *NOTE*
> *To avoid a mess, place a shop cloth at the end of the cable to catch the oil as it runs out.*

Table 4   FINAL DRIVE LUBRICANTS

Temperature	Type	Capacity
Above 41 °F (5 °C)	Hypoid gear oil SAE 90	5.8 oz. (170cc)
Below 41 °F (5 °C)	Hypoid gear oil SAE 80	5.8 oz. (170cc)
Zerk fitting	Molybdenum disulfide grease	1.5 oz. (45cc)

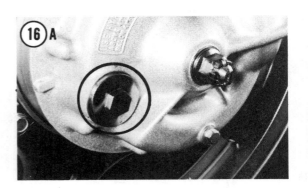

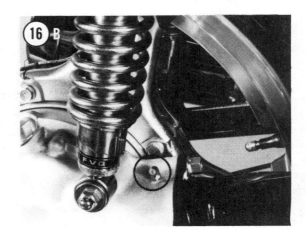

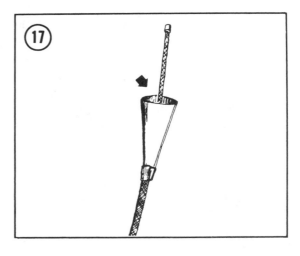

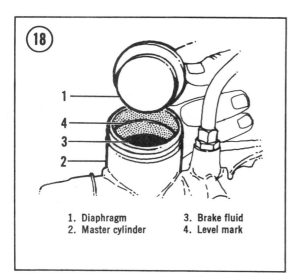

1. Diaphragm   3. Brake fluid
2. Master cylinder   4. Level mark

3

4. Remove the cone, reconnect the cable and adjust the cable(s) as described in Chapter Three in the main body of this book.

Lubricator method

1. Disconnect the cables from the clutch lever and the front brake lever.
2. Attach a lubricator following the manufacturer's instructions.
3. Insert the nozzle of the lubricant can in the lubricator, press the button on the can and hold it down until the lubricant begins to flow out of the other end of the cable.

> *NOTE*
> *Place a shop cloth at the end of the cable(s) to catch all excess lubricant that will flow out.*

4. Remove the lubricator, reconnect the cable(s) and adjust the cable(s) as described in this chapter.

PERIODIC MAINTENANCE

The hydraulic brake fluid level in the disc brake master cylinder should be checked every month or 1,800 miles and the brake pads should be checked for wear. Bleeding the hydraulic system, servicing the master cylinder, caliper, and disc and also replacing brake pads are covered in Chapter Eleven.

Front Disc Brake Fluid Level

1. Clean the outside of the reservoir cap thoroughly with a dry rag and unscrew it. Remove the washer and diaphragm.
2. The fluid level in the reservoir should be up to the upper level line (**Figure 18**). If necessary, correct the level by adding fresh brake fluid.

> *WARNING*
> *Use brake fluid clearly marked "DOT 3" only. Others may vaporize and cause brake failure.*

> *CAUTION*
> *Be careful not to spill brake fluid on painted or plated surfaces as it will destroy the surface. Wash immediately with soapy water and rinse thoroughly.*

3. Reinstall the washer, diaphragm and cap. Make sure that the cap is screwed on tightly.

Front Disc Brakes

Check brake lines between the master cylinder and the brake caliper. If there is any leakage, tighten the connections and bleed the brakes as described under *Bleeding the System* in Chapter Eleven. If this does not cure the leak, or if a line is obviously damaged, cracked or chafed, replace the line and bleed the brake.

Front Disc Brake Pad Wear

Inspect the brake pads for excessive or uneven wear, scoring, and oil or grease on the friction surface. If the pads are worn to the red line (**Figure 19**) they must be replaced.

> *NOTE*
> *Always replace both pads at the same time.*

If any of these conditions exist, replace the pads as described under *Brake Pad Replacement* in Chapter Eleven.

Front Disc Brake Fluid Change

Every time you remove the master cylinder reservoir cap, a small amount of dirt and moisture enters the brake fluid. The same thing occurs if there is a leak in the system or when any part of the hydraulic brake system is loosened or disconnected. Dirt can clog the system and cause unnecessary wear. Water in the fluid vaporizes at high temperatures, impairing the hydraulic action and reducing brake performance.

To maintain peak performance, change the brake fluid every 21,000 miles or 2 years.

1. Remove the dust cap from the caliper bleed valve (**Figure 20**) and connect the length of clear tubing to the bleed valve on the caliper. Place other end of the tube into a container (**Figure 21**).
2. Clean the top of the master cylinder of all dirt and foreign matter. Unscrew the reservoir cap and remove the washer and diaphragm.
3. Slowly apply the brake lever several times. Hold the lever in the applied position. Open the bleed valve about one-half turn. Allow the lever to travel to its limit. When this limit is reached, tighten the bleed screw. As the fluid leaves the system, the level will drop in the reservoir.

WARNING
Do not reuse brake fluid which has been drained from a brake system.

4. Continue to pump the lever until almost all old fluid has been expelled from the reservoir.

NOTE
Do not allow the reservoir to empty during this operation or air will enter the system.

5. Hold the lever, tighten the bleed valve, remove the bleed tube and install the bleed valve dust cap.
6. Add fresh brake fluid to correct the level in the reservoir. It should be to the level mark (**Figure 18**).

WARNING
Use brake fluid clearly marked "DOT 3" only. Others may vaporize and cause brake failure.

7. Install the washer, diaphragm and reservoir cap and bleed the the system. Refer to *Bleeding The System* in Chapter Eleven.

Front Disc Brake Adjustment

The front disc brake requires no adjustment, but the pads and fluid should be inspected as described under *Front Disc Brake* in this chapter.

Rear Brake Adjustment

The rear brake pedal should be adjusted so that there is 3/4-1 1/4 in. (20-30 mm) of brake

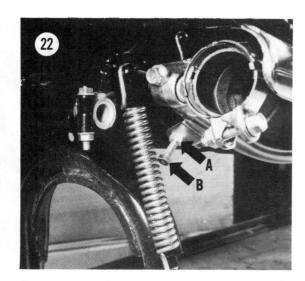

3

pedal movement required to actuate the brake, but it must not be so closely adjusted that the brake shoes contact the drum with the pedal relaxed.

1. Place the motorcycle on the centerstand.

2. Loosen the locknut (A, **Figure 22**) and turn the adjustment bolt (B, **Figure 22**) until the brake pedal is horizontal. Tighten the locknut and adjust switch as described under *Rear Brake Light Switch Adjustment* in Chapter Seven.

3. At the brake plate on the wheel, adjust the nut (**Figure 23**) on the brake rod until the correct amount of free play can be achieved.

> *NOTE*
> *Be sure that the adjustment nut is properly seated on the brake arm pin after adjustment is complete.*

4. When the two arrows (**Figure 24**) on the brake arm and the brake plate align, the brake shoes must be replaced. Refer to Chapter Eleven.

Clutch Free Play Adjustment

In order for the clutch to fully engage and disengage, there must be 3/8-3/4 in. (10-20 mm) free play at the lever end (**Figure 25**).

1. Loosen the locknut (A, **Figure 26**) and turn the adjuster (B, **Figure 26**) in or out to obtain the correct amount of free play. Tighten the locknut (A).

> *CAUTION*
> *Do not screw the adjuster out so that there are more than 0.3 in. (8 mm) of threads exposed between it and the locknut.*

2. Start the engine, pull the clutch lever in and shift into first gear. If shifting is difficult, if bike

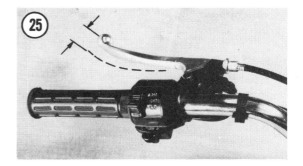

creeps when stopped or the clutch slips when accelerating in high gear, the clutch will have to be adjusted at the clutch housing.

3. At the clutch lever, loosen the locknut (A, **Figure 26**) and screw the adjuster (B, **Figure 26**) in all the way toward the hand grip. Tighten the locknut (A).

4. At the clutch housing, loosen the locknut (C, **Figure 27**) and turn the adjuster (D, **Figure 27**) in or out to obtain the correct amount of free play and tighten the locknut (C).

5. If necessary, do some final adjusting at the clutch lever as described in Step 1.

6. Road test the bike to make sure the clutch fully disengages when the lever is pulled in; if it does not, the bike will creep in gear when stopped. Also, make sure that clutch fully engages; if it does not, clutch will slip, particularly when accelerating in high gear.

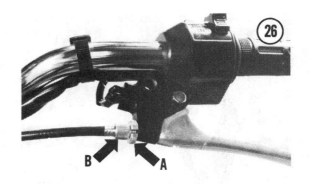

Throttle Operation/Adjustment

The throttle grip should have 0.08-0.24 in. (2-6mm) rotational play (**Figure 28**). If adjustment is necessary, loosen the pull cable locknut (A, **Figure 29**) and turn the adjuster (B, **Figure 29**) in or out to achieve the proper play. Tighten the locknut (A).

Check the throttle cables from grip to carburetors. Make sure they are not kinked or chafed. Replace them if necessary.

Make sure that the throttle grip rotates smoothly from fully closed to fully open. Check at center, full left, and full right positions of the steering.

Cooling System Inspection

Every 7,200 miles, check the following items.

1. Have radiator cap and the system pressure tested. This can be done at your Honda dealer or most service stations. The radiator cap relief pressure should be 12.8 ± 2.1 psi (0.9±1.5 kg/cm²). The radiator and cooling system should be pressurized up to, but not exceeding, 14.9 psi (1.05 kg/cm²). The system should be able to maintain this pressure for at least 6 seconds. Replace or repair any part that fails this test.

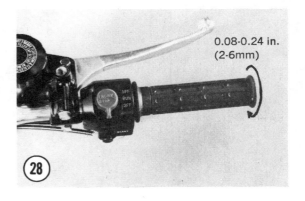

0.08-0.24 in. (2-6mm)

CAUTION
Test pressure exceeding that specified may damage the radiator.

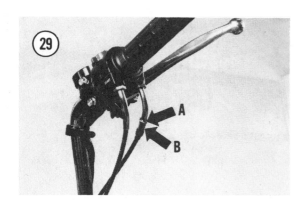

2. Check the specific gravity of coolant with an antifreeze tester to ensure adequate temperature and corrosion protection. The system must have at least a 50/50 mixture of antifreeze to water. Never let the mixture become less than 40/60 or corrosion protection will be impaired.

3. Check all hoses to make sure they are not damaged or deteriorated. Replace them if questionable. Make sure that clamps are tight. See **Figures 30, 31 and 32**.

> NOTE: *Figure 32 is shown with the engine removed. It is not necessary to remove the engine to perform this inspection.*

4. Clean the front of radiator. Remove the 4 screws **(Figure 33)** securing the radiator screen. Remove road dirt and bugs which limit air flow through the radiator.

Coolant Change

The coolant should be completely drained and refilled with at least 50/50 mixture of ethylene glycol antifreeze and water, every 21,000 miles or two years, whichever comes first.

> CAUTION
> *Use only a high quality ethylene glycol antifreeze specifically labeled for aluminum engines.*

In areas where freezing temperatures occur, add a higher percentage of antifreeze to protect the system to temperatures far below those likely to occur. **Table 5** lists the recommended amount of antifreeze to protect the CX500 at various temperatures.

The following procedure must be performed when the engine is cool.

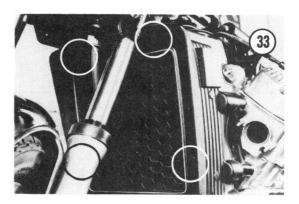

NOTE: *Figure 35 is shown with the exhaust system removed for clarity. It is not necessary to remove it.*

1. Remove the seat.

2. Turn the fuel shutoff valve to the OFF position (A, **Figure 34**) and remove the fuel line to the carburetors (B, **Figure 34**).

3. Remove rear bolt and rubber pad (**Figure 35**) securing the fuel tank at the rear, slide the tank to the rear, and remove it.

4. Remove the rubber plugs and screws, 2 on each side, (**Figure 36**) securing the radiator shroud. Slide the shroud forward and down and remove it.

5. Place a drip pan under the radiator and remove the drain plug (**Figure 37**).

6. Remove the radiator cap. This will speed up the draining process. Let coolant completely drain. Install the drain plug.

7. Remove the hose from the bottom of the recovery tank and completely drain the tank and hose. Install the hose.

8. Fill the radiator through the radiator filler neck, not the recovery tank. Use the recommended mixture of antifreeze. See **Table 5**.

> *WARNING*
> *Keep hands and tools away from the fan while the engine is running.*

9. Temporarily install the fuel tank and start the engine. Let it run at idle speed to remove

> CAUTION
> *Antifreeze can damage painted surfaces. If it does come in contact with any, rinse the area immediately with clean water.*

Table 5   ANTIFREEZE PROTECTION

Temperature	Antifreeze-to-Water Ratio
Above −25°F (−32°C)	45/55
−34°F (−37°C)	50/50
−48°F (−44.5°C)	55/45

any air from the system. Add additional coolant to the radiator if the level drops. Remove the fuel tank.

10. Install the radiator cap tightly.

11. Fill the recovery tank to the FULL mark **(Figure 38)**.

12. Install the radiator shroud, the fuel tank, and the seat.

Air Cleaner

The air cleaner element must be cleaned every 3,600 miles and replaced every 7,200 miles. It should be cleaned and changed more frequently if the bike is ridden in dusty areas.

1. Remove the seat.

2. Remove the air cleaner cover by turning it *counterclockwise*.

3. Remove the air cleaner element **(Figure 39)**.

4. Clean the element by tapping it lightly to loosen the dirt and dust. Apply compressed air to it to remove remaining dust.

5. Wipe out the interior of air box (**Figure 40**) with a shop rag and cleaning solvent. Remove any foreign matter that may have passed through a broken element.

6. Install by reversing the removal steps. Be sure to install the cover with the TOP mark facing to the front of the bike.

Wheel Bearings

The wheel bearings should be cleaned and repacked every 10,800 miles. The correct service procedures are covered in Chapters Nine and Ten.

Camshaft Chain Adjustment

1. Place the bike on the centerstand.

2. Remove the seat.

3. Remove rear bolt and rubber pad (**Figure 35**) securing the fuel tank at the rear. Slightly lift it up at the rear — do not remove it.

4. Remove the rubber plugs and screws, 2 on each side (**Figure 36**) securing the radiator shroud. Slide the shroud forward and down and remove it.

5. Remove the left-hand spark plug wire and cap (A, **Figure 41**).

6. Remove the 2 bolts securing the left-hand valve cover (B, **Figure 41**) and remove it.

7. Remove the crankshaft front cover cap (**Figure 42**).

8. Remove the timing inspection hole cover cap (A, **Figure 43**).

9. Rotate the crankshaft *clockwise* until the left-hand piston is at top dead center (TDC) on

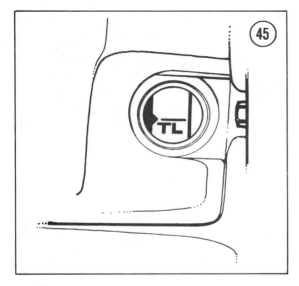

the compression stroke. Use the bolt on the front of the crankshaft (**Figure 44**) for turning with a suitable size socket.

> NOTE: *A cylinder at* TDC *will have both its rocker arms loose, indicating that the exhaust valves and intake valves are closed.*

10. Make sure that the TL mark on the alternator rotor aligns with the index mark on the crankcase (**Figure 45**).

11. Loosen the cam chain tensioner lock bolt (B, **Figure 43**). The camshaft chain tensioner will automatically adjust to the correct tension.

12. Tighten lock bolt (B, **Figure 43**) securely.

13. Install all items removed by reversing the above steps.

Crankcase Breather

Every 3,600 miles, or sooner if a considerable amount of riding is done at full throttle or in the rain, remove the 2 drain plugs (**Figure 46**) and drain out all residue. Install the caps.

Side Stand Rubber

The rubber tip on the side stand kicks the stand up if you should forget. If it wears down to the molded line (**Figure 47**), replace the rubber as it will no longer be effective.

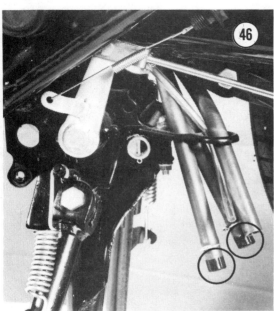

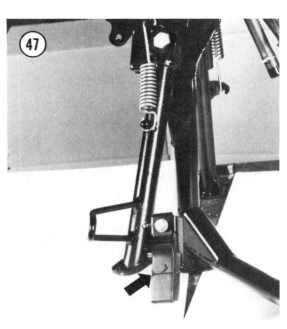

TUNE-UP

A complete tune-up should be performed every 3,600 miles of normal riding. More frequent tune-ups may be required if the motorcycle is ridden primarily in stop-and-go traffic.

The spark plugs should be routinely replaced at every other tune-up or if the electrodes show signs of erosion. In addition, this is a good time to clean the air cleaner element. Have the new parts on hand before you begin.

Because different systems in an engine interact, the procedures should be done in the following order:

   a. Tighten the cylinder head bolts.
   b. Adjust the valve clearances.
   c. Check the engine compression.
   d. Check the ignition system.
   e. Adjust the carburetors.

Cylinder Head Bolts

1. Place the bike on the centerstand and remove right- and left-side covers (**Figure 48**).

2. Remove the seat.

3. Turn the fuel shutoff valve to the OFF position (A, **Figure 49**) and remove the fuel line to the carburetors (B, **Figure 49**).

4. Remove the rear bolt and rubber pads (**Figure 50**) securing the fuel tank at the rear, slide the tank to the rear and remove it.

5. Remove both spark plug wires and caps (A, **Figure 51**).

6. Remove the bolts (B, **Figure 51**) securing the valve covers and remove them.

7. Tighten the bolts in the sequence shown in **Figure 52**. Torque the bolts to 33-40 ft.-lb. (45-54 N•m). The fuel tank and valve covers

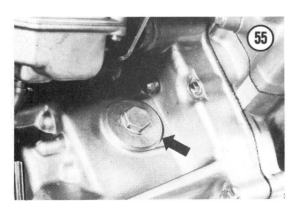

should be left off at this time for the following procedures.

Valve Clearance Adjustment

Valve clearance adjustment must be made with the engine cold. The intake valve clearance is 0.003 in. (0.08 mm) and the exhaust valve clearance is 0.004 in. (0.10 mm). Exhaust valves are at the front of the engine; intake valves are at the rear of the engine.

1. Remove the spark plugs from the cylinder heads.

2. Remove the rubber plugs and screws, 2 on each side (**Figure 53**), securing the radiator shroud. Slide the shroud forward and down and remove it.

3. Remove the crankshaft front cover cap (**Figure 54**).

4. Remove the timing inspection hole cover cap (**Figure 55**).

5. Rotate the crankshaft *clockwise* until the left-hand piston is at top dead center (TDC) on the compression stroke. Use the bolt on the front of the crankshaft (**Figure 56**) for turning with a suitable size socket.

> NOTE: *A cylinder at* TDC *will have both its rocker arms loose, indicating that the exhaust valves and intake valves are closed.*

6. Make sure that the TL mark on the alternator rotor aligns with the index mark on the crankcase (**Figure 57**).

7. Check the clearance of all 4 valves on that cylinder by inserting a flat feeler gauge between

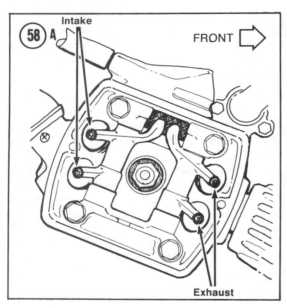

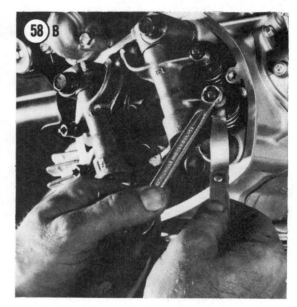

the adjusting screw and the valve stem. When the clearance is correct, there will be a slight resistance on the feeler gauge when it is inserted and withdrawn. Refer to **Figure 58A** for valve locations.

8. To correct the clearance, back off the locknut and screw the adjuster in or out far enough until a slight resistance can be felt on the gauge. Hold the adjuster to prevent it from turning further and tighten the locknut (**Figure 58B**). Recheck the clearance to make sure the adjuster did not turn after the correct clearance was achieved.

9. Rotate the crankshaft *clockwise* until the TR mark on the alternator rotor aligns with the mark on the crankcase (**Figure 59**). The right-hand cylinder must be at TDC on the compression stroke (see NOTE after Step 5).

10. Repeat Steps 7 and 8 for the right-hand cylinder valves.

11. When all clearances have been checked and adjusted, install all items removed by reversing the above steps.

NOTE: *Prior to installing the valve covers, coat the rubber bushings on the*

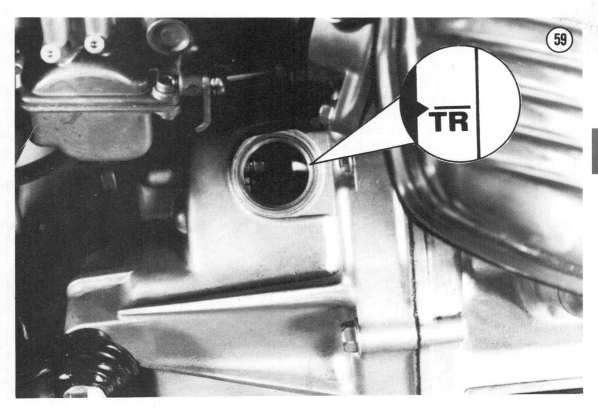

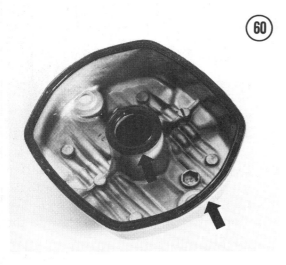

bolts with engine oil. Make sure the gaskets are in good condition and in place (Figure 60).

Compression Test

Every 6,000 miles, check cylinder compression. Record the results and compare them at the next 6,000 mile check. A running record will show trends in deterioration so that corrective action can be taken before complete failure.

The results, when properly interpreted, can indicate general cylinder, piston ring, and valve condition.

1. Warm the engine to normal operating temperature. Ensure that the choke valve and throttle valve are completely open.

2. Remove the spark plugs.

3. Connect compression tester to one cylinder following manufacturer's instructions.

4. Have an assistant crank the engine over until there is no further rise in pressure.

5. Remove the tester and record the reading.

6. Repeat Steps 3-5 for the other cylinder.

When interpreting the results, actual readings are not as important as the difference between the readings. Both readings should be from about 171 ± 20 psi (12 ± 2.0 kg/cm²). A maximum difference of 57 psi (4 kg/cm²) between the 2 cylinders is acceptable. Greater differences indicate worn or broken rings, leaky or sticky valves, blown head gaskets or a combination of all.

If compression reading does not differ between cylinders by more than 10 psi, the rings and valves are in good condition.

If a low reading (10% or more) is obtained on one of the cylinders, it indicates valve or ring trouble. To determine which, pour about a teaspoon of engine oil through the spark plug hole onto the top of the piston. Turn the engine over once to clear some of the excess oil, then take another compression test and record the reading. If the compression returns to normal, the valves are good but the rings are defective on that cylinder. If compression does not increase, the valves require servicing. A valve could be hanging open but not burned or a piece of carbon could be on a valve seat.

Correct Spark Plug Heat Range

Spark plugs are available in various heat ranges, hotter or colder than plugs originally installed at the factory.

Select plugs of a heat range designed for the loads and temperature conditions under which the bike will run. Use of incorrect heat ranges can cause seized pistons, scored cylinder walls, or damaged piston crowns.

In general, use a hot plug for low speeds, low loads, and low temperatures. Use a cold plug for high speeds, high engine loads, and high temperatures.

In areas where seasonal temperature variations are great, the factory recommends a "two-plug system" — a cold plug for hard summer riding and a hot plug for slower winter operation. Refer to **Table 6**.

The reach (length) of a plug is also important. A longer than normal plug could interfere with the valves and pistons causing permanent and severe damage. Refer to **Figure 61**.

Spark Plug Cleaning and Replacement

Spark plugs should be inspected and cleaned every 3,600 miles and replaced every 7,200 miles or sooner if necessary.

1. Grasp the spark plug leads as near the cap as possible and pull them off the plugs.

2. Blow away any dirt and moisture that has accumulated in the spark plug wells. Clean out the drain hole (**Figure 62**) in each head.

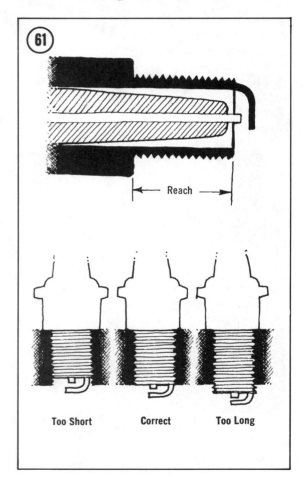

Table 6   SPARK PLUG HEAT RANGE

	NGK	ND	AC	CHAMPION
U.S. Models				
Standard	D8EA	X24ES-U	S121 XL	A-8Y
Cold climate	D7EA	X22ES-U	S123 XL	R-8, R-6
High speed	D9EA	X27ES-U	—	—
Canadian Models				
Standard	DR 8ES-L	X24ESR-U	—	—

CAUTION
Dirt could fall into the cylinders when the plugs are removed, causing serious engine damage.

3. Remove spark plugs with a spark plug wrench.

NOTE: *If plugs are difficult to remove, apply penetrating oil, like WD-40 or Liquid Wrench, around base of plugs and let it soak in about 10-20 minutes.*

4. Inspect spark plugs carefully. Look for plugs with broken center porcelain, excessively eroded electrodes, and excessive carbon or oil fouling. Replace such plugs. If deposits are light, plugs may be cleaned in solvent with a wire brush or cleaned in a special spark plug sandblast cleaner.

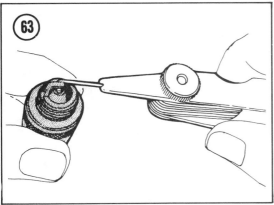

5. Gap plugs to 0.024-0.028 in. (0.6-0.7mm) with a *wire* feeler gauge. See **Figure 63**.

6. Install plugs with a *new* gasket. First, apply a *small* drop of oil or aluminum antiseize compound to threads. Tighten plugs finger-tight, then tighten with a spark plug wrench an additional 1/2 turn. If you must reuse an old gasket, tighten only an additional 1/4 turn.

NOTE: *Do not overtighten. This will only squash the gasket and destroy its sealing ability.*

Reading Spark Plugs

Much information about engine and spark plug performance can be determined by careful examination of the spark plugs. This information is only valid after performing the following steps.

1. Ride the bike a short distance at full throttle in any gear.

2. Turn the kill switch to OFF before closing the throttle and simultaneously pull in the clutch; coast to a stop.

3. Remove the spark plugs and examine them. Compare them to those shown in **Figure 64**.

If insulator is white or burned, the plug is too hot and should be replaced with a colder one.

A too-cold plug will have sooty deposits ranging in color from dark brown to black. Replace with a hotter plug and check for too-rich carburetion or evidence of oil blow-by at the piston rings.

If any one plug is found unsatisfactory, discard both.

Capacitor Discharge Ignition

The Honda CX500 is equipped with a capacitor discharge ignition (CDI). This system uses no breaker points or other moving parts.

Since there are no components to wear, adjusting the ignition timing is not necessary even after engine disassembly. The timing should not change for the life of the bike.

The two items that could cause the timing to vary are the CDI unit and/or the alternator. Check the timing with the following procedure; if it is incorrect, check out both of these units as described in Chapter Seven.

SPARK PLUG CONDITION

NORMAL

- Identified by light tan or gray deposits on the firing tip.
- Can be cleaned.

GAP BRIDGED

- Identified by deposit buildup closing gap between electrodes.
- Caused by oil or carbon fouling. If deposits are not excessive, the plug can be cleaned.

OIL FOULED

- Identified by wet black deposits on the insulator shell bore and electrodes.
- Caused by excessive oil entering combustion chamber thorugh worn rings and pistons, excessive clearance between valve guides and stems, or worn or loose bearings. Can be cleaned. If engine is not repaired, use a hotter plug.

CARBON FOULED

- Identified by black, dry, fluffy carbon deposits on insulator tips, exposed shell surfaces and electrodes.
- Caused by too cold a plug, weak ignition, dirty air cleaner, too rich a fuel mixture, or excessive idling. Can be cleaned.

LEAD FOULED

- Identified by dark gray, black, yellow, or tan deposits or a fused glazed coating on the insulator tip.
- Caused by highly leaded gasoline. Can be cleaned.

WORN

- Identified by severely eroded or worn electrodes.
- Caused by normal wear. Should be replaced.

FUSED SPOT DEPOSIT

- Identified by melted or spotty deposits resembling bubbles or blisters.
- Caused by sudden acceleration. Can be cleaned.

OVERHEATING

- Identified by a white or light gray insulator with small black or gray brown spots and with bluish-burnt appearance of electrodes.
- Caused by engine overheating, wrong type of fuel, loose spark plugs, too hot a plug, or incorrect ignition timing. Replace the plug.

PREIGNITION

- Identified by melted electrodes and possibly blistered insulator. Metallic deposits on insulator indicate engine damage.
- Caused by wrong type of fuel, incorrect ignition timing or advance, too hot a plug, burned valves, or engine overheating. Replace the plug.

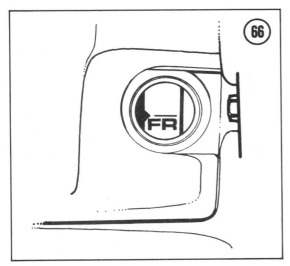

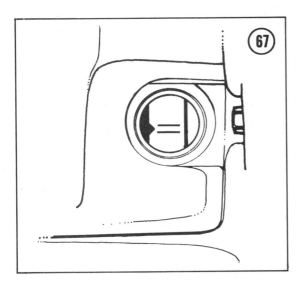

The only other item that could affect ignition timing is the pulser stator alignment in the rear engine cover. This is a very remote possibility but it is worth checking out if all else fails. Refer to Step 16 and related NOTE, *Alternator Removal/Installation* in Chapter Seven. The two screws may have worked loose causing the pulser stator to shift.

> NOTE: *Before starting on this procedure, check all electrical connections related to the ignition system. Make sure all connections are tight and free of corrosion and that all ground connections are tight.*

1. Remove the timing inspection hole cover cap (**Figure 65**).

2. Connect a portable tachometer to the engine following the manufacturer's instructions. The bike's tachometer is not correct enough at very low rpm.

3. Attach a timing light to right-hand spark plug lead.

4. Place the bike on the centerstand and start the engine. Let it warm up and idle at $1,100 \pm 100$ rpm; adjust if necessary as described under *Carburetor Idle Speed Adjustment* in this chapter.

5. Direct the timing light to the timing marks on the alternator flywheel. The timing is correct if the FR on the alternator flywheel aligns with the index mark on the crankcase (**Figure 66**).

6. Increase engine speed and check that the advance timing marks (**Figure 67**) align with the index mark on the crankcase at 5,000-6,000 rpm.

7. Repeat Steps 2-5 for the left-hand cylinder. In Step 4 the timing is correct if the FL on the alternator flywheel aligns with the index mark on the crankcase (**Figure 68**).

Carburetor Idle Adjustment

Carburetor idle adjustment should be checked every 3,600 miles.

Before making this adjustment, the air cleaner must be clean and the engine must have adequate compression; see *Compression Test* in this chapter. Otherwise this procedure cannot be done properly.

1. Start the engine and let it warm up to operating temperature. Make sure the choke knob is all the way in and open (**Figure 69**).

2. Connect a portable tachometer to the engine following the manufacturer's instructions.

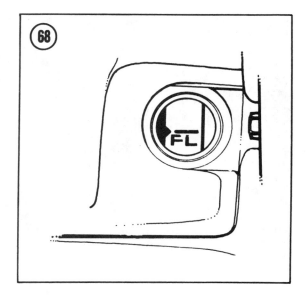

NOTE
The correct idle speed is 1,100 +/-100 rpm. The bike's tachometer is not correct enough at very low rpm.

3. Rotate black idle adjust screw (**Figure 70**), located between the 2 carburetors, *clockwise* to increase idle speed and *counterclockwise* to decrease idle speed.

Carburetor Synchronization

When the carburetors are properly synchronized the engine will warm up faster and there will be an improvement in throttle response, performance and mileage.

Prior to synchronizing the carburetors, the air cleaner must be clean and the ignition timing and valve clearance must be properly adjusted.

This procedure requires 2 special tools. First you will need a mercury manometer (carb-sync tool). This is a tool that measures the manifold vacuum for both cylinders simultaneously. A carb-sync tool can be purchased from a Honda dealer, motorcycle supply store, or mail order firm starting at about $25.

NOTE
When purchasing this tool check that it is equipped with restrictors. These restrictors keep the mercury from being drawn into the engine when engine rpm is increased during the adjustment procedure. If the mercury is drawn into the engine the tool will have to be replaced.

The second special tool needed is a carburetor adjusting wrench, also available from a Honda dealer. It is the Carburetor Adjusting Wrench.

1. Place the bike on the centerstand, start the engine and warm it up to normal operating temperature.

2. Remove both side covers and remove the seat.

3. Turn the fuel shutoff valve to the OFF position and remove the fuel line to the carburetors.

4. Remove the bolt securing the rear of the fuel tank, pull the tank to the rear and remove it.

5. Remove the vacuum plug (consisting of a screw and flat washer) from both of the intake tubes in the cylinder head (**Figure 71**).

6. Connect the vacuum lines from the carb-sync tool, following the manufacturer's instructions. Most carb-sync tools are designed for use with a maximum of 4 cylinders. Use the hoses and gauges for the No. 1 and No. 2 cylinders. Most carb-sync tools have the cylinder number indicated on them adjacent to each tube containing mercury.

NOTE
The No. 1 carburetor (left-hand side) has no synchronization screw; the No. 2 (right-hand side) carburetor must be synchronized to it.

7. Start the engine and let it idle at 1,100 rpm +/-100 rpm. There should be enough fuel in the float bowls to run the bike for this procedure.

WARNING
Do not rig up a temporary fuel supply as this presents a real fire danger.

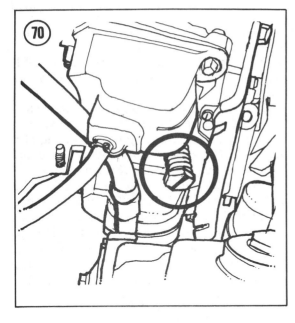

screw until the reading is the same as that on the No. 1 carburetor. Tighten the locknut. Open the throttle a little and close it back down after each adjustment.

> *CAUTION*
> *If your carb-sync tool is not equipped with restrictors, open and close the throttle very gently to avoid sucking mercury into the engine. If this happens, it will not harm the engine but will render the tool useless.*

> *NOTE*
> *To gain the utmost in performance and efficiency from the engine, adjust the carburetors so that the gauge readings are as close to each other as possible.*

8. If you start to run out of fuel during the test, shut off the engine. Reinstall the fuel tank and refill the carburetor float bowls; remove the fuel tank, restart the engine and proceed with the test.

9. If the difference in gauge readings is 1.6 in. Hg (40 mm Hg) or less between the 2 cylinders, the carburetors are considered synchronized. If not, proceed as follows.

10. Using the special tool described in the introduction to the procedure, loosen the locknut and turn the adjusting screw on the No. 2 carburetor (**Figure 72**). Turn the adjusting

11. After the carburetors are adjusted properly make sure the locknut is tight.

12. Shut off the engine and remove the vacuum lines. Install the screws and washers into the vacuum ports in the cylinder head (**Figure 71**). Make sure they are in tight to prevent a vacuum leak.

13. Install the fuel tank, seat and side covers.

14. Restart the engine and readjust the idle speed if necessary; refer to *Carburetor Idle Adjustment* in this chapter.

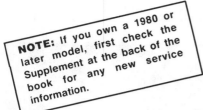

NOTE: If you own a 1980 or later model, first check the Supplement at the back of the book for any new service information.

CHAPTER FOUR

ENGINE

The engine is a liquid-cooled, 4-stroke, 80° V-twin with four overhead valves per cylinder. Two main bearings support the counterbalanced crankshaft. The camshaft, driven by a Hy-Vo chain, operates the valves via short pushrods and upper and lower rocker arms. Both sets of valves in each cylinder are operated by their own single rocker arm. Each valve has its own adjuster.

The oil pump supplies oil under pressure throughout the engine and is chain driven by the crankshaft.

This chapter provides complete service and overhaul procedures for the Honda CX500. **Tables 1-6**, at the end of this chapter, provide complete specifications for the engine. Although the clutch and transmission are mounted within the engine, they are covered separately in Chapter Five to simplify the presentation of this material.

ENGINE PRINCIPLES

Figure 1 explains how the engine works. This will be helpful when troubleshooting or repairing your engine.

SERVICING ENGINE IN FRAME

The following components can be serviced while the engine is mounted in the frame:

a. Cylinder heads
b. Upper rocker arm assemblies
c. Oil filter
d. Clutch
e. Carburetors
f. Electrical systems — except for the alternator
g. Radiator and thermostat

It is recommended that prior to engine removal and disassembly, the majority of parts be removed from the engine while it is still in the frame.

ENGINE

Removal/Installation

1. Place the bike on the centerstand. Remove the right- and left-hand side covers (**Figure 2**) and accessories such as fairings and crash bars.

2. Disconnect negative battery lead (**Figure 3**).

3. Remove the seat.

4-STROKE OPERATING PRINCIPLES ①

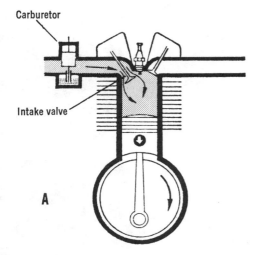

Carburetor

Intake valve

A

As the piston travels downward, the exhaust valve is closed and the intake valve opens, allowing the new fuel/air mixture from the **carburetor** to be drawn into the cylinder. When the piston reaches the bottom of its travel (BDC), the **intake valve** closes and remains closed for the next revolution-and-a-half of the crankshaft.

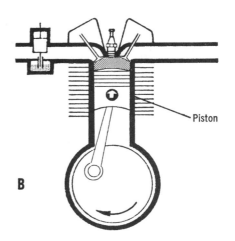

Piston

B

While the crankshaft continues to rotate, the **piston** moves upward, compressing the fuel/air mixture.

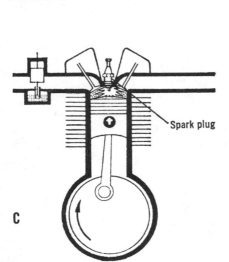

Spark plug

C

As the piston almost reaches the top of its travel, the **spark plug** fires, igniting the compressed fuel/air mixture. The piston continues to top dead center (TDC) and is pushed downward by the expanding gases.

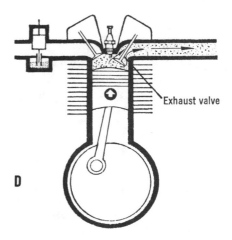

Exhaust valve

D

When the piston almost reaches BDC, the **exhaust valve** opens and remains open until the piston is near TDC. The upward travel of the piston causes the exhaust gases to be pushed out of the cylinder. After the piston has reached TDC, the exhaust valve closes and the cycle starts all over again.

4

4. Turn the fuel shutoff valve to the OFF position (A, **Figure 4**), and remove the fuel line from the carburetors (B, **Figure 4**).

5. Remove rear bolt and rubber pad **(Figure 5)** securing the fuel tank at the rear, slide the tank to the rear and remove it.

6. Remove the exhaust system as described under *Exhaust System Removal/Installation* in Chapter Six.

7. Drain the cooling system and remove the radiator and shroud as described under *Radiator Removal/Installation* in Chapter Eight.

8. Drain the engine oil as described under *Changing Engine Oil and Filter* in Chapter Three.

9. Loosen rear brake adjuster screw **(Figure 6)** and pivot the brake pedal arm down.

10. Remove the fuel tank rubber mounts and right-hand cable clip **(Figure 7)**.

11. Remove the wiring harness clips. Disconnect the coil electrical connectors (pink — right-hand coil, yellow — left-hand coil) from the CDI unit. See **Figure 8**.

4

12. Disconnect all electrical connectors at the terminal blocks (**Figure 8**). Disconnect the thermostat and oil pressure sending unit electrical cables.

13. Remove the through bolts securing the coils to the frame (A, **Figure 9**) and remove the coils.

14. Pull the wiring harness clear of the frame.

CAUTION
Do not pull hard on the harness as damage will occur to the wires and connectors.

15. Remove the 3 bolts and nuts (B, **Figure 9**) securing the upper engine mounting plates and remove them.

16. Remove the crankcase breather tubes (**Figure 10**) from the heads.

17. Remove the 2 upper bolts and nuts (A, **Figure 11**) securing the front engine cradle to the frame. The front bolt secures the electrical clip on the left-hand side.

18. Remove the 2 upper bolts and 2 lower nuts (B, **Figure 11**) securing the front engine cradle to the engine and remove it.

19. Remove carburetors as described under *Carburetor Removal/Installation* in Chapter Six.

20. Remove the 2 bolts (**Figure 12**) securing the starter motor to the crankcase. Pull it to the rear, rotate it slightly and pivot it down.

21. Disconnect the electrical cable (**Figure 13**) and remove the starter.

22. Loosen the bolt securing the shift lever (**Figure 14**) and remove the shift lever.

23. Loosen the tachometer cable set screw and withdraw the cable from the engine.

24. Disconnect the clutch cable at the clutch housing (**Figure 15**).

25. Pull back the rubber protective boot (**Figure 16**) on the drive shaft and remove the locating bolt (**Figure 17**). Push the drive shaft to the rear to disengage the shaft splines from the output shaft of the engine.

26. Take a final look all over the engine to make sure everything has been disconnected.

27. Place a suitable size jack, with a piece of wood on it to protect the crankcase, under the engine (**Figure 18**). Apply a *small amount* of jack pressure up on the engine.

4

CAUTION
The following steps can be performed by one person but it is advisable to have an assistant to stabilize the engine during removal from the frame. The engine weighs 141 lbs. (64 kg).

28. Loosen the 2 upper short bolts and nuts and lower long through bolt and nut (**Figure 19**) securing the rear of the engine. Leave the upper ones in place until the lower through bolt is withdrawn. Remove the upper bolts and slide the engine slightly forward.

CAUTION
Make sure the drive shaft splines are completely disengaged from the output shaft of the engine.

29. Lower the jack and remove the engine from the frame. Either place the engine in an engine stand or set it on a work bench for disassembly.
30. Install by reversing these removal steps.

31. After the engine is installed in the frame, pull the drive shaft forward and mesh the splines onto the output shaft of the engine. Install the locating bolt and tighten to 13-18 ft.-lb. (18-25 N•m).
32. Torque all bolts and nuts to the torque values in **Table 5**.
33. Fill the engine with the recommended type and quantity of engine oil and coolant. Refer to Chapter Three.
34. Start the engine and check for leaks.

CYLINDER HEAD

Removal

The cylinder heads can be removed with the engine in the frame. The engine must be cool prior to removing the heads.

1. Place the bike on the centerstand. Remove the right- and left-hand side covers (**Figure 20**) and accessories such as fairings and crash bars.

2. Remove the seat. Disconnect the negative battery lead (**Figure 21**).

3. Turn the fuel shutoff valve to the OFF position (A, **Figure 22**) and remove the fuel line to the carburetors (B, **Figure 22**).

4. Remove rear bolt and rubber pad **(Figure 23)** securing the fuel tank at the rear, slide the tank to the rear and remove it.

5. Remove the exhaust system as described under *Exhaust System Removal/Installation* in Chapter Six.

6. Drain the cooling system as described under Steps 4-6, *Coolant Change* in Chapter Three.

7. Remove the coils' rear attachment bolt (A, **Figure 24**) and 3 bolts and nuts (B, **Figure 24**) securing the upper engine mounting plates and remove them.

8. Remove the air dam attachment bolts and remove the dam.

9. Disconnect the thermostat switch and oil pressure sending unit electrical cables.

10. Remove 4 bolts, 2 on each side **(Figure 25)**, securing the thermostat housing and outlet pipes to the heads.

11. Remove the small rubber hose from the top of the water pump **(Figure 26)**.

> NOTE: *Figure 26 is shown with the engine removed for clarity only.*

12. Remove the thermostat assembly.

13. Remove the spark plug leads.

14. Remove the crankcase breather tubes (A, **Figure 27)** from the heads.

15. Remove the valve covers and loosen the carburetor band screw (B, **Figure 27)**.

> NOTE: *Steps 16-21 are shown with the engine removed for clarity.*

16. Rotate the crankshaft *clockwise* until the left-hand piston is at top dead center (TDC) on the compression stroke. Use the bolt on the front of the crankshaft **(Figure 28)** for turning with a suitable size socket.

> NOTE: *A cylinder at TDC will have both its rocker arms loose, indicating that the exhaust valves and intake valves are closed.*

17. Remove the 2 short 6mm bolts toward the centerline of the engine on the left-hand cylinder.

18. Remove the 4 left-hand cylinder head bolts, using the sequence shown in **Figure 29**. Loosen the bolts in two or more steps to avoid warping the head.

19. Remove rocker arm assembly **(Figure 30)** and the pushrods (A, **Figure 31)**.

NOTE: *Do not lose the 2 locating dowels (B, Figure 31).*

20. Loosen the head by tapping around the perimeter with a rubber or plastic mallet. *Do not use a metal hammer.*

21. Remove the cylinder head.

22. Remove the cylinder head gasket, 2 locating dowels (A, **Figure 32**) and the oil control orifice (B, **Figure 32**).

23. To remove the right-hand head, repeat Steps 16-21. In Step 16, rotate the crankshaft *clockwise* until the *right-hand piston is at* TDC.

Inspection

1. Remove all traces of gasket material from the head and cylinder mating surfaces.

2. Without removing the valves, remove all carbon deposits from the combustion chambers with a wire brush. A blunt screwdriver or chisel may be used if care is taken not to damage the head or valves.

3. After all carbon is removed from the combustion chamber and valve intake and exhaust ports, clean the entire head in solvent.

4. Clean away all carbon on the piston crowns. *Do not remove the carbon ridge at the top of the cylinder bore.*

5. Check for cracks in the combustion chamber and exhaust ports. A cracked head must be replaced.

6. Check the condition of the valves and valve guides as described under *Valve and Valve Seats* in this chapter.

Installation

Prior to installation of the head, make sure that the cylinder is at top dead center (TDC).

NOTE: *A cylinder at* TDC *will have the piston at the top of its stroke, **both lower** rocker arms (Figure 33) will be at the farthest down position, and the timing mark on the alternator rotor (TR for right-hand cylinder, Figure 34, and TL for the left-hand cylinder, Figure 35) will align with the index mark on the crankcase.*

1. Install a new head gasket, 2 locating dowels (A, **Figure 32**) and the oil control orifice (B, **Figure 32**).

2. Install the cylinder head.

3. Apply molybdenum disulfide grease to both ends of the pushrods.

4. Install the pushrods (A, **Figure 31**) into the lower rocker arm retainers.

5. Install the 2 locating dowels (B, **Figure 31**).

6. Loosen the valve adjusting screws. Install the rocker arm assembly (**Figure 30**). Be sure the 2 locating dowels (**Figure 36**) on the bottom of the assembly are in position.

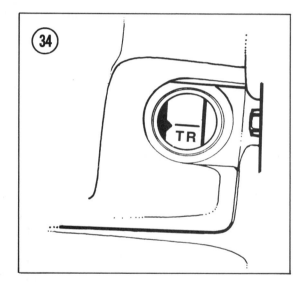

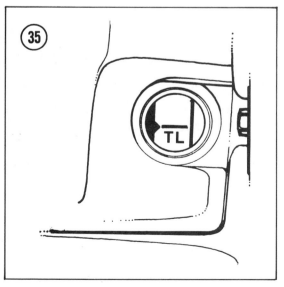

7. Install the 4 cylinder head bolts. Tighten the bolts in the sequence shown in **Figure 29**, tighten in 2 to 3 steps to a final torque of 33-40 ft.-lb. (45-54 N•m).

8. Install the short 6mm bolts and torque to 6-8 ft.-lb. (8-11 N•m).

CAUTION
*Before proceeding, rotate the crankshaft several revolutions with a wrench on the bolt shown in **Figure 28**. If there is any binding, **stop**. Determine the cause before assembling beyond this point.*

9. Complete the installation by reversing *Removal* Steps 1-15.

10. Adjust the valves as described under *Valve Clearance Adjustment* in Chapter Three.

11. Torque all bolts and nuts to torque values in **Table 5**.

12. Fill the engine with the recommended type and quantity of engine oil and coolant. Refer to Chapter Three.

13. Start the engine and check for leaks.

VALVE AND VALVE SEATS

Removal

1. Remove cylinder heads as described under *Cylinder Head Removal*.

2. Compress springs with a valve spring compression tool **(Figure 37)**, remove the valve keepers and release compression.

3. Remove the valve spring caps, springs, and valves **(Figure 38)**.

> CAUTION
> *Remove any burrs from the valve stem grooves before removing the valve. Otherwise the valve guides will be damaged.*

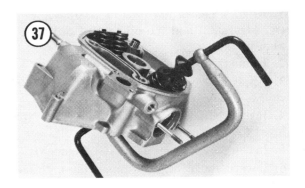

Inspection

1. Clean valves with a wire brush and solvent.

2. Inspect the contact surface of each valve for burning **(Figure 39)**. Minor roughness and pitting can be removed by lapping valve as described under *Valve Lapping* in this chapter. Excessive unevenness to the contact surface is an indication that the valve is not serviceable. Contact surface of the valve may be ground on a valve grinding machine, but it is best to replace a burned or damaged valve with a new one.

Inspect the valve stems for wear and roughness and measure the vertical runout of the

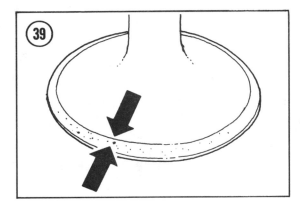

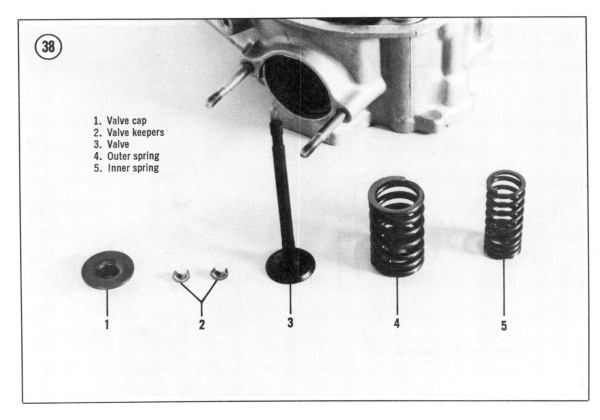

1. Valve cap
2. Valve keepers
3. Valve
4. Outer spring
5. Inner spring

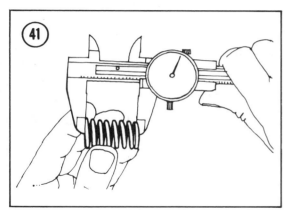

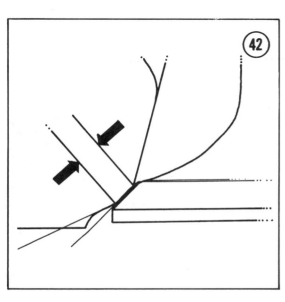

valve stem as shown in **Figure 40**. The runout should not exceed 0.001 in. (0.025mm).

3. Measure the valve stems for wear. Compare with specifications in **Table 6** at the end of the chapter.

4. Remove all carbon and varnish from the valve guides with a stiff spiral wire brush.

5. Insert each valve in its guide. Hold the valve just slightly off its seats and rock it sideways. If it rocks more than slightly, the guide is probably worn and should be replaced. As a final check, take the head to a dealer and have the valve guides measured.

6. Measure the valve spring heights with a vernier caliper (**Figure 41**). All should be of length specified in **Table 6** without bends or other distortions. Replace defective springs.

7. Check the valve spring retainer and valve keepers. If they are in good condition, they may be reused.

8. Inspect and measure valve seats (**Figure 42**). Compare with specifications in **Table 6** at end of the chapter. If the seats are too wide, too narrow, or worn or burned, they must be reconditioned. This should be performed by your dealer or local machine shop, although the procedure is described later in this section. Seats and valves in near-perfect condition can be reconditioned by lapping with fine carborundum paste. Lapping, however, is always inferior to precision grinding.

Installation

1. Coat the valve stems with molybdenum disulphide paste and insert them into cylinder head.

2. Install bottom spring retainers and new seals.

3. Install valve springs, with the narrow pitch end (end with coils closest together) facing the head, and upper valve spring retainers.

4. Push down on upper valve spring retainers with the valve spring compressor and install valve keepers.

Valve Guide Replacement

When guides are worn so that there is excessive stem-to-guide clearance or valve tipping, they must be replaced. Replace all, even if only one is worn. This job should only be done by a Honda dealer as special tools are required.

Valve Seat Reconditioning

This job is best left to your dealer or local machine shop. They have the special equipment and knowledge for this exacting job. You can still save considerable money by removing the cylinder head and taking just the head to the shop.

Valve Lapping

Valve lapping is a simple operation which can restore the valve seal without machining if the amount of wear or distortion is not too great.

1. Coat the valve seating area in the head with a lapping compound such as carborundum or Clover Brand.

2. Insert the valve into the head.

3. Wet the suction cup of the lapping stick (**Figure 43**) and stick it onto the head of the valve. Lap the valve to the seat by rotating the lapping stick in both directions. Every 5 to 10 seconds, rotate the valve 180° in the seat; continue lapping until the contact surfaces of the valve and the valve seat are a uniform grey. Stop as soon as they are, to avoid removing too much material.

4. Thoroughly clean the valves and cylinder head in solvent to remove all grinding compound. Any compound left on the valves or the cylinder head will end up in the engine and will cause damage.

UPPER ROCKER ARM ASSEMBLIES

The upper rocker arms are activated by pushrods which are driven by a secondary set of rocker arms that ride on the camshaft.

The upper rocker arm assemblies can be removed with the engine in the frame but the cylinder heads have to be removed.

Removal/Installation

Remove and install the cylinder heads as described under *Cylinder Head Removal/Installation* in this chapter.

Disassembly/Assembly

It is important that all parts be assembled in their original positions. Refer to **Figure 44**. Therefore, before disassembling, mark the parts in some way to remind you later.

Refer to **Figure 45** for this procedure.

1. Push one of the rocker shafts out of the holder.

2. Remove the spring washer and rocker arm.

3. Push the other rocker shaft out and remove the spring washer and rocker arm.

4. Clean all the parts thoroughly in cleaning solvent.

5. Carefully inspect the rocker arm bore and bearing surfaces for signs of wear or scoring. Measure the inside diameter of the rocker arm bore (A, **Figure 46**) with a micrometer and check against measurements given in **Table 6**. Replace them if defective.

6. Inspect the rocker shafts for signs of wear or scoring. Measure the outside diameter (B,

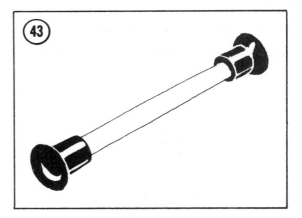

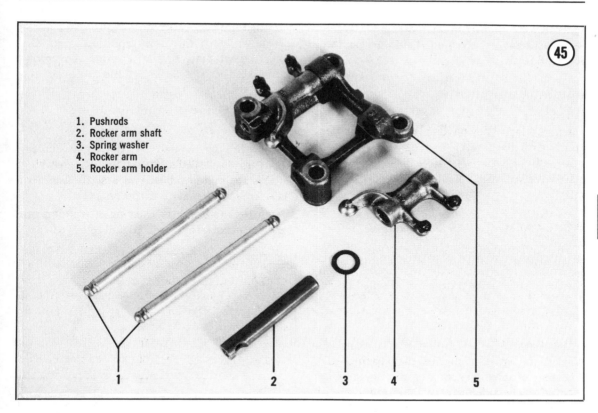

1. Pushrods
2. Rocker arm shaft
3. Spring washer
4. Rocker arm
5. Rocker arm holder

4

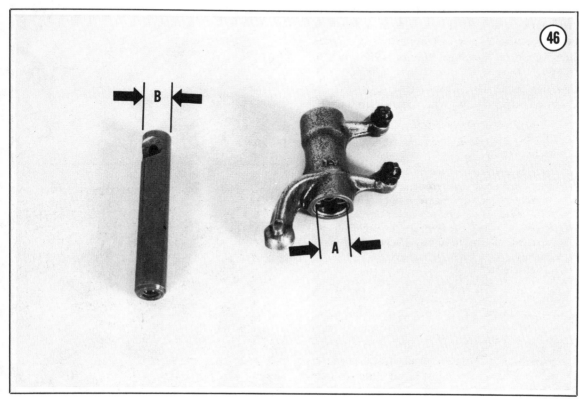

Figure 46) with a micrometer and check against the measurements given in **Table 6**. Replace them if defective.

7. Check the spring washers for breakage or distortion. Replace if necessary.

8. Coat the rocker shafts, holder bores, and rocker arm bores liberally with assembly oil or clean engine oil.

9. Slide the rocker shaft into the holder while assembling the rocker arm and spring washer.

> NOTE: *Be sure to install the rocker shaft with the locating notch toward the side of the head where the pushrods are located.*

10. Rotate the shaft so the notch aligns with the hole in the holder for the cylinder head bolt.

CAMSHAFT

The camshaft is driven by a Hy-Vo chain off of the timing sprocket on the crankshaft.

Due to problems encountered with the bolt securing the stationary cam chain guide on all 1978 models, the factory has modified the affected parts. They consist of a new stationary cam chain guide and its securing bolt, a small set plate, and a new tensioner cover. *These parts must be installed on all 1978 models CX500's — frame serial No. 2000001 — 2034366 inclusive.* Subsequent models are equipped at the factory with the modified parts.

> CAUTION
> *If the bolt securing the cam chain guide works loose the engine will develop a ticking noise. Prolonged operation with the loose bolt will cause the bolt to break, increasing engine noise. If the bike is ridden beyond this point the cam chain may break, locking up the engine, possibly causing total loss of control of the bike.*

All 1978 models that have been corrected with the new parts are supposed to be identified by the Honda dealer that performed the work. The identification consists of three marks in a triangular configuration (**Figure 47A**) on the left side of the engine serial number plate, located on the lower left-hand side of the crankcase.

In the following procedure, **Figures 56 and 58** are shown with the new modified parts. If either the set plate or the tensioner cover on your bike does not look like the ones shown, consult your Honda dealer for correct parts replacement.

Removal

1. Remove the engine as described under *Engine Removal/Installation* in this chapter. Remove the cylinder heads as described under *Cylinder Head Removal* in this chapter.

2. Remove the 2 clamps securing the water pipe to cylinder block (**Figure 47B**) and remove it.

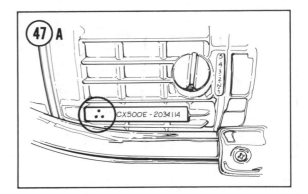

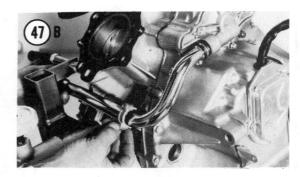

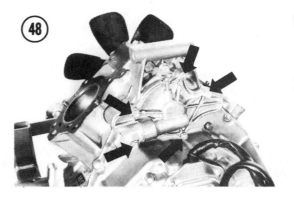

3. Remove the 5 bolts (**Figure 48**) securing the water pump housing and remove it.

NOTE: *Do not lose the 2 locating dowels (A, Figure 49).*

4. Remove the cap nut and copper washer (B, **Figure 49**) securing the water pump impeller and remove it.

5. Remove the 17 bolts securing the rear engine cover. Hold the shift lever shaft in position and remove the cover.

NOTE: *Do not lose the 2 locating dowels and O-rings (Figure 50).*

6. Remove the bolt (**Figure 51**) securing the alternator pulser rotor and remove the rotor.

7. Remove the bolt (**Figure 52**) securing the alternator rotor to the crankshaft with a socket.

NOTE: *To prevent the flywheel from turning while removing the bolt, secure it with a strap wrench as shown in Figure 53.*

8. Screw a flywheel puller in all the way until it stops (**Figure 54**).

4

9. Hold the flywheel with the strap wrench and rotate the puller *clockwise* until the flywheel disengages from the crankshaft. Remove the flywheel, starter gear (**Figure 55**) and the needle bearing (**Figure 56**).

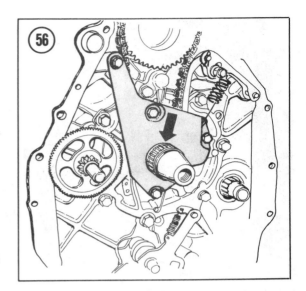

CAUTION
*Be careful not to damage the pulser pickup (**Figure 57**) on the outer surface of the flywheel.*

10. Remove the chain tensioner spring (A, **Figure 58**).

11. Remove the 4 bolts (B, **Figure 58**) securing the tensioner cover and remove it.

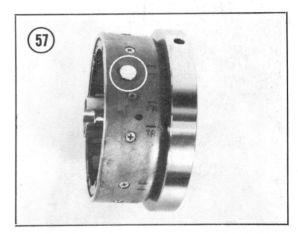

CAUTION
*If the tensioner cover on the bike does not look like the one shown in **Figure 58**, refer to detailed information at the beginning of this procedure for correct parts replacement.*

12. Unscrew chain tensioner bolt (**Figure 59**) and slide the tensioner assembly off of the 2 locating pins (**Figure 60**).

13. Remove the bolt (A, **Figure 60**) securing the stationary cam chain guide and remove it and the small set plate.

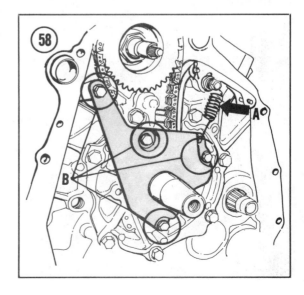

CAUTION
If the bike is not equipped with the small set plate, refer to detailed information at the beginning of this procedure for correct parts replacement.

14. Remove the 2 bolts (**Figure 61**) securing the cam sprocket to the camshaft.

15. Remove the sprocket and chain (**Figure 62**).

16. Remove the 27mm nut (**Figure 63**) securing the cam sprocket boss with a deep socket. Remove the nut, washer, and sprocket boss.

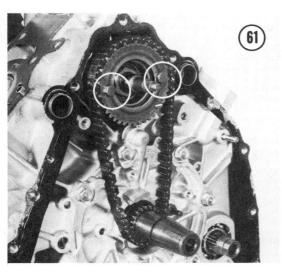

17. Remove the bolt **(Figure 64)** on the fan.

18. Remove the fan with a puller **(Figure 65)**. Screw in the puller until the fan disengages; remove the puller and the fan.

19. Remove the 3 bolts **(Figure 66)** securing the camshaft holder and tachometer drive, and remove it.

20. Withdraw the camshaft and thrust washer from the front of the engine.

CAUTION
Raise all lower rocker arms up off of the cam during removal. Use a piece of wire to hold them up.

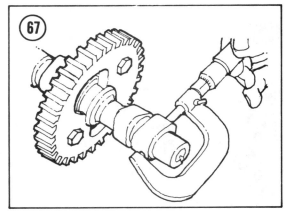

Camshaft Inspection

1. Check the bearing journals for wear and scoring.

2. Check cam lobes for wear. The lobes should not be scored and the edges should be square. Slight damage may be removed with a silicon carbide oilstone. Use No. 100-120 grit initially, then polish with a No. 280-320 grit.

3. Measure the height of each cam lobe with a micrometer as shown in **Figure 67**. Replace the shaft if worn beyond the serviceable limit (measurements less than those given in **Table 6**).

4. Check camshaft bearing bores in the camshaft holder and the cylinder block. Measure the inside diameter with a micrometer and check against measurements given in **Table 6**. Bores should not be excessively worn or scored.

Installation

1. Lubricate the camshaft journals with molybdenum disulfide grease and apply assembly oil to the cam lobes.

2. Install the thrust washer to the end of the camshaft.

3. Insert the camshaft from the front of the engine.

4. Install the O-ring and collar (**Figure 68**). Inspect the gasket on the camshaft holder, if its condition is in doubt, replace it.

5. Lubricate the camshaft holder oil seal with engine oil and install the holder (**Figure 66**).

6. Install the fan and bolt (**Figure 64**).

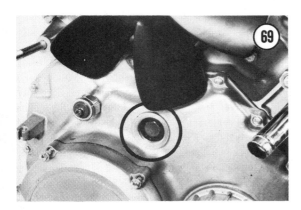

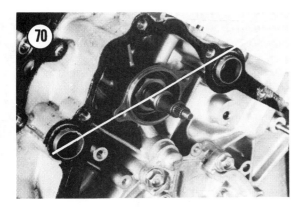

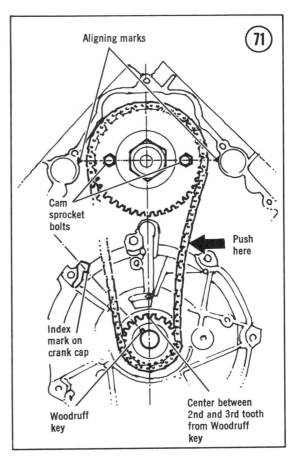

7. Install the camshaft sprocket boss. Align the cutout with the locating pin on the camshaft.

8. Install the lockwasher, with the mark OUT-SIDE facing out, and the locknut. Torque the nut to 58-72 ft.-lb. (79-98 N•m).

9. Rotate the crankshaft until the left-hand piston is at top dead center (TDC). Use the bolt on the front of the crankshaft (**Figure 69**) for turning with a suitable size socket.

10. Verify that the piston is at TDC by checking the following:

   a. The holes in the camshaft sprocket boss (**Figure 70**) are horizontal and align with the punch marks on the cylinder block. Also refer to **Figure 71**.

   b. Check that the Woodruff key on the crankshaft is aligned with the index mark on the crankshaft cap (**Figure 71**).

11. Install the camshaft sprocket and chain (**Figure 62**).

12. Install the 2 bolts (**Figure 61**) and tighten them to 12-14 ft.-lb. (16-19 N•m).

13. After the chain has been installed, press on the chain on the right-hand side so that the tensioner side of the chain is tight. Check again that all items in **Figure 71** are aligned as shown. Proper valve timing depends on the proper relationship of all of these parts.

CAUTION
Very expensive damage to the engine could result from improper installation. Before proceeding, rotate the crankshaft several revolutions with a wrench on the bolt shown in Figure 69. If there is any binding, stop. Determine the cause before assembling beyond this point.

14. Install the set plate (**Figure 72A**) on the guide bolt boss.

NOTE: *Make sure it will not interfere with the installation of the new rear engine cover gasket.*

15. Install the cam chain stationary guide.

16. Install the cam chain tensioner onto the 2 locating pins (**Figure 72B**).

17. Install the lock bolt and O-ring (**Figure 59**). *Do not tighten the bolt at this time.*

18. Install the tensioner cover and center it to ensure even clearance around the crankshaft. Install the 3 lower 6 X 16mm flange bolts and upper left-hand 6 X 30mm flange bolt (B, **Figure 58**). Tighten all 4 bolts to 6-9 ft.-lb. (8-12 N•m). Install the chain tensioner spring (A, **Figure 58**).

19. Install the needle bearing (**Figure 56**), starter gear (**Figure 55**), and the alternator rotor. Install the rotor bolt (**Figure 52**) and tighten it to 58-72 ft.-lb. (79-97 N•m).

> NOTE: *To prevent the flywheel from turning while tightening the bolt, secure it with a strap wrench as shown in Figure 53).*

20. Install alternator pulser rotor (**Figure 51**).

> NOTE: *Align the rotor locating tab with notch in the flywheel when installing the rotor.*

21. Install the 2 locating dowels and O-rings (**Figure 73**), a new rear engine cover gasket and install the rear engine cover. Tighten the 6 mm bolts to 6-9 ft.-lb. (8-12 N•m) and 8 mm bolts to 13-18 ft.-lb (18-25 N•m).

22. Install the water pump impeller, copper washer, and cap nut (B, **Figure 49**).

23. Make sure 2 locating dowels (A, **Figure 49**) are in place.

24. Inspect the O-ring seal (**Figure 74**) on the water pump housing. If it is cracked or deteriorated, replace it. Make sure it is properly seated in the groove, and install the housing.

25. Pour about 3¼ oz. (100cc) of clean engine oil into the oil pockets (**Figure 75**) in the lower rocker arm area.

26. Install the water pipe and clamps to the cylinder block.

> NOTE: *Be sure the O-ring is properly seated between the 2 ribs on the water pipe (Figure 76).*

27. Install the cylinder heads as described under *Cylinder Head Installation* in this chapter.

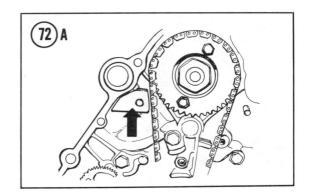

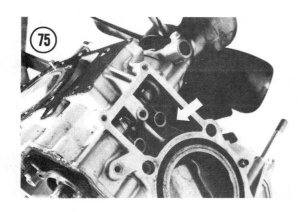

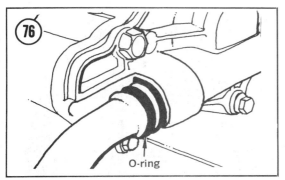

O-ring

28. Install the engine as described under *Engine Removal/Installation* in this chapter.

29. Adjust the valve clearance as described under *Valve Clearance Adjustment* in Chapter Three.

30. Adjust the camshaft chain tension as described under *Camshaft Chain Adjustment* in Chapter Three.

31. Start the engine and check for leaks.

CAMSHAFT CHAIN AND TENSIONER

Replacement

In order to replace the camshaft chain and/or the camshaft chain tensioner, it is necessary to remove the engine from the frame and disassemble it.

Remove the camshaft chain and/or the tensioner as described in Steps 1-15, *Camshaft Removal* in this chapter.

Install by following Steps 9-31, *Camshaft Installation* in this chapter.

LOWER ROCKER ARM ASSEMBLIES

The lower rocker arms ride on the camshaft and activate the pushrods.

In order to gain access to the lower rocker arms it is necessary to remove the engine from the frame and disassemble it.

Removal/Installation

It is important that all parts be assembled in their original positions. Therefore, before disassembling, mark the parts in some way to remind you later.

1. Remove all parts as described in Steps 1-15, *Camshaft Removal* in this chapter.

2. Remove the rocker arm shaft lock bolts (**Figure 77**).

3. Screw in a 6mm bolt into the end of the rocker arm shaft (**Figure 78**) and withdraw the rocker shaft.

4. Remove the rocker arms and springs.

5. Remove the other rocker arm shaft, and remove the rocker arms and springs.

6. Clean all the parts thoroughly in cleaning solvent.

7. Carefully inspect the rocker arm bore and bearing surfaces for signs of wear or scoring. Measure the inside diameter of the rocker arm bore with a micrometer and check the measurements given in **Table 6**. Replace them if defective.

8. Inspect the rocker shafts for signs of wear or scoring. Measure the outside diameter with a micrometer and check against the measurements given in **Table 6**. Replace them if found defective.

9. Check the springs for breakage or distortion. Replace if necessary.

10. Coat the rocker shafts and rocker arm bores liberally with assembly oil or clean engine oil.

11. Install the rocker arms and springs into the cylinder block with the pushrod cup offset in *toward* the lock bolt **(Figure 79)**.

12. Install the rocker arm shaft with the threaded end facing the rear of the engine, toward the camshaft sprocket.

13. Rotate the rocker arm shaft with a screwdriver until the notch aligns with the lock bolt hole. Install the lock bolt.

14. Complete installation by following Steps 9-31, *Camshaft Installation* in this chapter.

PISTONS AND CONNECTING RODS

For removal of pistons and connecting rods it is necessary to remove the engine from the frame and disassemble it.

Removal

1. Remove the engine as described under *Engine Removal/Installation* in this chapter.

2. Remove the cylinder heads as described under *Cylinder Head Removal/Installation* in this chapter.

3. Remove the clutch as described under *Clutch Removal/Installation* in Chapter Five.

4. Remove the oil pump as described under *Oil Pump Removal/Installation* in this chapter.

5. Remove the transmission as described under *Transmission Removal/Installation* in Chapter Five.

6. Lightly mark the top of the piston with a L and R **(Figure 80)** so that they will be installed into the correct cylinder.

> NOTE: *The L and R relate to the engine as it sits in the bike frame.*

7. Scrape all deposits from the top of the cylinder.

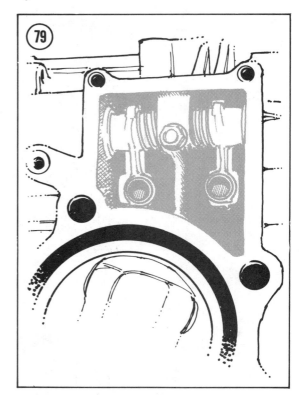

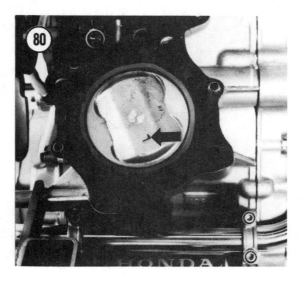

8. Rotate the crankshaft until one of the pistons is at the bottom of its travel. Place an oil-soaked cloth into the cylinder and over the piston to collect the cuttings, then remove the ridge and/or deposits from the upper edge of the cylinder bore with a ridge remover.

9. Turn crankshaft until that piston is at top dead center (TDC), remove cloth and cuttings.

CAUTION
*Make sure none of the cuttings fall into the water jacket (A, **Figure 81**), crankcase breather passageway (B), or lower rocker arm area (C).*

10. Repeat for the other cylinder.

11. Rotate the crankshaft until the piston being removed is at bottom dead center (BDC).

12. Remove the bearing cap nuts and bearing cap (**Figure 82**). Immediately after removal, mark the cap with a L or R so it will be installed on the correct connecting rod.

WARNING
*Protect your hands while working in the lower cylinder block area as there are a lot of sharp edges, especially in the area of rod cap removal (**Figure 83**).*

13. Slowly rotate the crankshaft until the piston is at TDC. Push up on the rod studs enough to push the piston out of the bore so it can be withdrawn from the top. Remove the piston/rod assembly.

14. Repeat Steps 11-13 for the other piston.

15. Remove bearing inserts from the connecting rods and bearing caps. Mark the backs of the bearings with the correct cylinder (L or R) and whether they were upper or lower bearings.

CAUTION
Bearing inserts may be reused if they are in good condition, but they must be reinstalled in their original position.

Disassembly

1. Remove the top ring first by spreading the ends with your thumbs just enough to slide it up over the piston (**Figure 84**). Repeat for the remaining rings.

> WARNING
> *The rail portions of the oil scraper can be very sharp. Be careful when handling them in order to avoid cut fingers.*

2. Before removing the piston, hold the rod tightly and rock the piston as shown in **Figure 85**. Any rocking motion (do not confuse with the normal sliding motion) indicates wear on the wrist pin, rod bushing, pin bore, or more likely, a combination of all three. Mark the piston, pin, and rod so that they will be reassembled into the same set.

3. Remove the circlips from the piston pin bores (**Figure 86**).

4. Heat the piston and pin with a small butane torch. The pin will probably drop right out. If not, heat the piston to about 140°F (60°C), i.e., until it is too warm to touch, but not excessively hot. If the pin is still difficult to push out, use a homemade tool as shown in **Figure 87**.

Piston Inspection

1. Carefully clean the carbon from the piston crown with a chemical remover or a soft scraper. *Do not* remove or damage the carbon ridge around the circumference of the piston above the top ring. If the pistons, rings and cylinders are found to be dimensionally correct

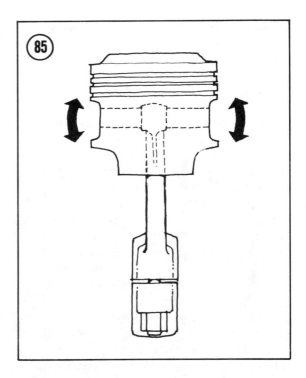

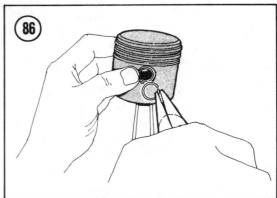

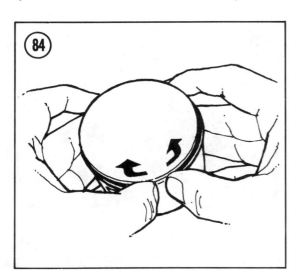

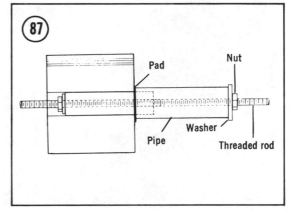

and can be reused, removal of the carbon ring from the tops of the pistons will promote excessive oil consumption.

> CAUTION
> *Do not wire brush piston skirts.*

2. Examine each ring groove for burrs, dented edges, and wide wear. Pay particular attention to the top compression ring groove, as it usually wears more than the others.

3. Measure piston-to-cylinder clearance as described under *Piston Clearance* in this chapter.

4. If damage or wear indicates piston replacement, select a new piston as described under *Piston Clearance* in this chapter.

5. Measure any parts marked in Step 2 of the *Piston Removal* procedure with a micrometer and dial bore gauge to determine which part or parts are worn. Check against measurements given in **Table 6**. Any machinist can do this for you if you do not have micrometers. Replace piston/pin set as a unit if either or both are worn.

Piston Clearance

1. Make sure the piston and cylinder walls are clean and dry.

2. Measure the inside diameter of the cylinder bore at a point ½ in. (13mm) from the upper edge with a bore gauge **(Figure 88)**.

3. Measure the outside diameter of the piston at a point ⅝ in. (15mm) from the lower edge of

the piston 90° to the piston pin axis **(Figure 89)**. Check against measurement given in **Table 6**.

Connecting Rod Inspection

1. Check each rod for obvious damage such as cracks and burns.

2. Check the piston pin bushing for wear or scoring.

3. Take the rods to a machine shop and have them check alignment for twisting and bending.

4. Examine the bearing inserts for wear, scoring, or burning. They are reusable if in good condition. Make a note of the bearing size (if any) stamped on the back of the insert if the bearing is to be discarded; a previous owner may have used undersize bearings.

5. Check bearing clearance and connecting rod side play as described under *Connecting Rod Bearing and Crankpin Inspection*.

Connecting Rod Bearing and Crankpin Inspection

1. Due to the confined space of the cylinder block in the area of the connecting rod cap, it is suggested that the crankshaft be removed as described under *Crankshaft Removal/Installation* in this chapter.

2. Install bearing inserts in the rod and cap.

> CAUTION
> *If the old bearings are reused, be sure that they are installed in their exact original locations.*

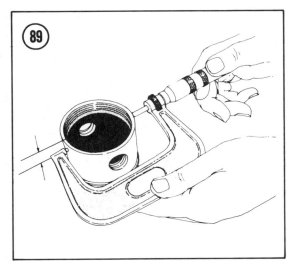

3. Wipe bearing inserts and crankpins clean. Check again that inserts and crankpins are in good condition.

4. Place a piece of Plastigage on one crankpin parallel to the crankshaft. Do not put Plastigage on top of oil holes.

5. Install rod cap and tighten nuts to 20-23 ft.-lb. (27-31 N•m).

CAUTION
Do not rotate crankshaft while Plastigage is in place.

6. Remove rod cap.

7. Measure width of flattened Plastigage according to the manufacturer's instructions. Measure at both ends of the strip. A difference of 0.001 in. (0.025mm) or more indicates a tapered crankpin, indicating that the crankshaft must be reground or replaced.

8. Reassemble the connecting rod (separate from crankshaft) with the bearings in place. Measure bearing ID with inside micrometers.

9. Measure the OD of the crankpin journal with micrometers. Also check the crankpin size code

letter. The inner letter (**Figure 90**) is for the crankpin journals (outer letters are for the main journals).

10. Select new bearings by cross referencing the crankpin journal letter code, horizontal column **Table 1**, to the ID of the rod bearing, vertical column **Table 1**. Where the two columns intersect, the new replacement bearing color is indicated. **Table 2** gives the bearing color and thickness.

11. After new bearings are installed, the clearance should be checked with Plastigage. Recommended clearance for new bearings is 0.008-0.0017 in. (0.020-0.044 mm). Used bearing clearance must not exceed 0.0031 in. (0.08 mm).

12. Repeat Steps 8-11 for the other rod.

13. Measure the inside diameter of the small ends of the connecting rods with an inside dial gauge. Check against measurements given in **Table 6**.

14. Lubricate bearings and crankpins and install rods and rod caps onto the crankshaft. Tighten the nuts to 20-23 ft.-lb. (27-31 N•m).

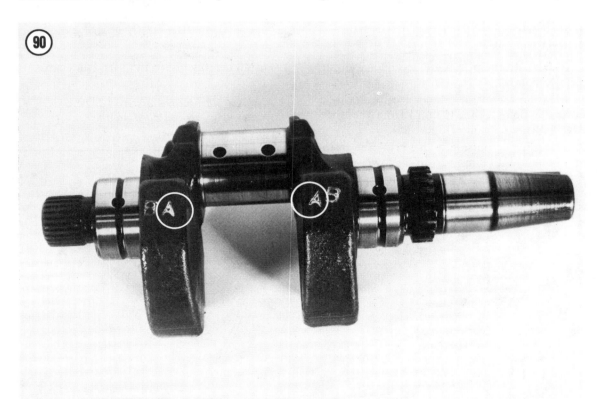

15. Rotate the crankshaft to be sure bearings are not too tight.

16. Insert feeler gauge between connecting rods. Side clearance should be between 0.006-0.007 in. (0.15-0.17mm). Replace any rod that exceeds the service limit of 0.014 in. (0.350mm).

17. Remove the connecting rods.

Assembly

1. Coat the connecting rod bushing, piston pin, and piston holes with assembly lubricant.

2. Place the piston over the connecting rod. If you are reusing the same pistons and connecting rods, match the pistons to the rod from which it came and orient it in the same way.

CAUTION
With the oil hole in the connecting rod facing up, the left-hand (L) piston must be assembled with the IN mark to the left side of the connecting rod and the right-hand (R) piston must be assembled with the IN mark to the right side of the con-

*necting rod. See **Figure 91**. Failure to do so will result in major engine damage.*

3. Insert the piston pin and tap it with a plastic mallet until it starts into the connecting rod bushing. If it does not slide in easily, heat the piston until it is too warm to touch but not excessively hot (140°F or 60°C). Continue to drive the piston in while holding the piston so that the rod does not have to take any shock. Otherwise, it may be bent. Drive the pin in until it is centered in the rod. If pin is still difficult to install, use the homemade tool (**Figure 87**) but eliminate the piece of pipe.

4. Install rings as described in Steps 3-8 under *Piston Ring Replacement*.

5. Insert bearing shells in connecting rod in the bearing cap with the locating tangs locked into place.

CAUTION
*If old bearings are reused, be sure they are installed in their exact original locations. Refer to marks made in Step 15, **Pistons and Connecting Rods-Removal**.*

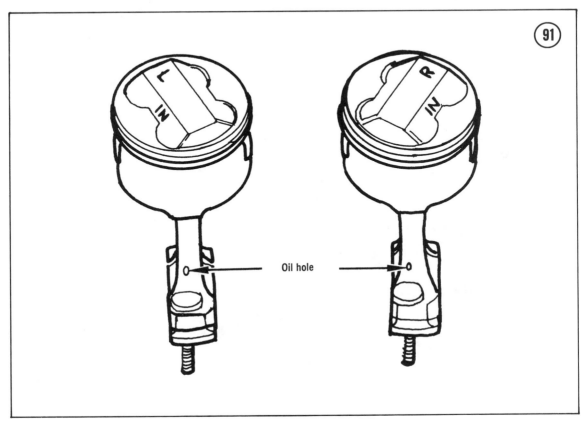

Oil hole

Piston Ring Replacement

1. Remove old rings with a ring expander tool or by spreading the ring ends with your thumbs and lifting the rings up evenly **(Figure 84)**.

2. Carefully remove all carbon from the ring grooves. Inspect grooves carefully for burrs, nicks, or broken and cracked lands. Recondition or replace piston if necessary.

3. Check end gap of each ring. To check ring, insert the ring into the bottom of the cylinder bore and square it with the wall by tapping with the piston. The ring should be in about $\frac{5}{8}$ in. (15mm). Insert a feeler gauge as shown in **Figure 92**. Compare gap with **Table 6**. If the gap is smaller than specified, hold a small file in a vise, grip the ends of the ring with your fingers, and enlarge the gap. See **Figure 93**.

4. Roll each ring around its piston groove as shown in **Figure 94** to check for binding. Minor binding may be cleaned up with a fine cut file.

NOTE: *Install all rings with their markings facing up.*

5. Install oil ring in oil ring groove with a ring expander tool or spread the ends with your thumbs.

6. Install 2 compression rings carefully with a ring expander tool or spread the ends with your thumbs.

7. Check side clearance of each ring as shown in **Figure 95**. Compare with specifications in **Table 6**.

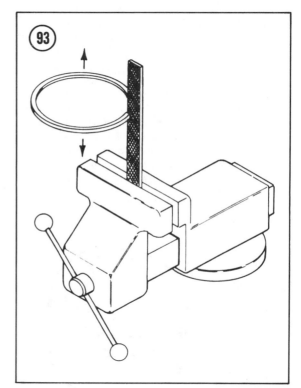

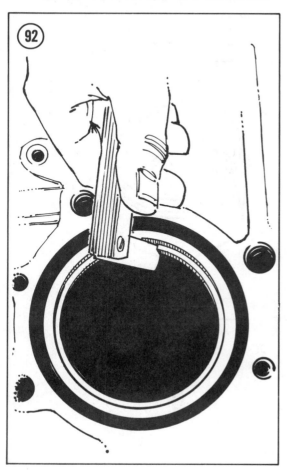

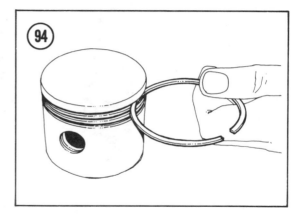

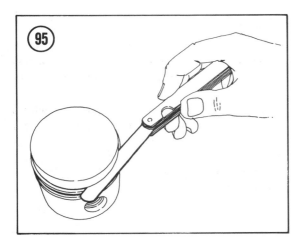

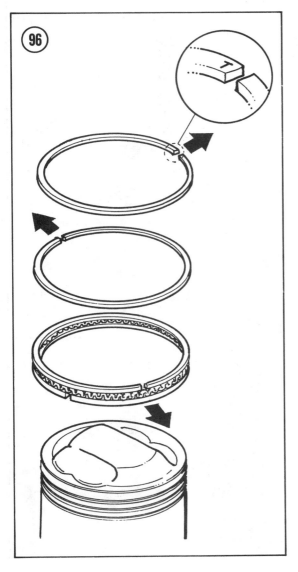

8. Distribute ring gaps around piston as shown in **Figure 96**. The important thing is that the ring gaps are not aligned with each other when installed.

Piston and Connecting Rod Installation

1. Install the crankshaft as described under *Crankshaft Installation* in this chapter.

2. Make certain that the rod bolt threads are clean, and lightly oil them.

3. Lubricate the rod bearings with molybdenum disulphide grease.

4. Rotate the crankshaft to TDC for the left-hand cylinder.

5. Lightly oil the cylinder bore and piston with clean engine oil.

6. Insert the piston/connecting rod assembly in through the top of the cylinder block.

7. Apply a ring compressor to the piston **(Figure 97)**.

CAUTION
Install the piston with the IN mark to the rear of the engine.

8. Insert the piston into the cylinder while guiding the connecting rod onto the crankshaft journal.

NOTE: *Jiggle the rod back and forth slightly so the sharp edge of the bearing insert will not gouge the crankshaft journal.*

9. Install the connecting rod cap and nuts.

CAUTION
Be sure to install the correct rod cap, marked "L" during the removal steps.

10. Tighten the nuts in two or three steps to a final torque of 20-23 ft.-lb. (27-31 N•m).

WARNING
Protect your hands while working in the lower cylinder block area as there are a lot of sharp edges, especially in the area of the rod cap installation (Figure 83).

11. Repeat Steps 4-10 for the right-hand cylinder.

CAUTION
Before proceeding, rotate the crankshaft several revolutions with a wrench on the bolt shown in Figure 69. If there is any binding, stop. Determine the cause before assembling beyond this point.

12. Complete installation by reversing Steps 1-5, *Pistons and Connecting Rods — Removal* in this chapter.

13. Fill the engine with the recommended type and quantity of engine oil and coolant. Refer to Chapter Three.

14. Start the engine and check for leaks.

ALTERNATOR

For removal of the alternator it is necessary to remove the engine from the frame and partially disassemble it.

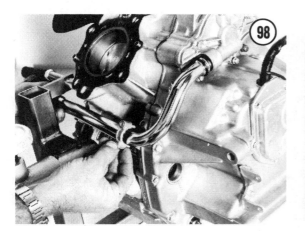

Removal/Installation

1. Remove the engine as described under *Engine Removal/Installation* in this chapter.

NOTE: *The following figures are shown with the cylinder heads removed, it is not necessary to remove them for this procedure.*

2. Remove the 2 clamps securing the water pipe to the cylinder block (**Figure 98**) and remove it.

3. Remove the 5 bolts securing the water pump housing (**Figure 99**) and remove it.

NOTE: *Do not lose the 2 locating dowels (A, Figure 100).*

4. Remove the cap nuts and copper washer (B, **Figure 100**) securing the water pump impeller and remove it.

5. Remove the bolts securing the rear engine cover. Hold the shift lever shaft in position and remove the cover.

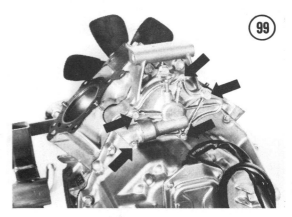

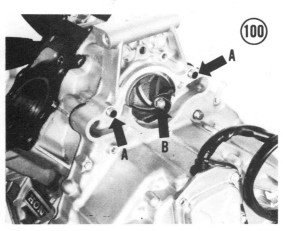

NOTE: *Do not lose the 2 locating dowels and O-rings (Figure 101).*

6. Remove the bolt **(Figure 102)** securing the alternator pulser rotor and remove it.

7. Remove the bolt **(Figure 103)** securing the alternator rotor (flywheel) to the crankshaft with a socket.

NOTE: *To prevent the flywheel from turning while removing the bolt, secure it with a strap wrench as shown in **Figure 104**.*

8. Screw a flywheel puller in all the way until it stops **(Figure 105)**.

9. Hold the flywheel with the strap wrench and rotate the puller *clockwise* until the flywheel disengages from the crankshaft. Remove the flywheel, starter gear **(Figure 106)** and the needle bearing (A, **Figure 107**).

CAUTION
*If the tensioner cover (B, Figure 107) on the bike does not look like the one shown, refer to detailed information, regarding factory replacement parts, at the beginning of the **Camshaft** section in this chapter.*

4

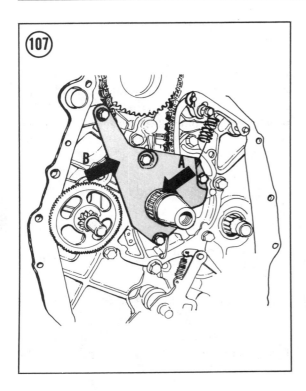

CAUTION
*Be careful not to damage the pulser pickup (**Figure 108**) on the outer surface of the flywheel.*

10. Remove the 5 bolts (**Figure 109**) securing the CDI pulser cover and remove it.

11. Disconnect the electrical wires at the pulser stator, remove the 2 screws (A, **Figure 110**) securing the pulser stator and remove it. Pull the rubber grommets (B, **Figure 110**) out of the rear engine cover.

12. Remove the 3 bolts (A, **Figure 111**) securing the alternator stator and the 2 bolts (B, **Figure 111**), securing the right and left pulsers.

13. Carefully pull the electrical wires through the hole in the rear engine cover.

CAUTION
Do not pull too hard on the stator as it may damage electrical connections where the wires attach to the stator.

14. Install by reversing these removal steps and secure the alternator rotor bolt to 58-72 ft.-lb. (79-97 N•m). Be sure that the Woodruff key, on the crankshaft, is in place and correctly seated prior to installing the rotor.

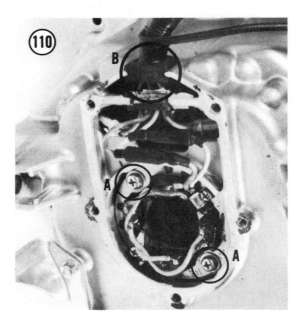

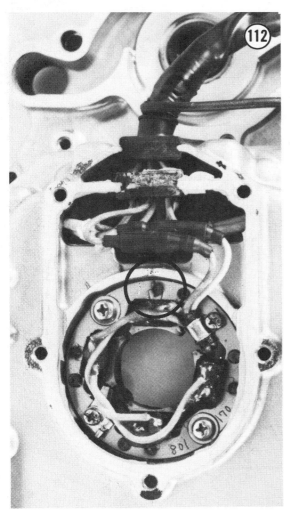

NOTE: *To prevent the flywheel from turning while installing the bolt, secure it with a strap wrench as shown in* **Figure 104.**

15. Be sure the rubber grommet (B, **Figure 110**) is securely in place and that none of the electrical wires are pinched between the stator and the rear engine cover. Make sure the wires are correctly routed.

16. Install the pulser stator and align the index mark on the stator and the rear engine cover **(Figure 112)**.

NOTE: *If the marks are not aligned properly, the ignition timing will be incorrect. Do not try to modify ignition timing by altering the alignment of these marks. This is not the purpose of these marks — they are to be always aligned correctly.*

17. Install the pulsers with their holding tabs facing to the right-hand side, toward the timing inspection hole.

Inspection

The alternator rotor (flywheel) is permanently magnetized and cannot be remagnetized. If it is dropped, the magnetism can be lost. There is no way to check it except by replacing it with a good one.

OIL PUMP

The oil pump can be removed with the engine in the frame.

This sequence is shown with the engine and clutch assembly removed for clarity. It is not necessary to remove them to perform this procedure.

Removal/Installation

1. Remove the radiator assembly as described under *Radiator Removal/Installation* in Chapter Eight.

2. Disconnect the electrical wire from the oil pressure sending switch.

3. Drain the engine oil as described under *Changing Oil and Filter* in Chapter Three.

4. Remove the clutch cable from the clutch lever **(Figure 113)**.

5. Remove the 13 bolts **(Figure 114)** securing the front engine cover and remove it.

6. Remove the bolt securing the oil pump drive sprocket **(Figure 115)**.

7. Remove sprocket and drive chain **(Figure 116)**.

8. Remove the 3 bolts **(Figure 117)** securing the oil pump assembly and remove it **(Figure 118)**.

9. Install by reversing these removal steps.

10. Adjust the drive chain tension to 1/16-1/8 in. (2.0-3.5 mm). See **Figure 119**. Adjust by loosening the bolts (A, **Figure 119**) and pivot the oil pump assembly to right or left until the correct slack is achieved; tighten the bolts.

11. Use a new gasket and make sure the small locating dowel (A, **Figure 120**) and the large dowel and O-ring (B, **Figure 120**) are in place.

12. Fill the engine with the recommended type and quantity of engine oil and coolant. Refer to Chapter Three.

13. Start the engine and check for leaks.

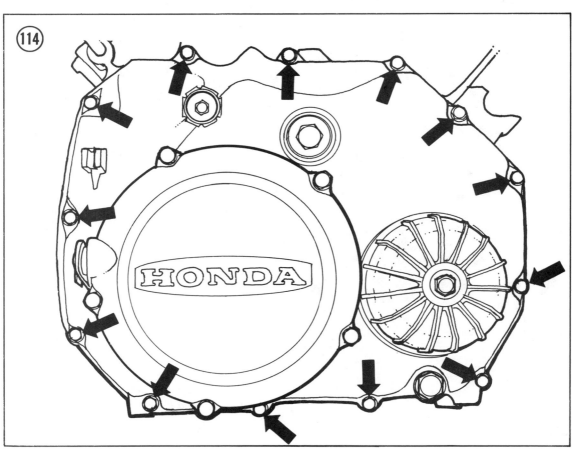

1/16-1/8 in. (2.0-3.5mm)

4

Inspection

1. Check the housing for cracks. Replace if necessary.

2. Remove the 3 screws (A, **Figure 121**) securing the cover and remove it.

3. Measure the clearance between the outer rotor and the body with a flat feeler gauge. If the clearance is 0.014 in. (0.35mm) or greater, the worn part must be replaced.

4. Measure the clearance between the inner and outer rotor with a flat feeler gauge (**Figure 122**). If the clearance is 0.004 in. (0.10 mm) or greater, the worn part must be replaced. Install the cover and tighten the screws securely.

5. Remove the 2 bolts (**Figure 123**) securing the pick-up assembly and remove it.

6. Clean the pick-up assembly in cleaning solvent and thoroughly dry with compressed air. Inspect the screen; if damaged, it should be replaced. Install the pick-up assembly and tighten the bolts securely.

7. Make sure the O-ring (B, **Figure 121**) is in good condition; if the condition is doubtful, replace it.

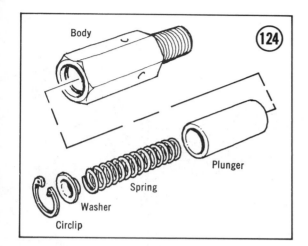

Body

Plunger

Spring

Washer

Circlip

(124)

(125)

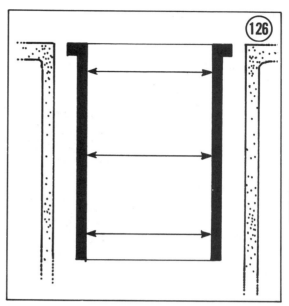

(126)

OIL PRESSURE RELIEF VALVE

Removal/Inspection/Installation

To gain access to the relief valve, follow the removal steps of *Oil Pump Removal/Installation* in this chapter.

1. Unscrew the relief valve from the oil pump.

2. From the backside of the valve, push on the plunger; it should move freely. It will take some effort to push it, though, as it would normally open at 71-85 psi (5.0-6.0 kg/cm²).

3. If it will not move, remove the circlip, washer, spring, and plunger **(Figure 124)** from the body.

4. Wash all parts in solvent and dry with compressed air. Make sure the relief holes in the body are clean.

5. If the spring is broken or the plunger body damaged, the entire unit should be replaced.

6. Coat all parts with assembly oil; reassemble and install on the oil pump.

7. Complete installation by reversing the removal steps of the oil pump.

CYLINDER BLOCK/CRANKCASE

To perform the following steps, turn to the procedure in this chapter for the major assembly indicated, e.g., cylinder head, and perform the removal procedure. To assemble, reverse the disassembly sequence and perform the installation procedure for the major assembly involved.

1. Remove the engine from the frame.

2. Remove the cylinder heads.

3. Remove the clutch.

4. Remove the transmission.

5. Remove the oil pump.

6. Remove the alternator.

7. Remove the camshaft, chain, tensioner, and lower rocker arm assemblies.

8. Remove the shift mechanism.

9. Remove the piston and connecting rod assemblies.

10. Remove the crankshaft.

Cylinder Inspection

Measure the cylinder bores, with a cylinder gauge **(Figure 125)** or inside micrometer, at the points shown in **Figure 126**.

Measure in 2 axes — in line with the wrist pin and at 90° to the pin. If the taper or out-of-round are 0.004 in. (0.10mm) or greater, the cylinders must be rebored to the next oversize and new pistons installed.

> NOTE: *The new pistons should be obtained first before the cylinders are bored so that pistons can be measured; slight manufacturing tolerances must be taken into account to determine the actual size and the working clearance. Piston-to-cylinder clearance should not exceed the service limit of 0.004 in. (0.10mm).*

Cylinder Block Inspection

1. Remove all traces of gasket material from all surfaces. Thoroughly clean the block with cleaning solvent and dry with compressed air.

> NOTE: *Be sure to remove all traces of solvent, as residue will contaminate the engine's oil and cooling systems.*

2. Check the condition of the transmission ball-bearings, the camshaft and crankshaft bearings. Replace if necessary.

3. Check the block for indications of cracks and fatigue. Also check for imperfections in the sealing surfaces of the front and rear engine cover.

CRANKSHAFT

Removal

1. Remove the engine as described under *Engine Removal/Installation* in this chapter.

2. Remove the cylinder heads, pistons, and connecting rod assemblies as described under *Pistons and Connecting Rods Removal/Installation* in this chapter.

3. Remove the alternator and camshaft chain as described in Steps 1-14, *Camshaft Removal* in this chapter.

4. Remove the bolt on the fan (**Figure 127**).

5. Remove the fan with a puller (**Figure 128**). Screw in the puller until the fan disengages; remove the puller and fan.

6. Remove the bolt securing the primary drive gear, oil pump sprocket and side plates from the front of the camshaft.

7. Remove the 7 bolts (**Figure 129**) securing the crankshaft cap and remove it.

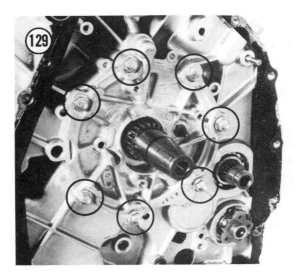

CAUTION
*Prior to removing the crankshaft and cap, wrap the splines of the primary timing gear (**Figure 130**) with vinyl tape to prevent damage to the splines.*

8. Carefully tap the crankshaft and cap assembly out of the cylinder block with a plastic or rubber mallet (**Figure 131**).

CAUTION
Do not use a metal hammer as it will damage the splines and end of shaft.

Installation

1. Coat the bearing surfaces of the crankshaft and cap (**Figure 132**) with molybdenum disulfide grease.

2. Install the crankshaft in the cylinder block (**Figure 133**).

CAUTION
*Be sure that the primary timing gear splines (**Figure 130**) are still wrapped with vinyl tape; if not, retape.*

NOTE: *Be sure the dowel and O-ring are in place (**Figure 133**).*

3. Install the crankshaft cap on partway and start all 7 bolts (**Figure 134**). They are used to guide the cap on so it will not get tilted during installation.

4. Tap around the perimeter of the cap with a plastic or rubber mallet (**Figure 135**) until it is completely seated.

CAUTION
Do not use a metal hammer as it will damage the cap.

5. Tighten cap bolts to 14-17 ft.-lb. (19-23 N•m).

CAUTION

After tightening the bolts, rotate the crankshaft. Make sure it rotates freely, if not, tap the end with a plastic mallet which should free it.

6. Complete assembly by reversing Steps 1-6, *Crankshaft Removal.*

7. Tighten all bolts and nuts to torque values in **Table 4.**

Crankshaft Inspection

1. Clean crankshaft thoroughly with solvent. Clean oil holes with rifle cleaning brushes; flush thoroughly and dry with compressed air. Lightly oil all journal surfaces immediately to prevent rust.

2. Carefully inspect each journal for scratches, ridges, scoring, nicks, etc. Very small nicks and scratches may be removed by grinding — a job for a machine shop.

3. If the surface finish on all journals is satisfactory, take the crankshaft to your dealer or local machine shop. They can check out-of-roundness, taper, and wear on the journals. They can also check crankshaft alignment and inspect for cracks. Check against measurements given in **Table 6.**

4. Check the bearing inserts for evidence of wear, abrasion, and scoring. If the bearings are good, they may be reused. If either insert is questionable, replace both of them.

5. Measure the inner diameter (ID) of the cylinder block bearing support and the crankshaft cap bearing support **(Figure 136)** with inside micrometers.

6. Determine the main journal outer diameter code letters **(Figure 137)**. The outer letters are for the main journals (inner letters are for the crankpins).

7. Select new bearings by cross referencing the main journal codes (A or B), horizontal column in **Table 3**, to the bearing support ID, vertical column in **Table 3**. Where the two columns intersect, the new replacement bearing color will be indicated. **Table 4** gives the bearing color and thickness.

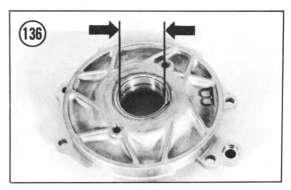

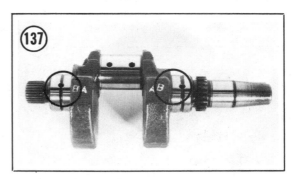

8. After the new bearings are installed the clearance should be checked with Plastigage. Recommended clearance for new bearings is 0.0008-0.0017 in. (0.020-0.044 mm). Used bearings must not exceed 0.0031 in. (0.08 mm).

STARTER GEARS AND CLUTCH

Refer to **Figure 138** for this procedure.

Removal/Installation

1. Remove alternator as described in Steps 1-9, *Alternator Removal/Installation*, this chapter.

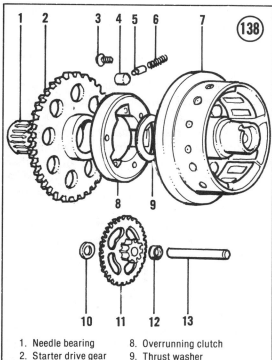

1. Needle bearing
2. Starter drive gear
3. Torx bolts (3)
4. Roller (3)
5. Plunger (3)
6. Spring (3)
7. Alternator flywheel
8. Overrunning clutch
9. Thrust washer
10. Thrust washer
11. Starter reduction gear
12. Thrust washer
13. Starter reduction gear shaft

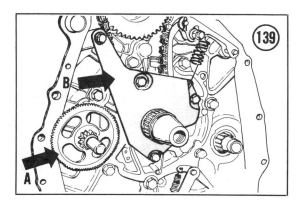

2. Remove starter reduction gear (**A, Figure 139**) and thrust washers.

CAUTION

*If the tensioner cover (B, **Figure 139**) on the bike does not look like the one shown, refer to detailed information, regarding factory replacement parts, at the beginning of the **Camshaft** section in this chapter.*

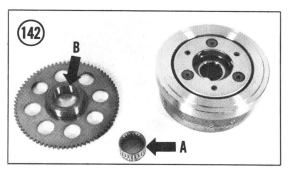

3. Remove the starter drive gear and thrust washer from the alternator flywheel.

NOTE

*A special tool is required for removal of the Torx bolts. The size is T-40 and it is available in the Allen wrench configuration as shown in **Figure 140** or a configuration similar to a screwdriver. These tools are manufactured by Proto and Apex and are available at most large hardware, automotive or motorcycle supply stores.*

4. Remove the 3 Torx bolts (**Figure 141**) securing the starter clutch to the alternator flywheel. Discard the Torx bolts; do not reuse them.

5. Inspect the gears for chipped or missing teeth. Look for uneven or excessive wear on the gear faces. Replace if necessary.

6. Check the rollers in the starter clutch for uneven or excessive wear; replace as a set if any are bad.

7. Check the condition of the bearing (A, **Figure 142**) and the bearing race in the gear (B, **Figure 142**). Replace either if necessary.

8. Install by reversing these removal steps. Apply Loctite Lock N' Seal, or equivalent, to new Torx bolts prior to installation and torque them to 14-17 ft.-lb. (19-23 N•m).

BREAK-IN

Following cylinder servicing (boring, honing, new rings, etc.) and major lower end work, the engine should be broken in just as though it were new. The performance and service life of the engine depend greatly on a careful and sensible break-in.

For the first 500 miles no more than one-third throttle should be used and speed should be varied as much as possible within the one-third throttle limit. Prolonged, steady running at one speed, no matter how moderate, is to be avoided, as is hard acceleration.

Following the 500-mile service increasingly more throttle can be used, but full throttle should not be used until the motorcycle has covered at least 1,000 miles, and then it should be limited to short bursts until 1,500 miles have been logged.

The mono-grade oils recommended for break-in and normal use provide a bedding pattern for rings and cylinders superior to that of multi-grade oils. As a result, piston ring and cylinder bore life are greatly increased. During this period, oil consumption will be higher than normal. It is therefore important to frequently check and correct the oil level. At no time, during break-in or later, should the oil level be allowed to drop below the bottom line on the dipstick; if the oil level is low, the oil will become overheated resulting in insufficient lubrication and increased wear.

500-Mile Service

It is essential that oil and filter be changed after the first 500 miles. In addition, it is a good idea to change the oil and filter at the completion of break-in (about 1,500 miles) to ensure that all of the particles produced during break-in are removed from the lubrication system. The small added expense may be considered a smart investment that will pay off in increased engine life.

Table 1   CONNECTING ROD BEARING SELECTION

Crankpin journal size code letter and dimension	Letter A: 1.5745-1.5748 in. (39.992-40.000mm)	Letter B: 1.5742-1.5745 in. (39.984-39.992mm)	Letter C: 1.5739-1.5742 in. (39.976-39.984mm)
Connecting rod ID code number and dimension	Color Identification		
No. 1: 1.6929-1.6932 in. (43.000-43.008mm)	Pink	Yellow	Green
No. 2: 1.6932-1.6935 in. (43.008-43.016mm)	Yellow	Green	Brown
No. 3: 1.6935-1.6939 in. (43.016-43.024mm)	Green	Brown	Black

Table 2   CONNECTING ROD BEARING THICKNESS

Color	Bearing Thickness Inches	Millimeters
Black	0.0592-0.0593	1.503-1.507
Brown	0.0590-0.0592	1.499-1.503
Green	0.0588-0.0590	1.495-1.499
Yellow	0.0587-0.0588	1.491-1.495
Pink	0.0585-0.0587	1.487-1.491

Table 3   MAIN JOURNAL BEARING SELECTION

Crankcase/Cap Bearing Support ID	Main Journal OD Code Letter A	B
1.8504-1.8508 in. (47.000-47.010mm)	Brown	Black
1.8508-1.8517 in. (47.010-47.020mm)	Black	Blue

Table 4   MAIN JOURNAL BEARING THICKNESS

Color	Inches	Millimeters
Brown	0.0783-0.0787	1.989-1.999
Black	0.0785-0.0789	1.994-2.004
Blue	0.0787-0.0791	1.999-2.009

Table 5   ENGINE TORQUE SPECIFICATIONS

Item	Foot-pounds (ft.-lb.)	Newton meters (N•m)
Cylinder head bolts		
6mm	6-9	8-12
12mm	33-40	45-54
Camshaft locknut	58-72	79-98
Camshaft sprocket bolts	12-14	16-19
Crankshaft end cap bolts	14-17	19-23
Rod bearing cap nuts	20-23	27-31
Cooling fan bolt	14-18	19-24
Oil filter bolt	14-18	19-24
Alternator rotor bolt	58-72	79-97
Clutch center nut	58-72	79-97
Radiator drain bolt	1-2	1.4-2.7

Table 6   ENGINE SPECIFICATIONS

Item	Specifications (new)	Wear Limit
General		
Number of cylinders	2	
Bore X stroke	3.071 × 2.047 in. (78 × 52mm)	
Displacement	30.3 cu.in. (496cc)	
Compression ratio	10:1	
Compression pressure (cold)	171 ± 20 psi (12 ± 2 kg/cm²)	
Cylinders		
Bore	3.0708-3.0714 in. (78.000-78.015mm)	3.0748 in. (78.10mm)
Cylinder/piston clearance	_____	0.004 in. (0.10mm)
Out-of-round	_____	0.004 in. (0.10mm)
Warpage	_____	0.004 in. (0.10mm)
Pistons		
Diameter	3.068-3.069 in. (77.940-77.960mm)	3.065 in. (77.860mm)
Clearance in bore	_____	0.004 in. (0.10mm)
Wrist pin bore	0.8268-0.8271 in. (21.002-21.008mm)	0.828 in. (21.040mm)
Wrist pin outer diameter	0.8265-0.8268 in. (20.994-21.000mm)	0.8261 in. (20.984mm)
Ring end gap		
Top	0.004-0.012 in. (0.1-0.3mm)	0.024 in. (0.60mm)
Second	0.004-0.012 in. (0.1-0.3mm)	0.024 in. (0.60mm)
Oil control ring	0.012-0.35 in. (0.3-0.9mm)	0.043 in. (1.10mm)
Ring side clearance		
Top	0.0006-0.0020 in. (0.015-0.050mm)	0.004 in. (0.10mm)
Second	0.0006-0.0020 in. (0.015-0.050mm)	0.004 in. (0.10mm)
Crankshaft		
Main bearing journal oil clearance	0.0008-0.0023 in. (0.020-0.060mm)	0.0033 in. (0.085mm)
Connecting Rods		
Side clearance	0.006-0.007 in. (0.150-0.170mm)	0.0138 in. (0.350mm)
Bearing clearance (large end)	0.0008-0.0017 in. (0.02-0.04mm)	0.003 in. (0.080mm)
Wrist pin inner diameter	0.8276-0.8283 in. (21.020-21.041mm)	0.8294 in. (21.068mm)
Camshaft		
Valve timing		
Intake	Opens 6° BTDC, closes 46° ABDC	_____
Exhaust	Opens 46° BBDC, closes 6° ATDC	_____
Cam lobe height		
Intake	1.4585 in. (37.046mm)	1.4196 in. (36.058mm)
Exhaust	1.4573 in. (37.015mm)	1.4184 in. (36.027mm)

(continued)

Table 6   ENGINE SPECIFICATIONS (continued)

Item	Specification (new)	Wear Limit
Cam holder inner diameter	0.866-0.867 in. (22.000-22.021mm)	0.868 in. (22.050mm)
Cam block journal inner diameter	1.023-1.024 in. (26.000-26.021mm)	1.03 in. (26.170 mm)
Valves		
Valve stem clearance		
Intake	————	0.004 in. (0.10mm)
Exhaust	————	0.004 in. (0.10mm)
Valve guide inner diameter		
Intake	0.259-0.261 in. (6.600-6.620mm)	0.264 in. (6.70mm)
Exhaust	0.259-0.261 in. (6.600-6.620mm)	0.264 in. (6.70mm)
Valve stem outer diameter		
Intake	0.2591-0.2594 in. (6.580-6.590mm)	0.257 in. (6.54mm)
Exhaust	0.2579-0.2583 in. (6.550-6.560mm)	0.2575 in. (6.54mm)
Valve seat width	0.04-0.05 in. (1.1-1.3mm)	0.08 in. (2.0mm)
Upper and Lower **Rocker Arm Assembly**		
Rocker arm bore inner diameter	0.5512-0.5522 in. (14.00-14.027 mm)	0.553 in. (14.05mm)
Rocker shaft outer diameter	0.5505-0.5512 in. (13.982-14.000mm)	0.549 in. (13.96mm)
Upper rocker arm holder inner diameter	0.5512-0.5522 in. (14.00-14.027mm)	0.553 in. (14.05mm)
Valve Springs		
Free length (inner)		
Intake	1.98 in. (50.3mm)	1.91 in. (48.5mm)
Exhaust	1.98 in. (50.3mm)	1.91 in. (48.5mm)
Free length (outer)		
Intake	1.98 in. (50.3mm)	1.91 in. (48.5mm)
Exhaust	1.98 in. (50.3mm)	1.91 in. (48.5mm)
Length under load (inner)		
Intake	1.49 in. @ 25.4 lb. (37.9mm @ 11.5 kg)	1.49 in. @ 23.2 lb. (37.9mm @ 10.5 kg)
Exhaust	1.49 in. @ 25.4 lb. (37.9mm @ 11.5 kg)	1.49 in. @ 23.2 lb. (37.9mm @ 10.5 kg)
Length under load (outer)		
Intake	1.57 in. @ 61.7 lb. (39.9mm @ 28.5kg)	1.566 in. @ 58.4 lb. (39.8mm @ 26.5 kg)
Exhaust	1.57 in. @ 61.7 lb. (39.9mm @ 28.5 kg)	1.566 in. @ 58.4 lb. (39.8mm @ 26.5 kg)

4

NOTE: If you own a 1980 or later model, first check the Supplement at the back of the book for any new service information.

CHAPTER FIVE

CLUTCH AND TRANSMISSION

CLUTCH

The clutch on the Honda CX500 is a wet multi-plate type which operates immersed in the engine oil.

All clutch parts can be removed with the engine in the frame. This sequence is shown with the engine assembly removed for clarity; it is not necessary to remove it to perform this procedure.

Figure 1 shows all clutch parts.

Removal

1. Place the bike on the centerstand.

2. Drain the engine oil as described under *Changing Oil and Filter* in Chapter Three.

3. Remove the exhaust system as described under *Exhaust System Removal/Installation* in Chapter Six.

4. Remove the rubber plugs and screws, 2 on each side (**Figure 2**) securing the radiator shroud. Slide the shroud forward and down and remove it.

5. Disconnect the clutch cable at the clutch housing (**Figure 3**).

6. Remove the 5 bolts (**Figure 4**) securing the clutch cover and remove it.

7. Remove the 4 bolts, in a crisscross pattern, securing the lifter plate and bearing (**Figure 5**).

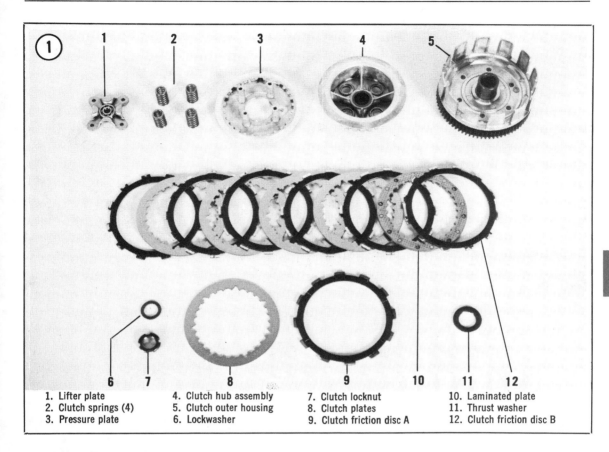

1. Lifter plate
2. Clutch springs (4)
3. Pressure plate
4. Clutch hub assembly
5. Clutch outer housing
6. Lockwasher
7. Clutch locknut
8. Clutch plates
9. Clutch friction disc A
10. Laminated plate
11. Thrust washer
12. Clutch friction disc B

5

8. Remove the 4 springs (**Figure 6**).

9. Loosen the clutch locknut with a drift and a hammer (**Figure 7**); remove it and the lockwasher.

10. Remove the clutch hub, the 6 clutch plates, the 7 friction discs, and the pressure plate as an assembly (**Figure 8**).

> NOTE: *The outermost friction disc ("B" disc) is thicker than the other 6 friction discs. Remember this when installing them.*

11. Remove the outer housing (A, **Figure 9**) and the bushing (B, **Figure 9**).

12. Remove the thrust washer.

Inspection

1. Clean all clutch parts in petroleum-based solvent such as kerosene and thoroughly dry with compressed air.

2. Measure the free length of each clutch spring as shown in **Figure 10**. New springs measure 1.3346 in. (33.90mm). Replace the springs that are 1.2795 in. (32.5mm) or less.

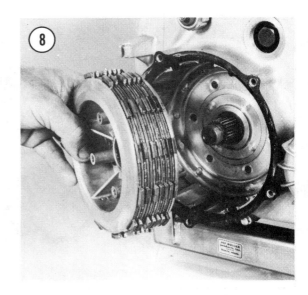

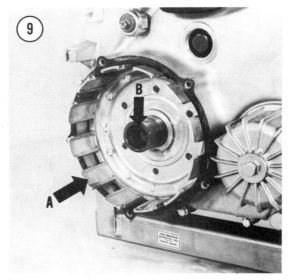

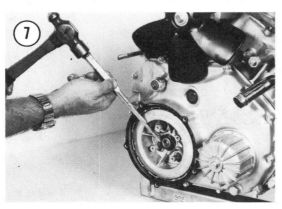

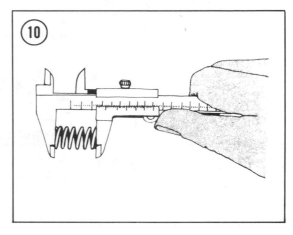

3. Measure the thickness of each friction disc at several places around the disc as shown in **Figure 11**. Compare them to the measurements in **Table 1**. Replace any that are worn to the wear limit. The "B" disc is the outermost friction disc, located against the clutch hub.

4. Check all other parts for signs of wear or other damage. Replace any parts as necessary.

Installation

Install by reversing the removal steps and noting the following steps. Refer to **Figure 1** for this procedure.

1. After installing the thrust washer, outer clutch housing and the pressure plate, alternate the 6 thin friction discs ("A" disc) and the 6 clutch plates as shown in **Figure 12**. The thicker

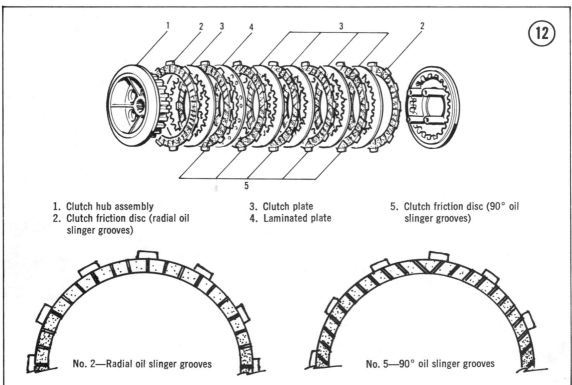

1. Clutch hub assembly
2. Clutch friction disc (radial oil slinger grooves)
3. Clutch plate
4. Laminated plate
5. Clutch friction disc (90° oil slinger grooves)

No. 2—Radial oil slinger grooves

No. 5—90° oil slinger grooves

Table 1   CLUTCH DISC THICKNESS

Type/Quantity	New	Wear Limit
A disc (6)	0.106 in. (2.7mm)	0.091 in. (2.3mm)
B disc (1)	0.138 in. (3.5mm)	0.122 in. (3.1mm)

friction disc ("B" disc) is the last one to be installed and the thicker laminated plate is the next to last to be installed.

> NOTE: *Note direction of oil slinger grooves in friction discs. See* ***Figure 12***.

> *CAUTION*
> *The clutch plates and discs must be installed in sequence shown in* ***Figure 12*** *or the clutch will be damaged.*

2. Install the lockwasher and locknut. Torque the nut to 58-72 ft.-lb. (79-97 N•m).

3. Adjust the clutch cable as described under *Clutch Cable Adjustment* in Chapter Three.

4. Fill the engine with the recommended type and quantity of engine oil; refer to Chapter Three.

CLUTCH CABLE

Removal/Installation

In time, the cable will stretch to the point where it is no longer useful and will have to be replaced.

1. Loosen the adjusting nut (**Figure 13**) and disconnect the cable from the hand lever.

2. Loosen the locknut and adjusting nut (A, **Figure 14**) at the front engine cover.

3. Disconnect the bottom end of the cable (B, **Figure 14**) from the operating lever.

> NOTE: *Prior to removing the cable, make a drawing of the cable routing through the frame. It is very easy to forget how it was, once it has been removed. Replace it exactly as it was, avoiding any sharp turns.*

4. Remove the rubber plugs and screws, 2 on each side (**Figure 2**) securing the radiator shroud. Slide the shroud forward and down and remove it.

5. Remove the cable from the frame and replace with a new one. Install the radiator shroud.

6. Adjust the cable free play as described under *Clutch Free Play Adjustment* in Chapter Three.

SHIFTING MECHANISM

The engine must be removed from the frame and partially disassembled to gain access to the shifting mechanism.

Refer to **Figure 15** for this procedure.

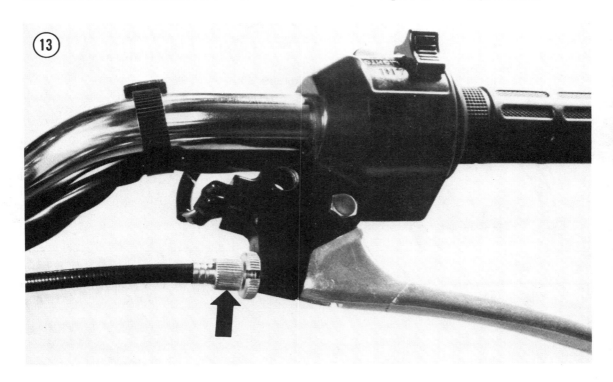

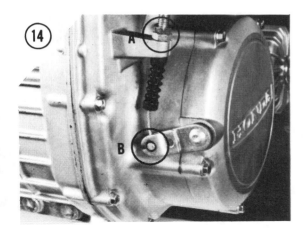

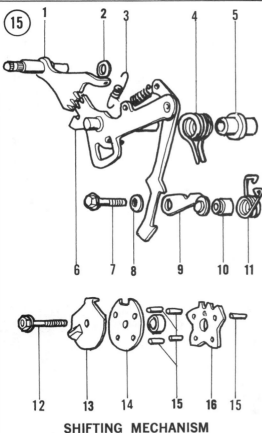

SHIFTING MECHANISM

1. Shift lever arm
2. Shift lever arm bushing
3. Shift lever arm spring
4. Gearshift return spring
5. Shift spindle collar
6. Shift arm/shift spindle
7. Bolt
8. Washer
9. Shift pawl
10. Spacer
11. Shift pawl spring
12. Bolt
13. Neutral switch plate
14. Center plate
15. Shift drum pins (5)
16. Shift drum cam plate

Removal/Installation

1. Remove the engine as described under *Engine Removal/Installation* in Chapter Four.

2. Remove the alternator as described under *Alternator Removal/Installation* in Chapter Four.

3. Shift transmission to neutral position.

4. Remove the shift lever arm and spindle (**Figure 16**).

5. Push the gear shift arm away from the shift drum and remove the gear shift arm, spindle return spring, and spindle collar (**Figure 17**).

6. Loosen approximately 3 to 4 turns, the bolt securing the detent arm (**Figure 18**).

5

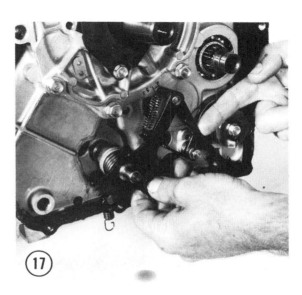

7. Flip the pawl out and off of the cam plate, remove bolt and remove the pawl and spring (**Figure 19**).

8. Remove the bolt securing the cam plate (**Figure 20**) and remove it.

9. Remove the cam (**Figure 21**) and the 5 pins.

10. Install by reversing these removal steps. Apply Loctite Lock N' Seal to the 6 mm bolt securing the cam plate (**Figure 22**).

11. Make sure the transmission is still in the neutral position. Make sure the teeth on the shift lever (A, **Figure 23**) and the gear shift lever (B, **Figure 23**) mesh properly.

12. Fill the engine with the recommended type and quantity of engine oil and coolant; refer to Chapter Three.

13. Start the engine and check for leaks.

TRANSMISSION

The transmission is a 5-speed constant mesh type; all components are shown in **Figure 24**.

Transmission specifications are covered in **Table 2**.

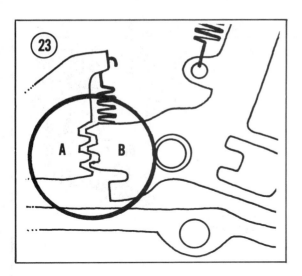

Disassembly

1. Remove the engine as described under *Engine Removal/Installation* in Chapter Four.

2. Remove the shifting mechanism as described under *Shifting Mechanism Removal/Installation* in this chapter.

3. Remove the clutch assembly as described under *Clutch Removal/Installation* in this chapter.

4. Remove the 13 bolts (**Figure 25**) securing the front engine cover and remove it.

> NOTE: *Figures 26 and 27 are shown with the oil pump assembly removed. It is not necessary to remove it to perform this procedure.*

5

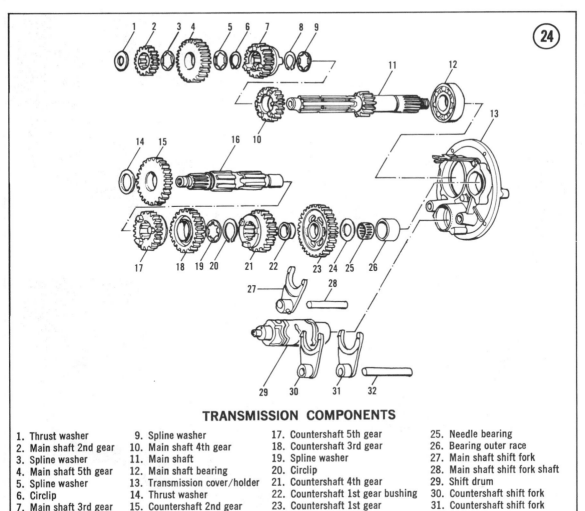

TRANSMISSION COMPONENTS

1. Thrust washer	9. Spline washer	17. Countershaft 5th gear	25. Needle bearing
2. Main shaft 2nd gear	10. Main shaft 4th gear	18. Countershaft 3rd gear	26. Bearing outer race
3. Spline washer	11. Main shaft	19. Spline washer	27. Main shaft shift fork
4. Main shaft 5th gear	12. Main shaft bearing	20. Circlip	28. Main shaft shift fork shaft
5. Spline washer	13. Transmission cover/holder	21. Countershaft 4th gear	29. Shift drum
6. Circlip	14. Thrust washer	22. Countershaft 1st gear bushing	30. Countershaft shift fork
7. Main shaft 3rd gear	15. Countershaft 2nd gear	23. Countershaft 1st gear	31. Countershaft shift fork
8. Circlip	16. Countershaft	24. Thrust washer	32. Countershaft shift fork shaft

Table 2   5-SPEED TRANSMISSION SPECIFICATIONS

Item	Standard Value	Wear Limit
Main shaft outer diameter	0.9819-0.9826 in. (24.940-24.959mm)	0.9823 in. (24.95mm)
Countershaft outer diameter At 1st gear location	0.7869-0.7874 in. (19.987-20.000mm)	0.7858 in. (19.96mm)
At 2nd gear location	1.0811-1.0819 in. (27.459-27.480mm)	1.0799 in. (27.43mm)
At 3rd and 4th gear location	0.9826-0.9835 in. (24.959-24.980mm)	0.9815 in. (24.93mm)
At 5th gear location	1.2579-1.2586 in. (31.950-31.975mm)	1.2526 in. (31.91mm)
1st gear bushing Outer diameter	0.9443-0.9451 in. (23.984-24.005mm)	0.9429 in. (23.95mm)
Inner diameter	0.7882-0.7890 in. (20.020-20.041mm)	0.7898 in. (20.06mm)
Gear-to-bushing clearance		0.006 in. (0.15mm)

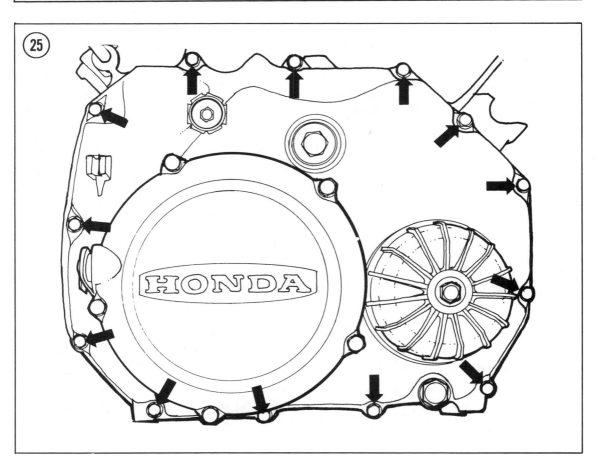

(25)

26

27

28

5. Remove the 3 bolts (**Figure 26**) securing the oil splash shield and remove it.

6. Remove the 3 remaining bolts (**Figure 27**) securing the transmission cover/holder.

7. Carefully pull the transmission assembly out of the cylinder block. It will come out as a complete assembly (**Figure 28**).

CAUTION
After removal, hold the assembly upright, with the cover to the bottom, as some of the parts may fall out.

8. Remove the 2 shift fork assemblies (**Figures 29 and 30**).

5

29

30

9. Remove the shift drum (**Figure 31**).

10. Remove countershaft assembly (**Figure 32**).

11. Remove main shaft assembly (**Figure 33**).

Assembly

Prior to assembly, coat all bearings and bearing surfaces with assembly oil.

1. Install the main shaft assembly (**Figure 33**) and countershaft assembly (**Figure 32**) into the transmission cover/holder.

> NOTE: *Hold the thrust washer in place while installing the countershaft.*

2. Tap on the ends of both shafts with a plastic or rubber mallet to make sure the shafts are completely seated.

3. Install the shift drum (**Figure 31**).

4. Slide the countershaft shift forks onto the long shaft. Insert the shift forks into the gears (**Figure 34**) and install the shaft into the transmission cover/holder (**Figure 35**).

5. Engage the main shaft shift fork onto the gear (**Figure 36**). Insert the short shaft onto the shift fork and into the transmission cover/holder (**Figure 37**).

6. Place transmission into neutral position.

7. Insert the transmission assembly into the cylinder block. Press the cover/holder into place while rotating the main shaft.

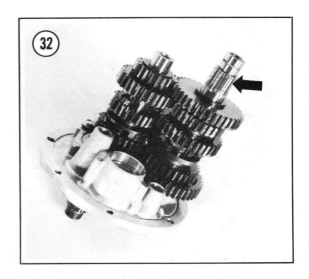

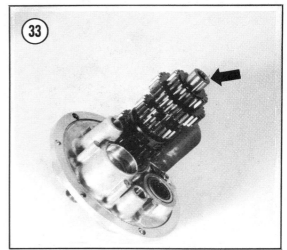

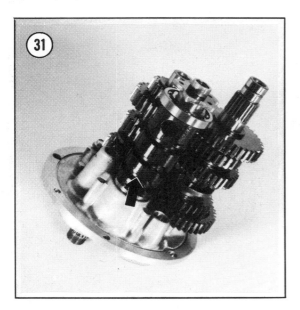

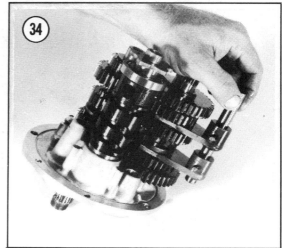

8. Install only the 3 bolts shown in **Figure 38**, securing the cover/holder.

9. Install the 3 bolts (**Figure 39**) securing the oil splash shield.

10. Install the front engine cover, using a new gasket, and the clutch assembly and the shift mechanism.

11. Install the engine.

12. Adjust the clutch cable as described under *Clutch Free Play Adjustment* in Chapter Three.

13. Fill the engine with the recommended type and quantity of engine oil and coolant; refer to Chapter Three.

14. Start the engine and check for leaks.

5

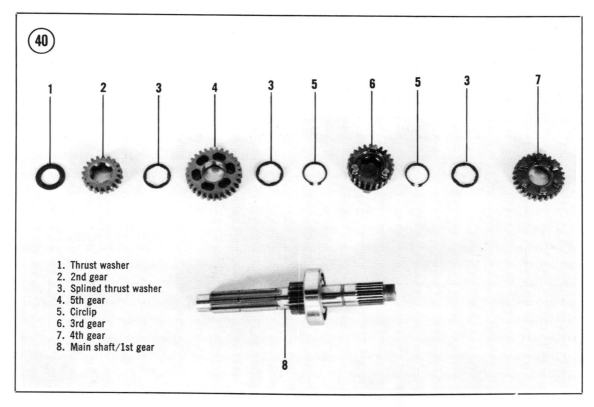

40

1. Thrust washer
2. 2nd gear
3. Splined thrust washer
4. 5th gear
5. Circlip
6. 3rd gear
7. 4th gear
8. Main shaft/1st gear

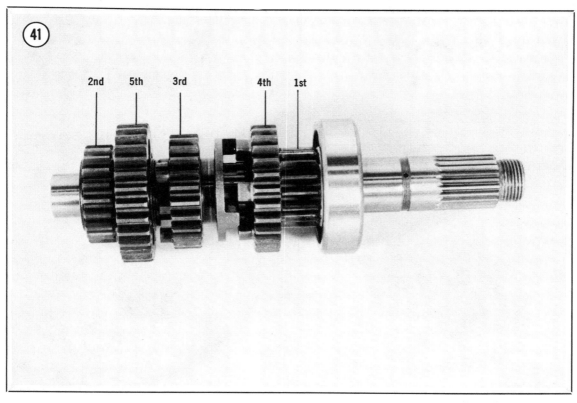

41

Main Shaft Disassembly

Refer to **Figures 40 and 41** for this procedure.

1. Slide off the thrust washer (A, **Figure 42**) and 2nd gear (B, **Figure 42**).

2. Remove spline washer (A, **Figure 43**) and 5th gear (B, **Figure 43**).

3. Remove the spline washer and circlip **(Figure 44)**.

4. Slide off 3rd gear **(Figure 45)**.

5. Remove the circlip (A, **Figure 46**), spline washer (B, **Figure 46**), and slide off 4th gear (C, **Figure 46**).

6. If necessary, remove the ball bearing from the shaft.

7. Clean all parts in solvent and thoroughly dry.

8. Check each gear for excessive wear, burrs, pitting, chipped or missing teeth. Make sure the lugs on ends of gears are in good condition.

NOTE: *Defective gears should be replaced, and it is a good idea to replace the mating gear on the countershaft even though it may not show as much wear or damage.*

9. Make sure that all gears slide smoothly on the main shaft splines.

10. Check the bearing. Make sure it operates smoothly with no signs of wear or damage.

11. Assemble by reversing the removal steps. Refer to **Figure 40** for correct positioning of gears. Make sure all snap rings are correctly seated in main shaft grooves.

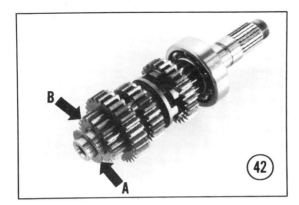

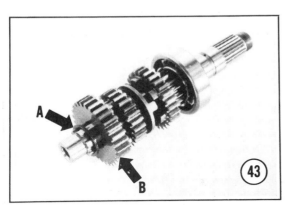

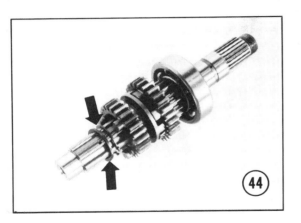

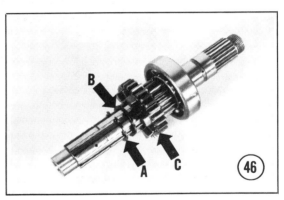

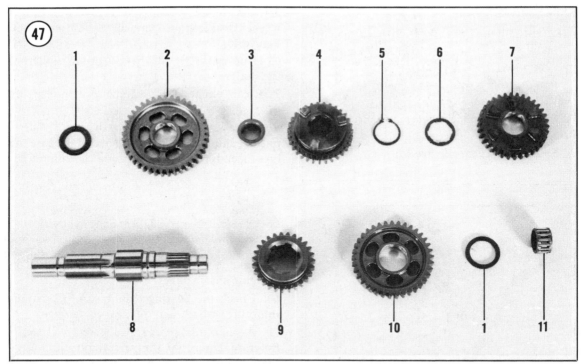

1. Thrust washer
2. 1st gear
3. 1st gear collar
4. 4th gear
5. Circlip
6. Splined thrust washer
7. 3rd gear
8. Countershaft
9. 5th gear
10. 2nd gear
11. Needle bearing

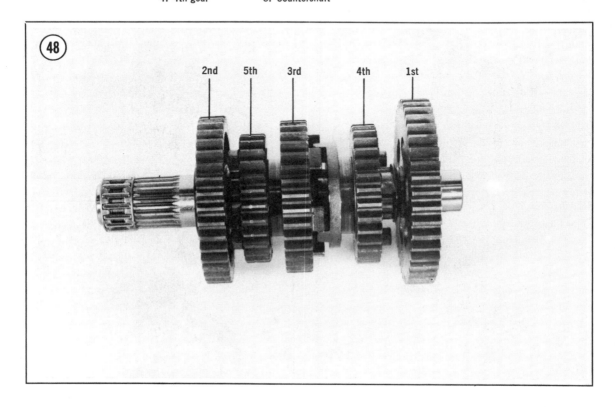

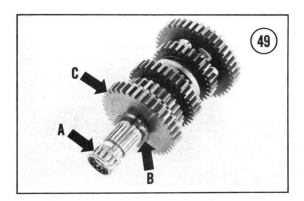

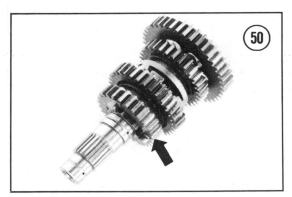

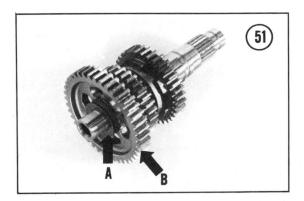

Countershaft Disassembly

Refer to **Figures 47 and 48** for this procedure.

1. Slide off the needle bearing (A, **Figure 49**), thrust washer (B, **Figure 49**) and 2nd gear (C, **Figure 49**).

2. Slide off 5th gear (**Figure 50**).

3. Slide off the thrust washer (A, **Figure 51**) and 1st gear (B, **Figure 51**).

4. Remove the 1st gear collar (**Figure 52**).

5. Slide off 4th gear (**Figure 53**).

6. Remove the circlip and thrust washer (**Figure 54**).

7. Slide off 3rd gear (**Figure 55**).

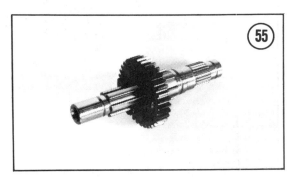

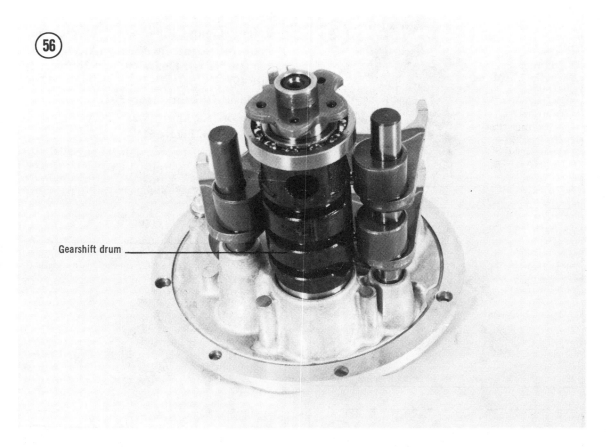

Gearshift drum

8. Clean all parts in solvent and thoroughly dry.

9. Check each gear for excessive wear, burrs, pitting, and for chipped or missing teeth. Make sure that the lugs on the ends of the gears are in good condition.

> NOTE: *Defective gears should be replaced, and it is a good idea to replace the mating gear on the main shaft even though it may not show as much wear or damage.*

10. Make sure that all gears slide smoothly on the countershaft splines.

11. Assemble by reversing the removal steps. Refer to **Figure 48** for correct positioning of gears. Make sure that the snap ring is correctly seated in the countershaft groove.

GEARSHIFT DRUM AND FORKS

Refer to **Figures 56 and 57** for this procedure.

Disassembly/Assembly

1. Perform Steps 1-9, *Transmission Disassembly* in this chapter.

2. Wash all parts in solvent and thoroughly dry.

3. Inspect as described later and assemble by performing Steps 3-14, *Transmission Assembly* in this chapter.

Inspection

1. Measure the inside diameter of the shift forks with an inside micrometer (**Figure 58**). Replace the ones worn beyond the wear limits given in **Table 3**.

2. Measure the width of the gearshift fingers with a micrometer (**Figure 59**). Replace the ones worn beyond the wear limit given in **Table 3**.

> NOTE: *Check for any arc shaped wear marks (Figure 60) on the shift forks. If this is apparent, the shift fork has come in contact with the gear, indicating the*

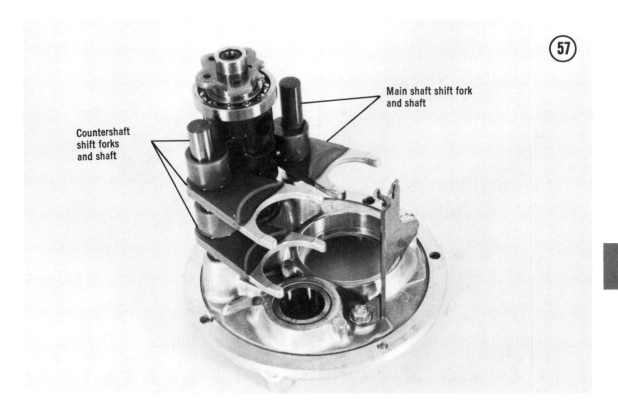

Main shaft shift fork and shaft

Countershaft shift forks and shaft

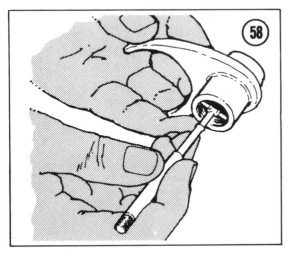

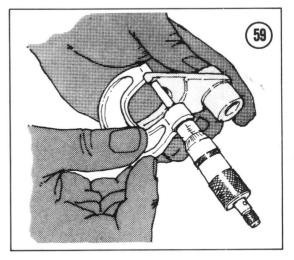

fingers are worn beyond use, and it must be replaced.

3. Measure the outside diameter of the shift fork shafts with a micrometer. Replace the ones worn beyond the wear limits given in **Table 3**.

4. Check the shift drum bearing (A, **Figure 61**). Make sure it operates smoothly without signs of wear or damage.

5. Check the grooves in the shift drum (B, **Figure 61**) for wear and chipping; replace if necessary.

6. Inspect the condition of all bearing surfaces **(Figure 62)** in the transmission cover/holder. Replace it if any are in questionable condition.

7. Inspect the bearings in the cylinder block. If necessary replace the main bearing (A, **Figure**

63) and countershaft bearing (B, **Figure 63**). Also check the condition of the shift drum bearing cavity (C, **Figure 63**).

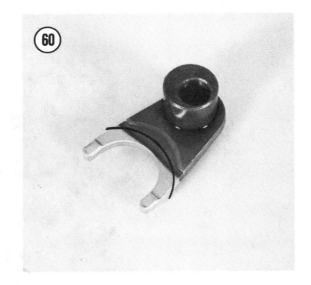

FINAL SHAFT

Do not try to disassemble the final shaft, as a press is required for this operation.

Removal/Installation

1. Remove the engine as described under *Engine Removal/Installation* in Chapter Four.

> NOTE: *Do not lose the 2 locating dowels (A, Figure 66).*

2. Remove the 2 clamps securing the water pump pipe to the cylinder block (**Figure 64**) and remove it.

3. Remove the 5 bolts securing the water pump housing (**Figure 65**) and remove it.

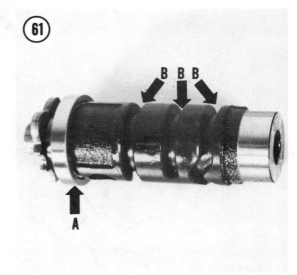

> NOTE: *The following figures are shown with the cylinder heads removed. It is not necessary to remove them for this procedure.*

4. Remove the cap nut and copper washers (B, **Figure 66**) securing the water pump impeller and remove it.

5. Remove the 17 bolts securing the rear engine cover. Hold the shift lever shaft in position and remove the cover.

> NOTE: *Do not lose the 2 locating dowels and O-rings (Figure 67).*

Table 3   GEARSHIFT DRUM AND FORK SPECIFICATIONS

Item	Standard Value	Wear Limit
Shift drum outer diameter	1.3760-1.3770 in. (34.950-34.975mm)	1.374 in. (34.90mm)
Case inner diameter	1.3780-1.3789 in. (35.00-35.025 mm)	1.380 in. (35.05mm)
Shift fork Finger width	0.233-0.236 in. (5.93-6.00mm)	0.217 in. (5.50mm)
Inner diameter	0.5118-0.5125 in. (13.000-13.018mm)	0.514 in. (13.05mm)
Shift fork shaft outer diameter	0.5105-0.5112 in. (12.966-12.984mm)	0.510 in. (12.95mm)

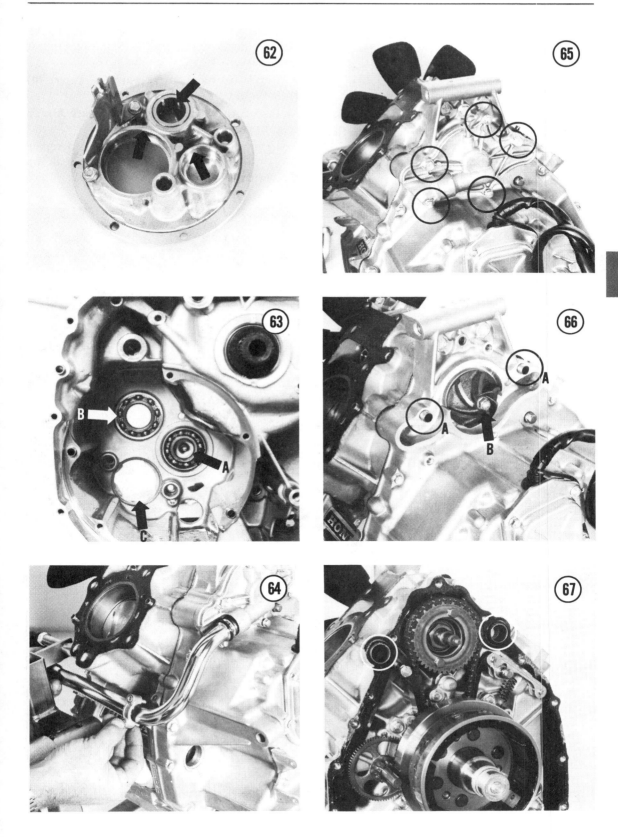

6. Withdraw final shaft from inside the rear engine cover.

7. Install by reversing these removal steps.

Inspection

1. Inspect condition of the oil seal **(Figure 68)** in the rear engine cover. Replace if necessary.

2. Check the condition of the bearing in the rear engine cover **(Figure 69)**. Make sure that it rotates freely. If not, it should be replaced.

3. Check inner and outer splines (A, **Figure 70**) for wear or damage.

4. Inspect the ramp surfaces (B, **Figure 70**) for wear or galling.

5. If any parts of the final shaft need repair take it to your Honda dealer for repair or replacement.

NOTE: If you own a 1980 or later model, first check the Supplement at the back of the book for any new service information.

CHAPTER SIX

FUEL AND EXHAUST SYSTEMS

The fuel system consists of the fuel tank, shutoff valve, fuel filter, two Keihin constant velocity carburetors and an air cleaner.

The exhaust system consists of two exhaust pipes, a common collector and two mufflers.

This chapter includes service procedures for all parts of the fuel and exhaust systems.

AIR CLEANER

The air cleaner must be cleaned every 3,600 miles and replaced every 7,200 miles, or more frequently in dusty areas.

Service of the air cleaner is described in Chapter Three.

CARBURETORS

Basic Principles

An understanding of the function of each of the carburetor components and their relationship to one another is a valuable aid for pinpointing a source of carburetor trouble.

The carburetor's purpose is to supply and atomize fuel and mix it in correct proportions with air that is drawn in through the air intake. At the primary throttle opening — at idle — a small amount of fuel is siphoned through the pilot jet by the incoming air. As the throttle is opened further, the air stream begins to siphon

fuel through the main jet and needle jet. The tapered needle increases the effective flow capacity of the needle jet as it is lifted with the air slide in that it occupies decreasingly less of the area of the jet. In addition, the amount of cutaway in the leading edge of the throttle slide aids in controlling the fuel/air mixture during partial throttle openings.

At full throttle, the carburetor venturi is fully open and the needle is lifted far enough to permit the main jet to flow at full capacity.

Service

The carburetor service recommended at 10,000-mile intervals involves routine removal, disassembly, cleaning, and inspection. Alterations in jet size, throttle slide cutaway, changes in needle position, etc., should be attempted only if you're experienced in this type of "tuning" work; a bad guess could result in costly engine damage or, at the very least, poor performance. If after servicing the carburetors and making the adjustments described in Chapter Three, the motorcycle does not perform correctly (and assuming that other factors affecting peformance are correct, such as ignition timing and condition, valve adjustment, etc.), the motorcycle should be checked by a Honda dealer or a qualified performance tuning specialist.

6

Due to U.S. Government emission controls, modification to the carburetor is not suggested. Refer to the Emission Information Label (**Figure 1**) on the frame, just above the right-hand muffler.

Removal/Installation

1. Remove the seat and the right- and left-hand side covers.

2. Turn the fuel shutoff valve to the OFF position (A, **Figure 2**). Remove the fuel line to the carburetors (B, **Figure 2**).

3. Remove rear bolt and rubber pad (**Figure 3**) securing the fuel tank at the rear, slide the tank to the rear and remove it.

4. Remove the bolts (**Figure 4**) securing the front intake tubes to the cylinder heads.

5. Loosen the clamping screws (**Figure 5**) and remove the front intake tubes.

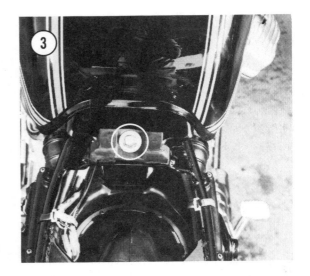

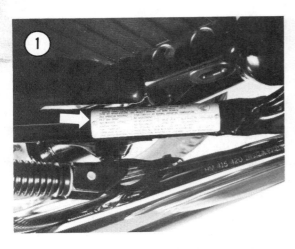

6. Loosen the clamping screws on the rear rubber boots (**Figure 6**) and slide the clamps away from the carburetors.

7. Pull the loose ends of the drain tubes free from the clamp (**Figure 7**) on the left-hand side near the kickstand.

8. Pull the carburetor assembly to the left and remove the choke (**Figure 8**) and throttle cables (**Figure 9**).

9. Install by reversing the removal steps. Do not mix the PULL and PUSH throttle cables when installing them.

10. Be sure the O-ring gaskets (**Figure 10**) in the front intake tubes are correctly seated in the groove prior to and during installation. If necessary, hold them in place with a small amount of non-hardening gasket sealer.

CAUTION
If the O-ring is not correctly seated it will allow a vacuum leak, thus leaning out the fuel/air mixture. This can cause serious damage to the intake valves.

Disassembly/Assembly

Refer to **Figure 11** for this procedure.

1. Remove the 3 screws securing the float bowl to the main body (**Figure 12**).

2. Lift the bowl off and remove the gasket and the overflow line (**Figure 13**).

3. Carefully push out the float pin (**Figure 14**).

4. Lift the float bowl assembly and the float valve needle out of the main body (**Figure 15**).

5. Unscrew the main jet (A, **Figure 16**) and the secondary jet (B, **Figure 16**).

> NOTE: *Do not remove or adjust the mixture jet or slow jet (C, Figure 16).*

6. Remove the idle adjust screw and spring (D, **Figure 16**).

7. Remove the 2 screws securing the top cover to the main body (**Figure 17**) and remove the cover.

8. Carefully pull out the spring (**Figure 18**) and the piston (**Figure 19**).

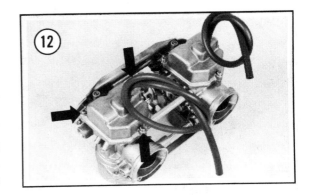

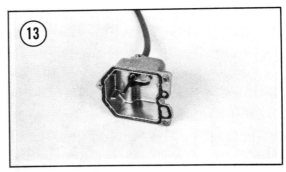

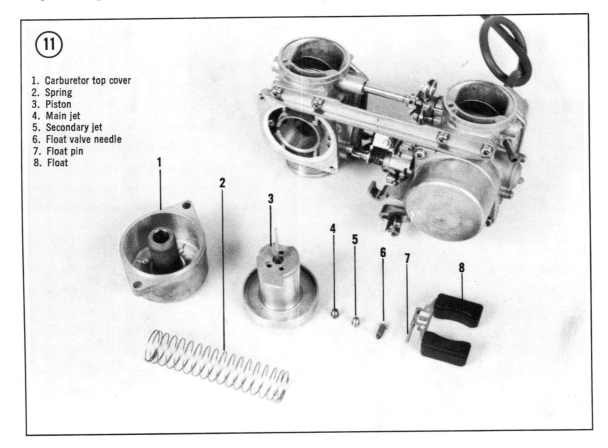

1. Carburetor top cover
2. Spring
3. Piston
4. Main jet
5. Secondary jet
6. Float valve needle
7. Float pin
8. Float

14

17

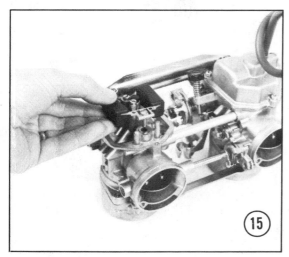

15

18

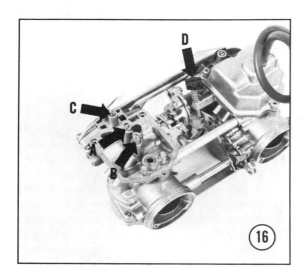

16

19

CAUTION
Do not bend the needle on the piston.

NOTE
Further disassembly is neither necessary nor recommended. If throttle shafts, choke shafts or butterflies are damaged, take the body to your dealer for replacement.

9. Repeat Steps 1-8 for the other carburetor. Do not intermix the parts—keep them separated.
10. Clean all parts, except rubber or plastic parts, in a good grade of carburetor cleaner. Follow the manufacturer's instructions for correct soak time (usually about 1/2 hour).

NOTE
It is recommended that one carburetor be cleaned at a time to avoid the interchange of parts.

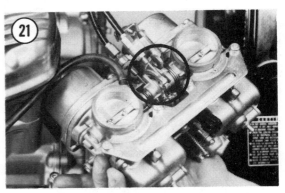

11. Remove the parts from the cleaner and blow dry with compressed air. Blow out the jets with compressed air. *Do not* use a piece of wire to clean them as minor gauges in a jet can alter the flow rate and upset the fuel/air mixture.
12. Assemble by reversing the disassembly steps.

THROTTLE CABLE REPLACEMENT

1. Remove the seat and fuel tank.
2. Disconnect the front brake light switch electrical connectors (A, **Figure 20**).
3. Remove the screws securing the halves of the right-hand switch/throttle housing (B, **Figure 20**).
4. Remove the switch housing from the handlebar and disengage the throttle cables from the throttle grip.
5. Partially remove the carburetor assembly as described in this chapter.

NOTE
It may not look like it, but it is practically impossible to remove the throttle cables from the carburetors with the carburetor assembly in place. There is not enough room for 2 hands within the area.

6. Loosen the throttle cable locknuts and remove both cables from the carburetor assembly (**Figure 21**).

NOTE
The piece of string attached in the next step will be used to pull the new throttle cables back through the frame so they will be routed in the exact same position as they were before.

7. Tie a piece of heavy string or cord (approximately 6-8 ft./1.8-2.4 m long) to the carburetor end of the throttle cables. Wrap this end with masking or duct tape. Do not use an excessive amount of tape as it will be pulled through the frame loop during removal. Tie the other end of the string to the frame or air box.
8. At the throttle grip end of the cables, carefully pull the cables (and attached string) out through the frame, past the electrical harness and from behind the headlight housing. Make sure the attached string follows the same path as the cables through the frame and behind the headlight.
9. Remove the tape and untie the string from the old cables.
10. Lubricate the new cables as described under *Control Cables* in Chapter Three.
11. Tie the string to the new throttle cables and wrap it with tape.
12. Carefully pull the string back through the frame routing the new cables through the same path as the old cables.
13. Remove the tape and untie the string from the cables and the frame.

CAUTION
*The throttle cables are the push/pull type and must be installed as described and shown in Steps 14 and 15. **Do not intermix the 2 cables**.*

14. Attach the throttle "pull" cable to the rear portion of the bracket. The other end is attached to the front receptacle (C, **Figure 20**) of the throttle/switch housing.
15. Attach the throttle "push" cable to the front portion of the bracket. The other end is attached to the rear receptacle (D, **Figure 20**) of the throttle/switch housing.
16. Tighten the nuts (**Figure 22**) securing the throttle cables to the carburetor assembly.

17. Install the throttle/switch housing. Make sure the pin on the lower portion of the switch housing is indexed into the hole in the handlebar.

CAUTION
Make sure that the electrical wires are not pinched between the switch housing and the handlebar.

18. Tighten the forward attachment screws first and then the rear screws. Attach the front brake light switch connectors.
19. Operate the throttle grip and make sure the carburetor throttle linkage is operating correctly and with no binding. If operation is incorrect or there is binding, carefully check that the cables are attached correctly and there are no tight bends in the cables.
20. Install the carburetor assembly, fuel tank and seat.
21. Adjust the throttle cables as described under *Throttle Operation/Adjustment* in Chapter Three.
22. Test ride the bike slowly at first and make sure the throttle is operating correctly.

CHOKE CABLE REPLACEMENT

1. Remove the seat and fuel tank.
2. Remove the carburetor assembly as described in this chapter.

NOTE
It may not look like it, but it is practically impossible to remove the choke cable from the carburetors with the carburetor assembly in place. There is just not enough room for 2 hands within the area.

3. Loosen the choke cable clamp screw (**Figure 23**) and remove the cable end from the choke linkage (**Figure 24**).

NOTE
The piece of string attached in the next step will be used to pull the new choke cable back through the frame so it will be routed in the same position as the old cable.

4. Tie a piece of heavy string or cord (approximately 6-8 ft./1.8-2.4 m long) to the carburetor end of the choke cable. Wrap this end with masking or duct tape. Do not use an

excessive amount of tape as it will be pulled through the frame loop during removal. Tie the other end of the string to the frame or air box.

5. Completely unscrew the locknut securing the choke knob assembly to the bracket.

6. At the choke knob end of the cable, carefully pull the cable (and attached string) out through the frame and from behind the headlight housing. Make sure the attached string follows the same path that the cable does through the frame and behind the headlight.

7. Remove the tape and untie the string from the old cable.

8. Lubricate the new cable as described under *Control Cables* in Chapter Three.

NOTE
Make sure the locknut is positioned on the string so it will be located below the mounting bracket when the cable is installed.

9. Tie the string to the new choke cable and wrap it with tape.

10. Carefully pull the string back through the frame routing the new cable through the same path as the old cable.

11. Remove the tape and untie the string from the cable and the frame.

12. Screw the locknut onto the choke cable knob assembly and tighten securely.

13. Attach the choke cable to the carburetor choke linkage as shown in **Figure 24**.

14. Operate the choke knob and make sure the carburetor choke linkage is operating correctly and with no binding. If operation is incorrect or there is binding carefully check that the cable is attached correctly and there are no tight bends in the cable.

15. Adjust the choke cable as described under *Choke Adjustment* in this section of the supplement.

16. Install the carburetor assembly, fuel tank and seat.

FUEL SHUTOFF VALVE

Removal/Installation

1. Turn the shutoff valve to the OFF position (A, **Figure 25**) and remove the flexible fuel line to the carburetor (B, **Figure 25**).

2. Place the loose end into a clean, sealable

metal container. This fuel can be reused if it is kept clean.

3. Open the valve to the RESERVE position (**Figure 26**) and remove the fuel fill cap. This will allow air to enter the tank and speed up the flow of fuel. Drain the tank completely.

4. Remove the fuel shutoff valve by unscrewing the locknut from the tank (A, **Figure 27**).

5. After removing the valve, insert a corner of a clean shop rag into the opening in the tank to stop the dribbling of fuel onto the engine and frame.

6. Remove the fuel filter (B, **Figure 27**) from the shutoff valve. Clean it with a medium soft toothbrush and blow out with compressed air. Replace it if defective.

7. Install by reversing the removal steps. Do not forget the gasket (C, **Figure 27**) between the valve and the tank. Tighten the locknut to 15-18 ft.-lb. (20-24 N•m).

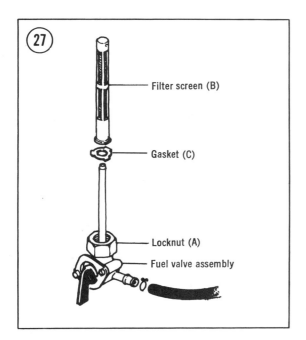

27

Filter screen (B)

Gasket (C)

Locknut (A)

Fuel valve assembly

28

6

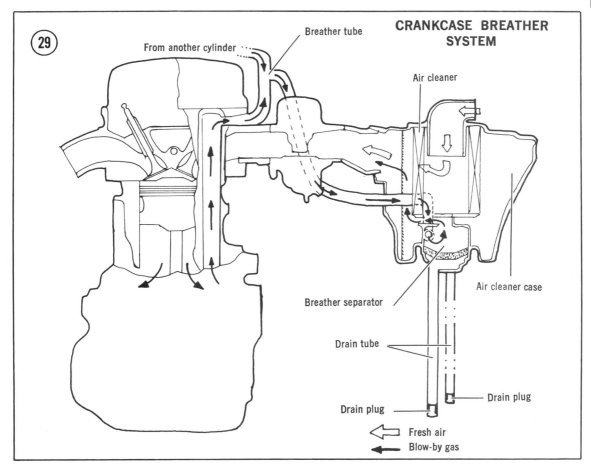

29

From another cylinder

Breather tube

CRANKCASE BREATHER SYSTEM

Air cleaner

Air cleaner case

Breather separator

Drain tube

Drain plug

Drain plug

⇦ Fresh air

◀ Blow-by gas

FUEL TANK

Removal/Installation

1. Remove the seat.
2. Turn the fuel shutoff valve to the OFF position (**Figure 25**), and remove the fuel line to the carburetors.
3. Remove rear bolt and rubber pad (**Figure 28**) securing the fuel tank at the rear, slide the tank to the rear, and remove it.
4. Install by reversing the removal steps.

Sealing (Pin-hole Size)

A small pin-hole size leak can be sealed with the use of a product called Thextonite Gas Tank Sealer Stick or equivalent. Follow the manufacturer's instructions.

Sealing (Small Hole Size)

This procedure requires the use of a non-petroleum based, non-flammable solvent. If you feel unqualified to accomplish it, take the tank to your dealer for service.

> *WARNING*
> *Before attempting any service on the fuel tank be sure to have a fire extinguisher rated for gasoline or chemical fires within reach. Do not smoke or work where there are any open flames. The work area must be well ventilated.*

1. Remove tank as described under *Fuel Tank Removal/Installation* in this chapter.
2. Mark the spot on the tank where the leak is visible with a grease pencil.
3. Turn the fuel shutoff valve to the RESERVE position and blow the interior of the tank *completely dry* with compressed air.
4. Turn the fuel shutoff valve to the OFF position and pour about 1 qt. (1 liter) of non-petroleum based solvent into the tank, install the fuel fill cap and shake the tank vigorously one or two minutes. This is used to remove all fuel residue.
5. Drain the non-petroleum based solvent into a safe storable container. This solution may be reused.
6. Remove the fuel shutoff valve by unscrewing the fitting from the tank. If necessary, plug the tank with a cork or tape it closed with duct tape.

7. Again blow the tank interior *completely dry* with compressed air.
8. Position the tank so that the point of the leak is located at the lowest part of the tank. This will allow the sealant to accumulate at the point of the leak.
9. Pour the sealant into the tank (a silicone rubber base sealer like Pro-Tech Fuel Tank Sealer or equivalent may be used). This is available at most motorcycle supply stores.
10. Let tank sit in this position for at least 48 hours.
11. After the sealant has dried, install the fuel shutoff valve, turn it to the OFF position and refill the tank with fuel.
12. After the tank has been filled, let it sit for at least two hours and recheck the leak area.
13. Install the tank on the motorcycle.

CRANKCASE BREATHER SYSTEM

In order to comply with air pollution standards the Honda CX500 is equipped with a crankcase breather system (**Figure 29**). The system draws the blow-by gases generated in the crankcase, and recirculates them into the fuel/air mixture and into the engine to be burned.

Inspection

Make sure the hose clamps (**Figure 30**) are tight at the cylinder heads and check the hoses for deterioration. Replace if necessary. Check that the hoses are not clogged or crimped.

> *NOTE*
> **Figure 30** *is shown with the engine upper mounting plates removed for clarity only.*

Remove the plugs (**Figure 31**) from the 2 drain hoses and clean out all residue.

> *NOTE*
> *Be sure to install the plugs and clamps.*

EXHAUST SYSTEM

The exhaust system consists of two exhaust pipes, a common collector and two mufflers.

Removal/Installation

1. Loosen the clamps securing the mufflers (A, **Figure 32**) to the collector. Remove bolts securing the rear footpegs and the mufflers (B, **Figure 32**). Slide the mufflers out of the collector and remove them.

2. Remove the 4 nuts and washers (**Figure 33**) securing the exhaust pipe flanges to the cylinder heads.

3. Loosen the clamps (A, **Figure 34**) securing the exhaust pipes to the collector inlet.

4. Remove the bolts on each side (B, **Figure 34**) securing the collector to the crankcase.

5. Pull the collector down and forward until the exhaust pipes are free from the cylinder heads and remove.

6. Install by reversing the removal steps.

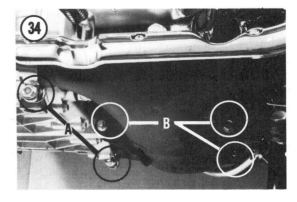

NOTE: If you own a 1980 or later model, first check the Supplement at the back of the book for any new service information.

CHAPTER SEVEN

ELECTRICAL SYSTEM

The electrical system includes the following systems (each is described in detail in this chapter):

a. Charging system
b. Ignition system
c. Lighting system
d. Directional signals
e. Horn

CHARGING SYSTEM

The charging system consists of the battery, alternator, and voltage regulator/rectifier (**Figure 1**).

The alternator generates an alternating current (AC) which the rectifier converts to direct current (DC). The regulator maintains the voltage to the battery and load (lights, ignition, etc.) at a constant voltage regardless of variations in engine speed and load.

Testing Charging System

Whenever a charging system trouble is suspected, make sure the battery is good before going any further. Clean and test the battery as described under *Battery Testing* in Chapter Three. Warm up engine prior to performing the test.

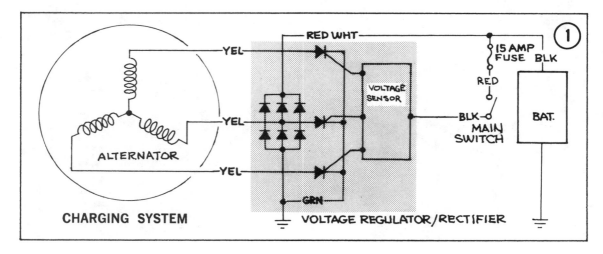

To test the charging system, connect a 0-15 DC voltmeter to battery as shown in **Figure 2**. Connect the positive voltmeter terminal to the positive battery terminal and the negative voltmeter terminal to ground.

NOTE: *Do not disconnect either the positive or negative battery cables; they are to remain in the circuit as is.*

Connect a 0-10 DC ammeter in line with the main fuse as shown in **Figure 3**. Use alligator clips on the test leads for good electrical connections. Pivot one end of the fuse out of the fuse holder and attach the positive ammeter terminal to the exposed end of the fuse. Attach the negative ammeter terminal to the exposed fuse clip within the fuse holder.

NOTE: *During the test if the needle of the ammeter reads in the opposite direction on the scale, reverse the polarity of the test terminals.*

CAUTION
In order to protect the ammeter, always run the test with the fuse in line in the circuit.

CAUTION
Do not try to test the system by connecting an ammeter between the positive battery terminal and the starter cable. The ammeter will burn out when the electric starter is operated.

Start the engine and run at 5,000 rpm. Minimum charging current should be 5 amperes. Voltage should read 14.5 volts.

NOTE: *All test measurements are to be made with the headlight on high beam.*

If the charging current is considerably lower than specified, check the alternator and voltage regulator/rectifier. Less likely is that the charging current is too high; in that case, the regulator is probably at fault.

Test the separate charging system components as described under the appropriate heading in the following section.

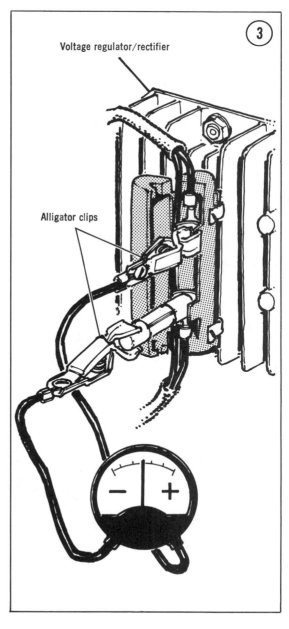

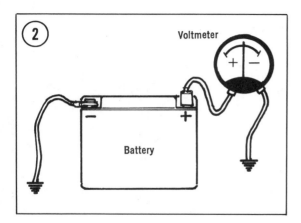

BATTERY

Care, Inspection, and Testing

For complete battery information refer to *Battery* in Chapter Three.

ALTERNATOR

An alternator is a form of electrical generator in which a magnetized field called a rotor revolves within a set of stationary coils called a stator. As the rotor revolves, alternating current is induced in the stator. The current is then rectified and used to operate the electrical accessories on the motorcycle and for charging battery. The rotor is permanently magnetized.

Removal/Installation

1. Remove the engine as described under *Engine Removal/Installation* in Chapter Four.

> NOTE: *Figures 4-18 are shown with the cylinder heads removed. However, it is not necessary to remove them for this procedure.*

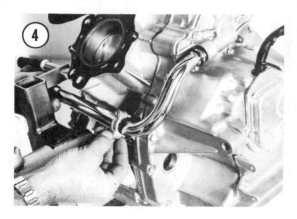

2. Remove the 2 clamps securing the water pump pipe to the cylinder block (**Figure 4**) and remove it.

3. Remove the 5 bolts securing the water pump housing (**Figure 5**) and remove it.

> NOTE: *Do not lose the 2 locating dowels (A, Figure 6).*

4. Remove the cap nuts and copper washers (B, **Figure 6**) securing the water pump impeller and remove it.

5. Remove the bolts securing the rear engine cover. Hold the shift lever shaft in position and remove the cover.

> NOTE: *Do not lose the 2 locating dowels and O-rings (Figure 7).*

6. Remove the bolt (**Figure 8**) securing the alternator pulser rotor and remove it.

7. Remove the bolt (**Figure 9**) securing the alternator rotor (flywheel) to the crankshaft with a sprocket.

> NOTE: *To prevent the flywheel from turning while removing the bolt, secure it with a strap wrench as shown in* **Figure 10**.

8. Screw a flywheel puller in all the way until it stops (**Figure 11**).

9. Hold the flywheel with the strap wrench and rotate the puller clockwise until the flywheel disengages from the crankshaft. Remove the flywheel, starter gear (**Figure 12**), and the needle bearing (A, **Figure 13**). Do not lose the Woodruff key.

7

CAUTION
*Honda recalled all 1978 CX500's to cor-
rect a serious cam tensioner problem. If
your tensioner cover does not look like
the one shown in B, **Figure 13**, your bike
has not been modified. Refer to the
Camshaft procedure in Chapter Four
for more details.*

CAUTION
*Be careful not to damage the pulser
pickup (**Figure 14**) on the outer surface
of the flywheel.*

10. Remove the 5 bolts **(Figure 15)** securing the
CDI pulser cover and remove it.

11. Disconnect the electrical wires at the pulser
stator, remove the 2 screws **(A, Figure 16)**
securing the pulser stator and remove it. Pull
the rubber grommet **(B, Figure 16)** out of the
rear engine cover.

12. Remove the 3 bolts **(A, Figure 17)** securing
the alternator stator and the 2 bolts **(B, Figure
17)** securing the right and left pulsers.

13. Carefully pull the electrical wires through
the hole in the rear engine cover.

CAUTION
*Do not pull too hard on the stator as it
may damage electrical connections
where the wires attach to the stator.*

14. Install by reversing these removal steps and
secure the alternator rotor bolt to 58-72 ft.-lb.
(79-97 N•m). Be sure that the Woodruff key,

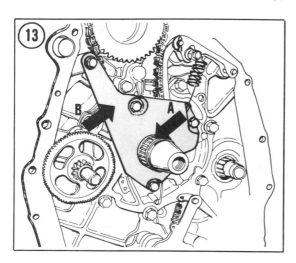

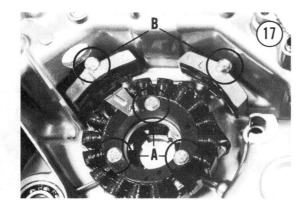

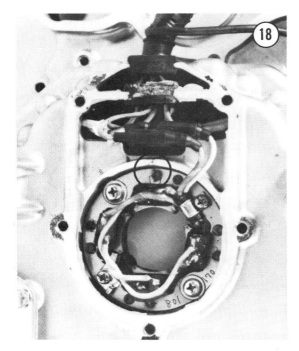

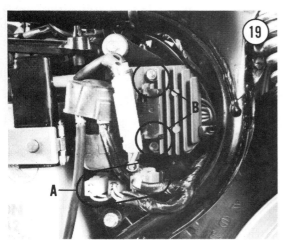

on the crankshaft, is in place and correctly seated prior to installing the rotor.

NOTE: *To prevent the flywheel from turning while installing the bolt, secure it with a strap wrench as shown in Figure 10.*

15. Be sure the rubber grommet (B, **Figure 16**) is securely in place and that none of the electrical wires are pinched between the stator and the rear engine cover. Make sure the wires are correctly routed.

16. Install the pulser stator and align the index mark on the stator and the rear engine cover (**Figure 18**).

NOTE: *If these marks are not aligned properly the ignition timing will be incorrect. Do not try to modify ignition timing by altering the alignment of these marks. This is not the purpose of these marks — they are to be always aligned correctly.*

17. Install the pulsers with their holding tabs facing to the right-hand side, facing toward the timing inspection hole.

Alternator Stator Testing

Disconnect the stator electrical leads at the voltage regulator/rectifier (A, **Figure 19**). Use an ohmmeter and measure the resistance between each yellow wire terminal and ground. If any connection shows continuity to ground, the stator must be replaced. Also measure the resistance between each pair of yellow wire terminals. There is no specified resistance, but there should be continuity present at each connection.

Alternator Rotor Testing

The rotor is permanently magnetized and cannot be tested except by replacement with a rotor known to be good. A rotor can lose magnetism from old age or a sharp blow. If defective, the rotor must be replaced; it cannot be remagnetized.

VOLTAGE REGULATOR/RECTIFIER

Removal/Installation

1. Remove the left-hand side cover.

2. Disconnect negative battery lead (**Figure 20**).

3. Remove the 2 bolts securing the voltage regulator/rectifier to the panel (B, **Figure 19**).

4. Disconnect wires from voltage regulator/ rectifier and remove it.

5. Install by reversing the removal steps.

Testing

To test the voltage regulator/rectifier, disconnect the plugs from the harness (A, **Figure 19**). Make the following measurements, using an ohmmeter set to RX10. Refer to **Figure 21** for this test.

1. Connect either ohmmeter lead to the green rectifier lead. Connect the other ohmmeter lead to each of the yellow leads. These 3 measurements must be the same, either all very high resistance (2000 Ω minimum) or very low resistance (5-40 Ω). If one or more differ, the voltage regulator/rectifier is bad and the entire unit must be replaced.

2. Reverse ohmmeter leads and repeat Step 1. This time, the readings must also be the same, but just the opposite from the measurements in Step 1. For example, if all readings in Step 1 were low, all readings in this step must be high, and vice versa. Replace the voltage regulator/ rectifier if these measurements are not correct.

3. Connect either ohmmeter lead to the red/white voltage regulator/recitifer lead. Connect the other ohmmeter lead to each of the yellow leads. These 3 measurements must be the same, either all very high or all very low. Replace the voltage regulator/rectifier if these measurements are not correct.

Voltage Regulator Performance Test

Connect a voltmeter to the battery negative and positive terminals (**Figure 22**). Leave the battery cables attached. Start the engine and let it idle; increase engine speed until the voltage going to the battery reaches 14.0-15.0 volts. At

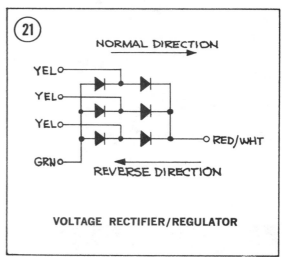

VOLTAGE RECTIFIER/REGULATOR

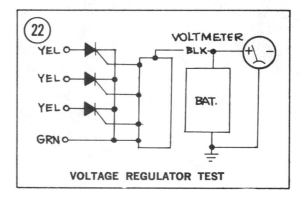

VOLTAGE REGULATOR TEST

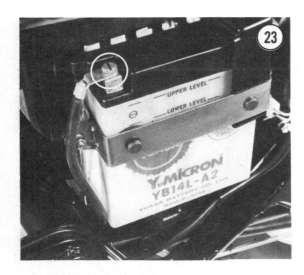

this point, the voltage regulator/rectifier should prevent any further increase in voltage. If this does not happen and voltage increases above specifications, the voltage regulator/rectifier is faulty and must be replaced.

IGNITION SYSTEM

The ignition system consists of an ignition coil, a capacitor discharge ignition (CDI) unit and spark plugs.

IGNITION COIL

Removal/Installation

1. Remove the seat. Disconnect the negative battery lead (**Figure 23**). Disconnect the spark plug leads (**Figure 24**).

2. Turn the fuel shutoff valve to the OFF position (A, **Figure 25**) and remove the fuel line to the carburetors (B, **Figure 25**).

3. Remove rear bolt and rubber pad (**Figure 26**) securing the fuel tank at the rear. Slide the tank to the rear and remove it.

4. Disconnect the coil electrical connectors (pink — right-hand coil, yellow — left-hand coil) from the CDI unit. See **Figure 27**.

7

5. Remove the 2 bolts **(Figure 28)** securing the coils to the frame and remove them.

6. Install by reversing the removal steps. Make sure to route the spark plug wires to the correct cylinder. The right-hand coil fires the right-hand spark plug and the left-hand coil fires the left-hand spark plug.

Testing

The only certain test for a suspected coil is to replace it with a known good coil. Interchange the two coils and see if the symptoms change.

CAPACITOR DISCHARGE IGNITION

The Honda CX500 is equipped with a capacitor discharge ignition (CDI) system. This solid state system uses no breaker points or other moving parts. **Figure 29** illustrates the capacitor discharge system.

Alternating current from the alternator is rectified and used to charge the capacitor. As the piston approaches the firing position, a

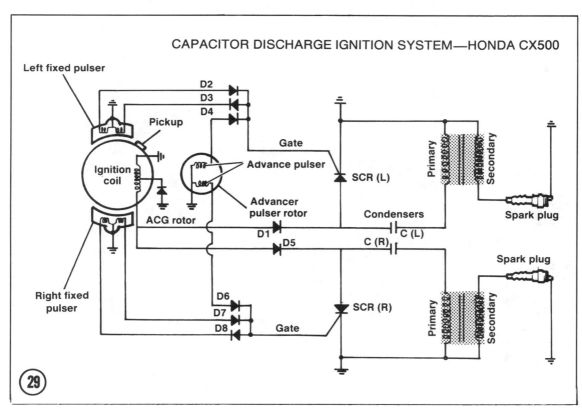

CAPACITOR DISCHARGE IGNITION SYSTEM—HONDA CX500

pulse from the signal coil is rectified, shaped, and then used to trigger the silicon controlled rectifier (SCR) which in turn allows the capacitor to discharge quickly into the primary circuit of the ignition coil, where the voltage is stepped up in the secondary circuit to a value sufficient to fire the spark plug.

CDI Cautions

Certain measures must be taken to protect the capacitor discharge system. Instantaneous damage to the semiconductors in the system will occur if the following precautions are not observed.

1. Never connect the battery backward. If battery polarity is wrong, damage will occur to the voltage regulator/rectifier, alternator, and CDI system.

Table 1   CDI TROUBLESHOOTING

Symptom	Probable Cause
Weak spark	Low battery
	Poor connections (clean and tighten)
	High voltage leakage (replace defective wire)
	Defective coil
No spark	Discharged battery
	Fuse burned out
	Wiring broken
	Defective coil
	Defective signal generating coil (replace)

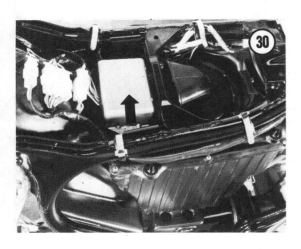

2. Do not disconnect the battery when the engine is running. A voltage surge will occur which will damage the voltage regulator/rectifier and possibly burn out the lights.

3. Keep all connections between the various units clean and tight. Be sure that the wiring connectors are pushed together firmly.

4. Do not substitute another type of ignition coil or battery.

5. Each unit is mounted with a rubber vibration isolator. Always be sure that the isolators are in place when replacing any units.

CDI Troubleshooting

Problems with the capacitor discharge system fall into one of the following categories. See **Table 1**.

   a. Weak spark

   b. No spark

CDI Testing

Tests may be performed on the CDI unit **(Figure 30)** but a good one may be damaged by someone unfamiliar with test equipment. To play it safe, have the tests performed by your Honda dealer or substitute a suspected unit with one known to be good.

SPARK PLUGS

The spark plugs recommended by the factory are usually the most suitable for your machine. If riding conditions are mild, it may be advisable to go to spark plugs one step hotter than normal. Unusually severe riding conditions may require slightly colder plugs. See Chapter Three for details.

STARTING SYSTEM

The starting system consists of the starting motor, starter solenoid and the starter button.

The layout of the starter system is shown in **Figure 31**. There are no provisions for a kickstarter on the CX500.

When the starter button is pressed, it engages the solenoid switch that closes the circuit. The electricity flows from the battery to the starter motor.

7

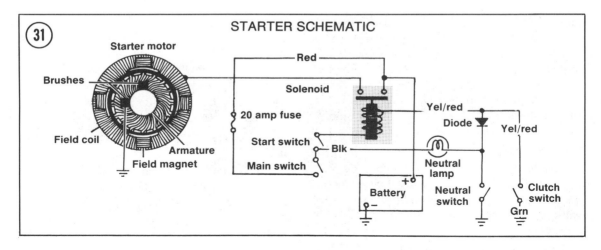

STARTER SCHEMATIC

CAUTION
Do not operate the starter for more than 5 seconds at a time. Let it rest for approximately 10 seconds, then use it again.

The starter gears are covered in detail under *Starter Gears and Clutch* in Chapter Four.

Starter Removal/Installation

1. Turn the ignition switch to the OFF position. Remove the left-hand side cover (**Figure 32**) and remove the negative battery cable from the battery (**Figure 33**).
2. Remove the 2 bolts (**Figure 34**) securing the starter to the crankcase. Pull it to the rear, rotate it slightly and pivot it down.
3. Disconnect the electrical cable (**Figure 35**) and remove the starter.
4. Install by reversing these removal steps. Take care when installing motor into crankcase. Make sure that gears mesh properly.

STARTER

Disassembly/Inspection/Assembly

The overhaul of a starter motor is best left to an expert. This procedure shows how to detect a defective starter.
1. Remove the case screws and separate the case and covers.

NOTE
Write down the number of shims used on the shaft next to the commutator. Be sure to install the same number when reassembling the starter.

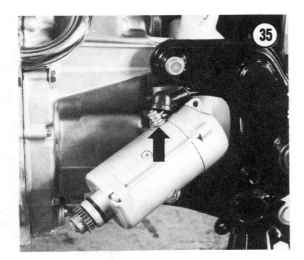

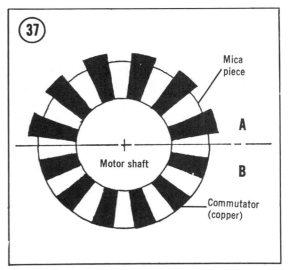

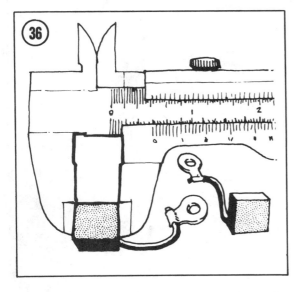

2. Clean all grease, dirt and carbon from the armature, case and end covers.

CAUTION
Do not immerse brushes or the wire windings in solvent as the insulation may be damaged. Wipe the windings with a cloth lightly moistened with solvent and dry thoroughly.

3. Remove the screws securing the brushes in their holders and remove both brushes. Measure the length of each brush with a vernier caliper (**Figure 36**). If the length is 0.21 in. (5.5 mm) or less it must be replaced. Replace both brushes as a set even though only one may be worn to this dimension.

4. Inspect the condition of the commutator (**Figure 37**). The mica in a good commutator (A) is below the surface of the copper bars. On a worn commutator (B) the mica and copper bars may be worn to the same level. This condition must be corrected by undercutting the mica but should be done by a specialist. Have this performed by a dealer or motorcycle or automotive electrical repair shop.

5. Inspect the commutator copper bars for discoloration. If a pair of bars are discolored grounded armature coils are indicated.

6. Use an ohmmeter and check for continuity between the commutator bars (**Figure 38**); there should be continuity between pairs of bars. Also check continuity between the commutator bars and the shaft (**Figure 39**); there should be no continuity. If the unit fails either of these tests the armature is faulty and must be replaced.

7. Use an ohmmeter and inspect the field coil by checking continuity between the starter cable terminal and the starter case; there should be no continuity. Also check continuity between the starter cable terminal and each brush wire terminal; there should be continuity. If the unit fails either of these tests the case/field coil assembly must be replaced.

8. Assemble the case; be sure to align the marks on both the case and end covers.

9. Inspect the condition of the gear and O-ring seal. If the gear is chipped or worn the armature must be replaced.

Starter Solenoid
Removal/Installation

1. Turn the ignition switch to the OFF position.

2. Remove the left-hand side cover **(Figure 32)** and remove negative battery cable **(Figure 33)**.

3. Slide up the rubber boot **(Figure 40)** and disconnect the electrical wires from the switch.

4. Pull the solenoid out of the rubber mount.

5. Install by reversing the removal steps.

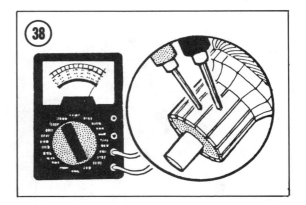

LIGHTING SYSTEM

The lighting system consists of the headlight, taillight/brakelight combination, directional signals, warning lights and speedometer and tachometer illumination lights. **Table 2** lists replacement bulbs for these components.

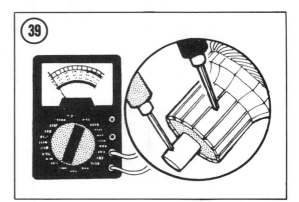

Headlight Replacement

1. Remove 2 mounting screws (A, **Figure 41**) on each side of the headlight housing.

2. Pull the trim bezel and sealed beam unit out and disconnect the electrical connector from the sealed beam.

3. Remove the 2 retaining screws (A, **Figure 42**) and the adjusting bolt, nut, and spring (B, **Figure 42**). Remove the inner rim and remove the sealed beam.

4. Install by reversing the removal steps. *Don't forget the spring on the adjusting bolt.*

5. Adjust the headlight as described under *Headlight Adjustment* in this chapter.

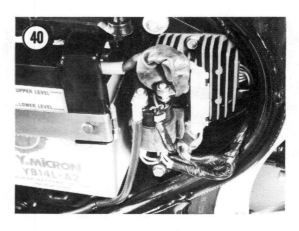

Headlight Adjustment

Adjust headlight horizontally and vertically according to Department of Motor Vehicle regulations in your area.

Table 2   LIGHT BULB REPLACEMENT

Item	Number	Wattage	Candle Power
Headlight	—	40/50	—
Tail/brakelight	SAE 1157	8/27	3/32
Directional signals			
Front	SAE 1034	23	32
Rear	SAE 1073	23	32
Instrument lights	SAE 57	3.4	2
Running light	SAE 1034	8	3

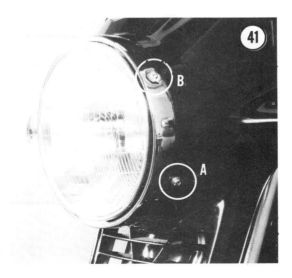

To adjust headlight horizontally, turn the upper left-hand screw (B, **Figure 41**). To adjust vertically, turn the lower right-hand screw.

Taillight Replacement

Remove the 2 screws securing the lens and remove it. Wash out the inside and outside of the lens with a mild detergent and wipe dry. Wipe off the reflective base surrounding the bulb with a soft cloth. Replace the bulb and install the lens; do not overtighten the screws or the lens may crack.

Directional Signal Light Replacement

Remove the 2 screws securing the lens and remove it. Wash the inside and outside of the lens out with a mild detergent. Replace the bulb and install the lens; do not overtighten the screws or the lens may crack.

Speedometer, Tachometer Illumination Light, and Indicator Light Replacement

Remove the 2 screws (**Figure 43**) securing the headlight nacelle; pull it down and out. Remove the upper portion to gain access to the bulbs. Pull the bulb holder out and replace the bulb(s).

Front Brake Light Switch Replacement

Pull back on the rubber boot (**Figure 44**). Pull the electrical wires from the connectors, remove the switch and replace it.

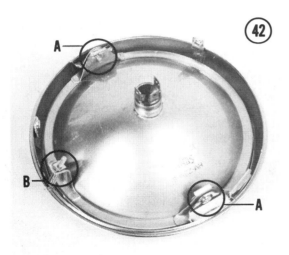

Rear Brake Light Switch Replacement

1. Remove the left-hand side cover.

2. Unhook the spring from the brake arm.

3. Unscrew the switch housing and locknut from the bracket (**Figure 45**).

4. Pull up the rubber boot and remove the electrical wires.

5. Replace the switch; reinstall and adjust as described under *Rear Brake Light Switch Adjustment* in this chapter.

Rear Brake Light Switch Adjustment

1. Turn the ignition switch to the ON position.

2. Depress the brake pedal. Light should come on just as the brake begins to work.

3. To make the light come on earlier, hold the switch body and turn adjusting locknut (**Figure 45**) *clockwise* as viewed from the back. Turn the nut *counterclockwise* to delay the light.

> NOTE: *Some riders prefer the light to come on a little early. This way, they can tap the pedal without braking to warn drivers who follow too closely.*

Flasher Relay Replacement

The flasher relay is located inside the headlight nacelle. Remove 2 screws (**Figure 43**) securing the nacelle, pull it down and out. Remove the wires from the bad unit and transfer wires to new relay. Install the nacelle.

Horn Replacement

1. Remove the 2 screws (**Figure 43**) securing the headlight nacelle; pull it down and out.

2. Disconnect horn connector (A, **Figure 46**) from the electrical harness.

3. Remove the bolt (B, **Figure 46**) securing the horn to the bracket and remove it.

4. Installation is the reverse of these steps.

Horn Testing

1. Disconnect the horn wires from the harness.

2. Connect the horn wires to a 12-volt battery. If it is good, it will sound. If not, replace it.

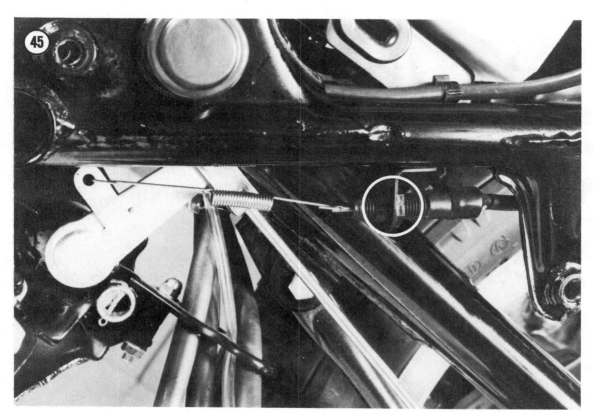

FUSES

There are three fuses used on the CX500. Two are located in the fuse box (**Figure 47**) at base of the handlebars. Remove the 2 screws and remove the cover (**Figure 48**). These are for headlight (10A) and taillight/brakelight (10A).

The main fuse (20A) is located under the left-hand side cover, next to the voltage regulator/ rectifier (**Figure 49**).

Inside each fuse compartment is a spare fuse; *always* carry spare fuses.

Whenever a fuse blows, find out the reason for failure before replacing the fuse. Usually, the trouble is a short-circuit in the wiring. This may be caused by worn-through insulation or a disconnected wire shorting to ground.

CAUTION
Never substitute tinfoil or wire for a fuse. Never use a higher amperage fuse than specified. An overload could result in fire and complete loss of the bike.

WIRING DIAGRAM

Full color wiring diagrams are located at the end of this book.

7

CHAPTER EIGHT

COOLING SYSTEM

COOLING SYSTEM

The pressurized cooling system consists of the radiator, water pump, thermostat, camshaft driven fan (running at one half the engine speed), and coolant recovery tank. **Figure 1** shows all components of the cooling system.

The system uses a 11-15 psi (0.75-1.05 kg/cm²) radiator filler cap and is designed to operate with a 180°F (82°C) thermostat, located on top of the cylinder block just behind the fan.

The centrifugal vane impeller water pump requires no particular care and the components can be serviced.

It is important that the coolant level be kept to the FULL mark on the coolant recovery tank **(Figure 2)**.

CAUTION
Drain and flush the cooling system with fresh water every 21,000 miles or 2 years, whichever comes first. Refill with a 50/50 mixture of a high quality ethylene glycol antifreeze and water (−20°F/−29°C coolant minimum). Do not reuse old coolant as it deteriorates with use. Do not operate with fresh water only (even in climates where antifreeze is not required). This is important

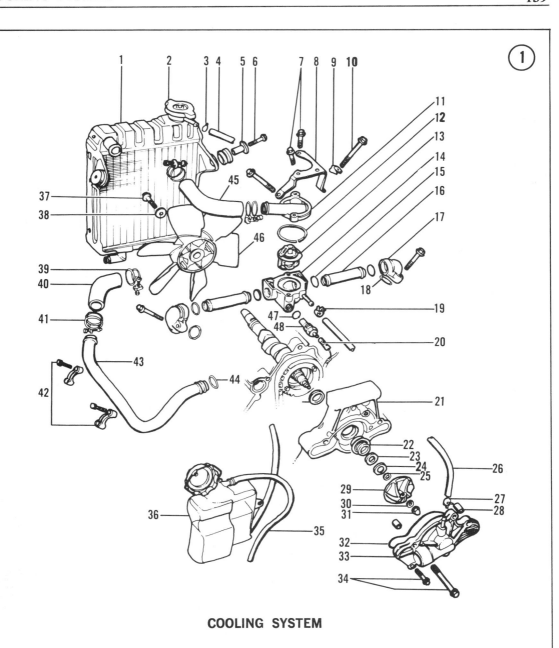

COOLING SYSTEM

1. Radiator
2. Radiator cap
3. Clamp
4. Overflow hose
5. Radiator mounting assembly (3)
6. Bolt (3)
7. Bolts (3)
8. Thermostat bracket
9. Spacer
10. Bolt (2)
11. Thermostat cover
12. Thermostat gasket

13. Thermostat
14. Thermostat housing
15. O-ring (4)
16. Water pipe (2)
17. Elbow (2)
18. O-ring (2)
19. Clamp (2)
20. Temperature sending unit electrical connector
21. Water pump housing
22. Water seal
23. Seal washer

24. Rubber seal
25. Collar
26. Bypass hose
27. Clamp
28. Locating dowel (2)
29. Impeller
30. Copper washer
31. Cap nut
32. O-ring
33. Water pump cover
34. Bolts (6)
35. Overflow hose

36. Coolant recovery tank
37. Bolt
38. Washer
39. Clamp (4)
40. Radiator lower hose
41. Clamp
42. Water pipe clamp
43. Water pipe
44. O-ring
45. Radiator upper hose
46. Fan
47. Seal
48. Temperature sending unit

because the CX500 engine is all alumi-num; it will not rust but it will oxidize and have to be replaced. Refer to Coolant Change in Chapter Three.

This chapter describes repair and replacement of cooling system components. **Table 1** at the end of the chapter lists all of the cooling system specifications. For routine maintenance of the system, refer to Chapter Three.

WARNING
Do not remove the radiator cap when the engine is hot. The coolant is very hot and is under pressure. Severe scalding could result if the coolant comes in contact with your skin.

The engine and cooling system must be cool prior to servicing *any component* in the system.

Cooling System Check

Two checks should be made before disassembly if a faulty cooling system is suspected.
1. Run the engine until it reaches operating temperature. While the engine is running, a pressure surge should be felt when the upper radiator hose is squeezed.
2. If substantial coolant loss is noted, the head gasket might be blown in one of the cylinders. In extreme cases sufficient coolant will leak into a cylinder when the bike is left standing for several hours so that engine cannot be turned by the starter. White smoke (steam) might also be observed at the muffler(s) when the engine is running. Coolant may also find its way into the oil. Check the dipstick; if it looks like a "chocolate malt" there is coolant in the system. If so, correct the cooling problem immediately.

CAUTION
After the cooling system is corrected, drain and thoroughly flush out the oil system to eliminate all coolant residue. Refill with fresh engine oil, refer to Chapter Three.

Pressure Check

If the cooling system requires repeated filling, it probably has a leak. The following procedure requires a cooling system pressure tester.

The check can be made by a Honda dealer or a service station.

The radiator cap should be tested for 11-15 psi (0.75-1.05 kg/cm^2). During the radiator test, if a leak is found in a hose, replace the hose and pressure test the system again. If a leak is found in the radiator core or in the top or bottom tank, remove radiator as described under *Radiator Removal/Installation* in this chapter. Have the radiator repaired by a shop specializing in radiator repair. When the radiator has been reinstalled, pressure test the system again to make sure all components are tight.

RADIATOR

Removal/Installation

1. Remove the exhaust system as described under *Exhaust System Removal/Installation* in Chapter Six.
2. Remove the seat and the fuel tank.
3. Remove the rubber plugs, screws, and metal spacers, 2 on each side (**Figure 3**) securing the radiator shroud in place.

NOTE: *Do not lose the 4 metal spacers; they may stick in the shroud after removal.*

4. Slide the shroud forward and down and remove it.
5. Remove the overflow tube at the radiator cap (A, **Figure 4**).

6. Place a drip pan under the radiator and remove the drain plug (**Figure 5**) at the base of the radiator. Remove the radiator cap; this will speed up the draining process. Completely drain the radiator; reinstall the drain plug and radiator cap.

7. Loosen the clamps on the upper (**Figure 6**) and lower (**Figure 7**) radiator hoses. Do not remove the hoses at this time.

8. Remove the upper and lower mounting bolt assemblies. See **Figure 8** and B, **Figure 4**.

9. Pull the radiator out at the bottom, slide it down and out of the bike frame. The hoses may stay either with the radiator or the engine.

CAUTION
Care must be taken when handling the radiator to avoid damaging the cooling fins and tubes.

10. After the radiator has been removed, inspect the fan shroud (**Figure 9**) for damage. Straighten it out or replace it if necessary.

11. Install by reversing these removal steps. Be sure to use the metal spacer with the screws when installing the shroud.

12. Fill radiator with recommended type and quantity of coolant; refer to Steps 8-11, *Coolant Change* in Chapter Three.

13. Install the fuel tank and seat, start the engine and check for leaks.

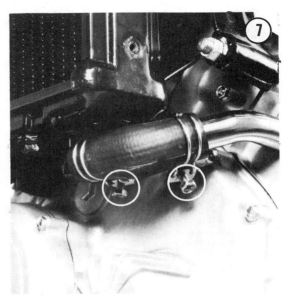

Inspection

Flush off the exterior of the radiator with a garden hose. Spray from both the front and back to remove all road dirt and bugs. Use a whisk broom or stiff paintbrush to remove any stubborn dirt.

Straighten out any bent cooling fins with a broad tipped screwdriver or putty knife.

CAUTION
Do not press too hard or the cooling fins and tubes will be damaged.

Check for cracks or signs of leakage (usually a moss-green colored residue) at the filler neck, the inlet and outlet hose fittings, and the upper and lower tank seams. See **Figure 10**. If radiator condition is in question, have it checked as described under *Pressure Check* in this chapter. It can be checked with the radiator removed from the bike.

FAN

Removal/Installation

1. Remove the radiator as described under *Radiator Removal/Installation* in this chapter.

NOTE: *Figures 11 and 12 are shown with engine removed for clarity only.*

2. Remove the bolt **(Figure 11)** on the fan.

3. Remove fan with a puller **(Figure 12)**. Screw in the puller until the fan disengages; remove the puller and the fan.

4. Inspect the fan blades. If any show signs of fatigue or cracking, the fan should be replaced. Severe damage can be done to the radiator if a blade breaks loose when the engine is running.

5. Install by reversing these removal steps. Torque the fan bolt to 14-18 ft.-lb. (19-24 N•m).

6. Refill the cooling system with the recommended type and quantity of coolant; refer to Steps 8-11, *Coolant Change* in Chapter Three.

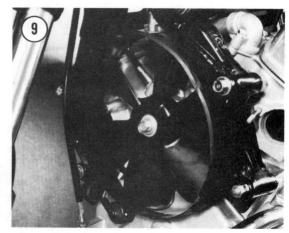

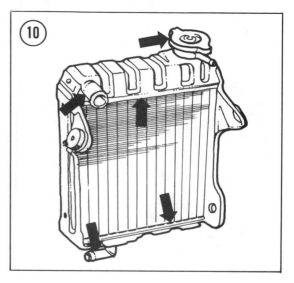

THERMOSTAT

Refer to **Figure 1** for this procedure.

Removal/Installation

1. Remove the radiator as described under *Radiator Removal/Installation* in this chapter.

2. Remove the fan as described under *Fan Removal/Installation* in this chapter.

> NOTE: *Figure 13 is shown with the engine removed for clarity. It is not necessary to remove it to perform this procedure.*

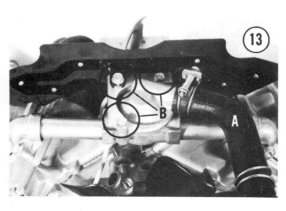

3. Remove upper radiator hose (A, **Figure 13**).

4. Remove the bolts securing the air dam and thermostat bracket (B, **Figure 13**). Remove the air dam and the bracket.

5. Remove the water outlet housing and gasket.

6. Lift out the thermostat.

7. Install by reversing these removal steps. Use a new gasket.

Thermostat Testing

Test the thermostat to insure proper operation. It should be replaced if it remains open at normal room temperature.

Place thermostat, on a small piece of wood, in a pan of water (**Figure 14**). Gradually heat and continue to stir the water until it reaches 180°F (82°C). At this temperature the thermostat valve should open.

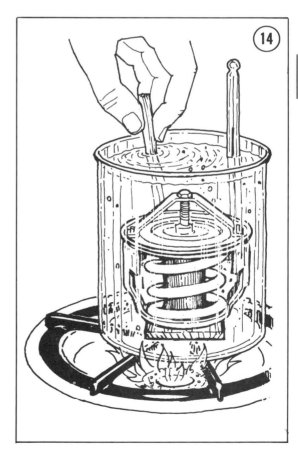

NOTE: *Valve operation is sometimes sluggish; it usually takes 3-5 minutes for the valve to work properly.*

If valve fails to open, it should be replaced. Be sure to replace it with one with the same temperature rating.

COOLANT CHANGE

The coolant should be completely drained and refilled with at least a 50/50 mixture of ethylene glycol antifreeze and water every 21,000 miles or 2 years, whichever comes first. Refer to *Coolant Change* in Chapter Three.

> **CAUTION**
> *Use only a high quality ethylene glycol antifreeze labeled specifically for aluminum engines.*

RADIATOR HOSES

Hoses deteriorate with age and should be replaced periodically or whenever they show signs of cracking or leakage. To be safe, replace the hoses every 21,000 miles or 2 years, whichever comes first. The spray of hot coolant from a cracked hose can injure the rider. Loss of coolant can also cause the engine to overheat causing damage.

Replacement

1. Remove the radiator shroud and drain the coolant as described in Steps 1-9, *Radiator Removal/Installation* in this chapter.

2. Remove the hoses. If a hose is difficult to remove, do not pull too hard as you may damage the hose fitting. Try to rotate it with your hand as you pull. If this does not work, cut the hose lengthwise with a sharp knife and peel if off the fitting.

> **CAUTION**
> *Do not press hard when cutting on the radiator fitting as it is brass and will damage easily.*

3. Install the hoses by reversing these steps.

4. Refill the cooling system with the recommended type and quantity of coolant; refer to Chapter Three.

5. Start the engine and check for leaks.

WATER PUMP

Refer to **Figure 1** for this procedure.

Removal/Installation

1. Remove the engine as described under *Engine Removal/Installation* in Chapter Four.

> NOTE: *The following procedure is shown with the cylinder heads removed. However, it is not necessary to remove them for this procedure.*

2. Remove the 2 clamps securing the water pipe to the cylinder block (**Figure 15**) and remove it.

3. Remove the 5 bolts (**Figure 16**) securing the water pump housing and remove it.

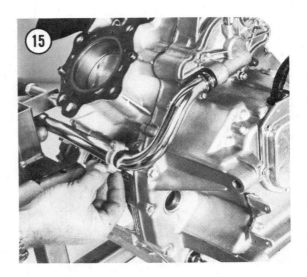

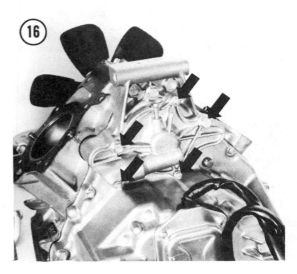

NOTE: *Do not lose the 2 locating dowels (A, Figure 17).*

4. Remove the cap nut and copper washer (B, **Figure 17**) securing the water pump impeller and remove it.

5. Remove the 17 bolts securing the rear engine cover. Hold the shift lever shaft in position and remove the cover.

NOTE: *Do not lose the 2 locating dowels and O-rings (Figure 18).*

6. Inspect the seal in the rear engine cover (**Figure 19**). Replace if necessary.

NOTE: *If there is water in the oil, one likely cause is a leaky seal in the rear engine cover.*

7. Install by reversing these removal steps. Torque impeller cap nut to 6-9 ft.-lb. (8-12 N•m).

8. When installing the water pipe, be sure the O-ring is properly seated between the 2 ribs on the water pipe (**Figure 20**).

9. Refill the cooling system with the recommended type and quantity of coolant, refer to Chapter Three.

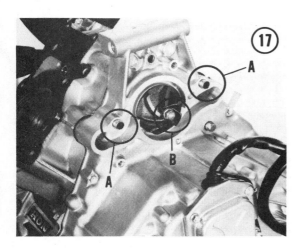

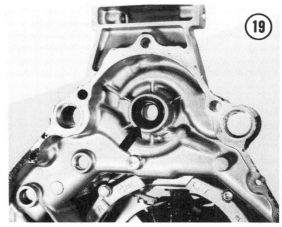

8

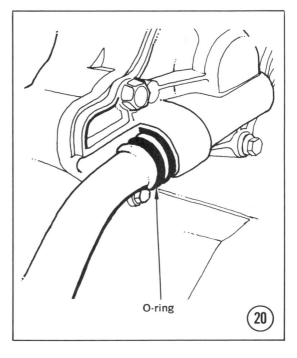

O-ring

Table 1   COOLING SYSTEM SPECIFICATIONS

Radiator cap relief pressure	10.7-14.9 psi (0.75-1.05 kg/cm^2)
Freezing point (hydrometer test)	
Water-to-antifreeze ratio	
55/45	$-25\,°F\,(-32\,°C)$
50/50	$-34\,°F\,(-37\,°C)$
45/55	$-48\,°F\,(-44.5\,°C)$
Cooling capacity	
Radiator and engine	1.9 U.S. qt. (1.9 liter)
Recovery tank	0.26 U.S. qt. (0.25 liter)
Total system	2.17 U.S. qt. (2.05 liter)
Thermostat	
Begins to open	176°-183°F (80°-84°C)
Fully open	199°-205°F (93°-97°C)
Valve lift	0.315 in. @ 203°F (8mm @95°C)
Boiling point — with 50/50 mixture	
Cap on, pressurized	258°F (125.6°C)
Unpressurized	226°F (107.7°C)

NOTE: If you own a 1980 or later model, first check the Supplement at the back of the book for any new service information.

CHAPTER NINE

FRONT SUSPENSION AND STEERING

This chapter describes repair and maintenance of the front wheel, forks, and steering components.

FRONT WHEEL

Refer to **Figure 1** for this procedure.

Removal

1. Place a wooden block under the crankcase to lift the front of the motorcycle off the ground.

2. Remove the setscrew securing the speedometer cable (A, **Figure 2**) and pull cable out.

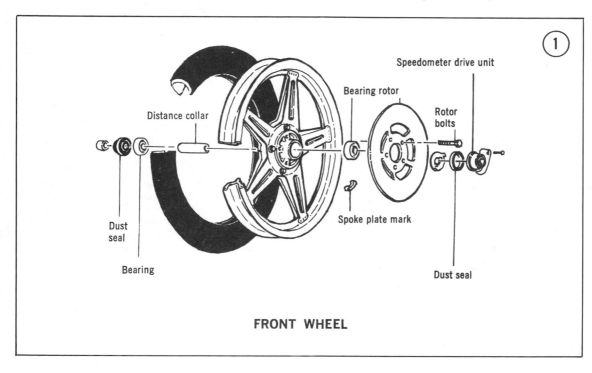

Speedometer drive unit

Bearing rotor

Rotor bolts

Distance collar

Dust seal

Bearing

Spoke plate mark

Dust seal

FRONT WHEEL

3. Remove the axle nut cotter pin (B, **Figure 2**) and discard it.

CAUTION
Never reuse a cotter pin.

4. Remove the axle nut (C, **Figure 2**).

5. Remove the 2 nuts securing the front axle holder (**Figure 3**) and remove it.

6. Push the axle out from the left side, with a drift or screwdriver, and remove it.

7. Remove the wheel; pull the wheel forward to disengage the disc from the caliper.

> NOTE: *Insert a piece of wood in the caliper in place of the disc. That way, if brake lever is inadvertently squeezed, the piston will not be forced out of the cylinder. If this does happen, the caliper might have to be disassembled to reseat the piston, and the system will have to be bled. By using the wood, bleeding the brake is not necessary when installing the wheel.*

Installation

1. Carefully insert the disc between the pads when installing the wheel.

2. Insert the axle from the right-hand side and install the axle holder and the 2 flat washers, lockwashers, and nuts (**Figure 3**).

> NOTE: *Install the axle holder with the arrow facing forward and the end of the*

axle flush with the outer surface of the fork.

3. Tighten the holder nuts to 13-18 ft.-lb. (18-24 N•m).

4. Install the axle nut and torque to 40-47 ft.-lb. (54-64 N•m). Install a *new* cotter pin.

CAUTION
Never reuse a cotter pin, always install a new one.

5. Insert the speedometer cable and install the setscrew (A, **Figure 2**).

> NOTE: *Rotate the wheel slowly when inserting the cable so that it will engage properly.*

6. After the wheel is installed, completely rotate it; apply the brake several times to make sure it rotates freely.

Inspection

Measure the wobble and runout of the wheel rim with a dial indicator as shown in **Figure 4**. The standard value for both wobble and runout is 0.02 in. (0.5mm). The maximum permissible limit is 0.08 in. (2mm).

If the runout exceeds the limit, it will have to be replaced as the ComStar wheel cannot be serviced.

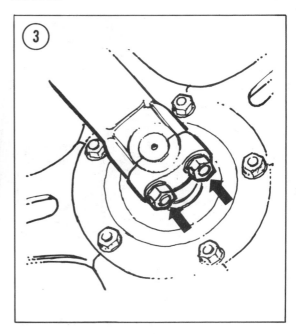

FRONT HUB

Disassembly

1. Remove the front wheel as described under *Front Wheel Removal* in this chapter.

2. Remove the dust seal.

3. Remove the 5 bolts securing the brake disc and remove it if necessary.

4. Remove the left-hand bearing.

5. Remove the distance collar.

6. Remove the right-hand bearing.

Inspection

1. Clean bearings thoroughly in solvent and dry with compressed air. Do not let the bearing spin while drying.

2. Clean the inside and outside of the hub with solvent. Dry with compressed air.

3. Turn each bearing by hand. Make sure bearings turn smoothly. Check balls for evidence of wear, pitting, or excessive heat (bluish tint). Replace bearings if necessary; always replace them as a complete set.

4. Check the axle for wear and straightness. Use V-blocks and a dial indicator as shown in **Figure 5**. If the runout is 0.008 in. (0.2mm) or greater, the axle must be replaced.

Assembly

1. Pack the bearings thoroughly with multipurpose grease. Work the grease in between the balls thoroughly.

2. Pack the wheel hub and distance collar with multipurpose grease.

3. Install the right-hand bearing.

4. Press in the distance collar.

5. Install the left-hand bearing.

NOTE: *Install the bearings with the sealed side facing outward.*

CAUTION
Tap the bearings squarely into place and tap on the outer race only. Do not tap on the inner race or the bearing might be damaged. Be sure that the bearings are completely seated.

6. Lubricate the dust seal with grease.

7. Install the dust seal and collar in the right-hand side.

8. Install the speedometer gear retainer in the hub on the left-hand side.

9. Lubricate the oil seal and install it.

10. Disassemble the speedometer gear box and lubricate the gears and sliding faces with multipurpose grease. Reassemble it.

11. Install brake disc, if removed, and tighten the bolts to 20-24 ft.-lb. (27-33 N•m).

12. Install the speedometer gear into the hub. Align the tangs of the gear with the notches in the wheel retainer.

WHEEL BALANCING

An unbalanced wheel results in unsafe riding conditions. Depending on the degree of unbalance and the speed of the motorcycle, the

9

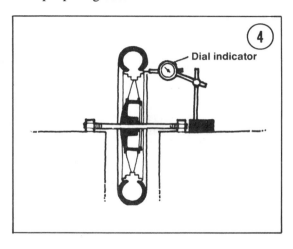

Dial indicator

④

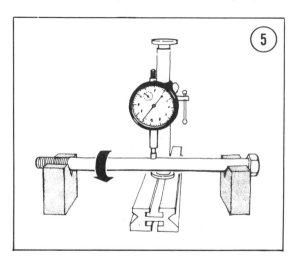

⑤

rider may experience anything from a mild vibration to a violent shimmy which may even result in loss of control.

On the ComStar wheels, weights are attached to the rim. A kit of Tape-A-Weight, or equivalent may be purchased from most motorcycle supply stores. This kit contains test weights and strips of adhesive-backed weights that can be cut to desired weight and attached directly to the rim.

Before you attempt to balance the wheel, check to be sure that the wheel bearings are in good condition and properly lubricated and that the brakes do not drag. *The wheel must rotate freely.*

1. Remove the wheel as described under *Front Wheel Removal* in this chapter.

2. Mount the wheel on a fixture such as the one in **Figure 6** so it can rotate freely.

3. Give the wheel a spin and let it coast to a stop. Mark the tire at the lowest point.

4. Spin the wheel several more times. If the wheel keeps coming to rest at the same point, it is out of balance.

5. Tape a test weight to the upper (or light) side of the wheel.

6. Experiment with different weights until the wheel, when spun, comes to rest at a different position each time.

7. Remove the test weight and install the correct size adhesive-backed weight.

TIRE CHANGING

The rim of the ComStar wheel is aluminum and the exterior appearance can easily be damaged. Special care must be taken with tire irons when changing a tire to avoid scratches and gouges to the outer rim surface.

Removal

1. Remove the valve core to deflate the tire.

2. Press the entire bead on both sides of the tire into the center of the rim.

3. Lubricate the beads with soapy water.

4. Insert the tire iron under the bead next to the valve (**Figure 7**). Force the bead on the opposite side of the tire into the center of the rim and pry the bead over the rim with the tire iron.

5. Insert a second tire iron next to the first to hold the bead over the rim. Then work around the tire with the first tire iron, prying the bead over the rim (**Figure 8**).

6. Stand the tire upright. Insert a tire iron between the second bead and the side of the rim

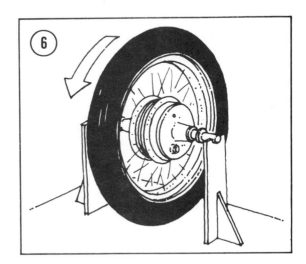

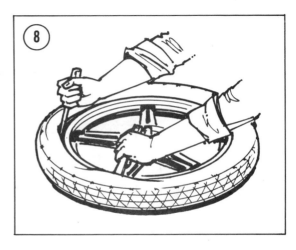

that the first bead was pried over **(Figure 9)**. Force the bead on the opposite side from the tire iron into the center of the rim. Pry the second bead off the rim, working around as with the first.

Installation

1. Carefully check the tire for any damage, especially inside.

2. A new tire may have balancing rubbers inside. These are not patches and should not be disturbed. A colored spot near the bead indicates a lighter point on the tire. This should be placed next to the valve or midway between the 2 rim locks if they are installed.

3. Lubricate the tire beads and rim with soapy water.

4. Press the lower bead into the rim center on each side of the valve, working around the tire in both directions **(Figure 10)**. Use a tire iron for the last few inches of bead **(Figure 11)**.

5. Press the upper bead into the rim opposite the valve **(Figure 12)**. Pry the bead into the rim on both sides of the initial point with a tire iron, working around rim to the valve **(Figure 13)**.

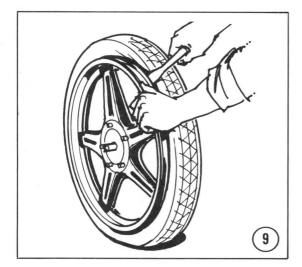

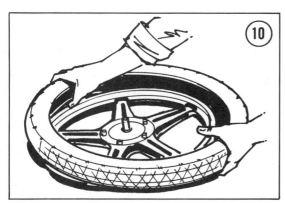

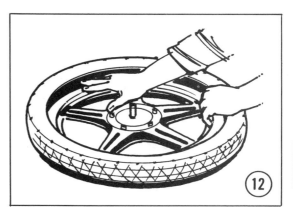

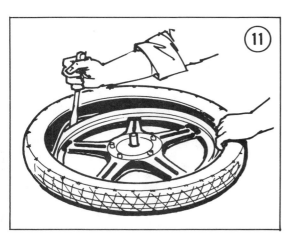

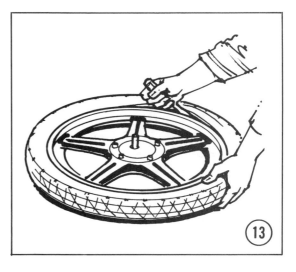

6. Check the bead on both sides of the tire for even fit around the rim. Inflate the tire slowly to seat the beads in the rim. It may be necessary to bounce the tire to complete the seating. Inflate to the required pressure. Balance the wheel as described previously.

HANDLEBAR

Removal/Installation

1. Remove the 2 bolts **(Figure 14)** securing the master cylinder and lay it on the fuel tank. It is not necessary to remove the hydraulic brake line.

> CAUTION
> *Cover the fuel tank with a heavy cloth or plastic tarp to protect it from accidental spilling of brake fluid. Wash any brake fluid off of any painted or plated surface immediately, as it will destroy the finish. Use soapy water and rinse thoroughly.*

2. Slacken the clutch cable **(Figure 15)** and disconnect it from the hand lever.

3. Separate the 2 halves of the start switch assembly. Disconnect the throttle cables from the twist grip **(Figure 16)**.

4. Remove the rear view mirrors and clamps securing electrical cables to the handlebar.

5. Remove the 4 rubber plugs (A, **Figure 17)** and 4 Allen bolts (B, **Figure 17)** securing the fuse/handlebar holder and remove it. Lay it over the fuel tank or the headlight nacelle.

6. Lift off the handlebars.

7. Install by reversing these steps. Align the punch marks on the handlebar with the line that separates the upper and lower fuse/handlebar holder.

8. Tighten the forward 2 Allen screws of the fuse/handlebar holder first, then the rear. Tighten to a torque of 13-18 ft.-lb. (18-24 N•m).

9. Align the punch mark on the handlebar with the lug on the master cylinder holder.

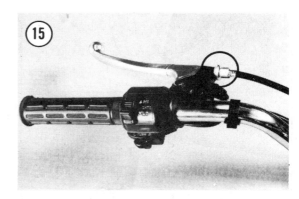

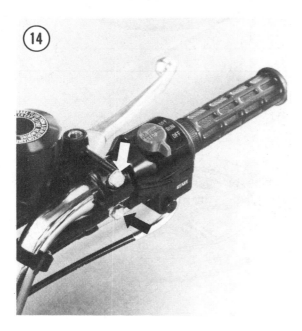

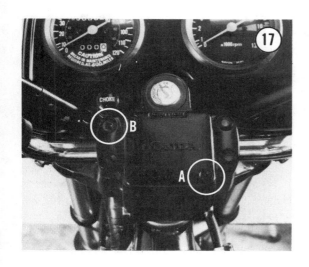

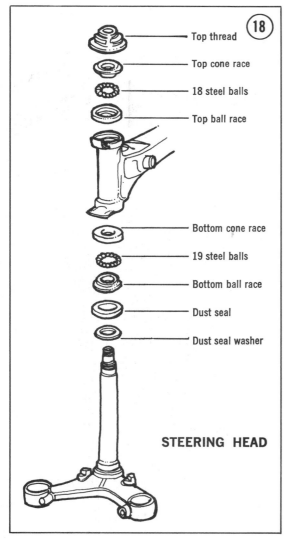

- Top thread
- Top cone race
- 18 steel balls
- Top ball race

- Bottom cone race
- 19 steel balls
- Bottom ball race
- Dust seal
- Dust seal washer

STEERING HEAD

STEERING HEAD

Disassembly

Refer to **Figure 18** for this procedure.

1. Remove the front wheel as described under *Front Wheel Removal* in this chapter.

2. Disconnect hydraulic brake line **(Figure 19)** at the caliper. Plug all exposed ends to prevent brake fluid spillage and to keep dirt and moisture out of the brake system.

> **CAUTION**
> *Do not spill brake fluid on painted or plated surfaces as it will ruin the finish. If you do spill it, wash the area immediately with soapy water and thoroughly rinse off.*

Remove the bracket securing the hydraulic brake line to fork tube.

3. Remove the headlight nacelle assembly.

4. Remove the handlebar as described under, *Handlebar Removal/Installation*, this chapter.

5. Unscrew the steering stem nut.

9

6. Loosen upper fork bridge bolts (**Figure 20**).

7. Loosen lower fork bridge bolts (**Figure 21**).

8. Slide entire fork and fender assembly out.

9. Remove the top fork bridge.

10. Remove the adjuster nut with the pin spanner, provided in the CX500 tool kit, or use an easily improvised unit (**Figure 22**).

11. Have an assistant hold a large pan under the steering stem to catch the loose ball-bearings and carefully lower the steering stem (**Figure 23**).

NOTE
There are 37 balls total—18 on the top and 19 on the bottom. The balls are all the same size.

Inspection

1. Clean the bearing races in the steering head, the steering stem races and all the ball-bearings with solvent.

2. Check for broken welds on the frame around the steering head.

3. Check each of the balls for pitting, scratches, or discoloration indicating wear or corrosion. *Replace them in sets if any are bad.*

4. Check upper and lower races in the steering head. See *Bearing Race Replacement* if races are pitted, scratched, or badly worn.

5. Check steering stem for cracks. Check bearing race on stem for pitting, scratches, or excessive wear.

6. Check inside of steering head adjuster (top ball race) for pitting, scratches, or excessive wear.

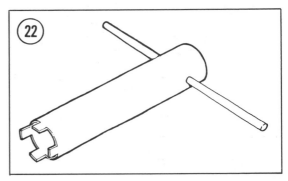

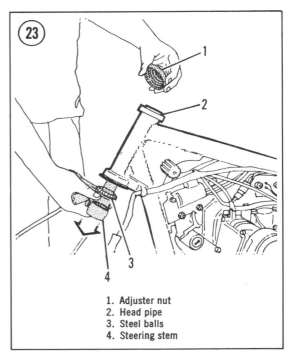

1. Adjuster nut
2. Head pipe
3. Steel balls
4. Steering stem

Bearing Race Replacement

The headset and steering stem bearing races are pressed into place. Because they are easily bent, do not remove them unless they are worn and require replacement. Take old races to the dealer to ensure exact replacement.

Headset bearing race removal/installation

To remove a headset race, insert a hardwood stick into the head tube and carefully tap the

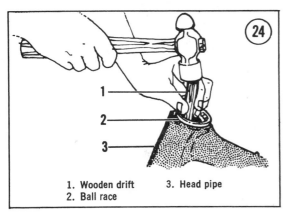

1. Wooden drift   3. Head pipe
2. Ball race

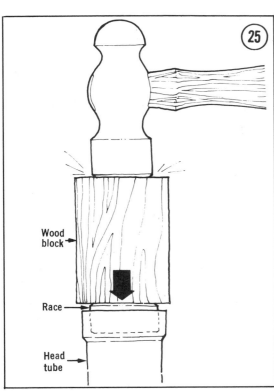

Wood block

Race

Head tube

race out from the inside (**Figure 24**). Tap all around the race so that neither the race nor the head tube are bent. To install a race, fit it into the end of the head tube. Tap it slowly and squarely with a block of wood (**Figure 25**).

> NOTE: *The upper and lower races are different. Be sure that you install them at the proper ends of the head tube.*

Steering stem race and dust seal removal/installation

To remove the steering stem race, try twisting and pulling it up by hand. If it will not come off, carefully pry it up with a screwdriver, while working around in a circle, prying a little at a time. Remove the dust seal and the washer.

Install the washer and new dust seal. Slide the race over the steering stem with the bearing surface pointing up. Tap the race down with a piece of hardwood; work around in a circle so that the race will not be bent. Make sure it is seated squarely and all the way down.

Assembly

Refer to **Figure 18** for this procedure.

1. Make sure the steering head and stem races are properly seated.

2. Install bottom bearing race cone over steering stem. Slide it down as far as possible.

3. Apply a coat of grease to bottom race cone and fit 19 ball bearings around it (**Figure 26**). The grease will hold them in place.

4. Fit 18 ball bearings into top race (**Figure 27**) in head tube. Grease will hold them in place.

5. Insert steering stem into head tube. Hold it firmly in place.

6. Install top bearing race cone.

7. Screw steering stem adjuster nut onto stem.

8. Tighten adjuster firmly to seat bearings. Use the pin spanner or tool shown in **Figure 22**.

9. Loosen adjuster until there is noticeable play in stem.

10. Tighten adjuster enough to remove all play, both horizontal and vertical (**Figure 28**), yet leaving it loose enough so that the assembly will turn to the locks under its own weight after an initial assist.

9

11. Install the top fork bridge.

12. Install the fork and fender assembly.

13. Tighten lower fork bridge bolts and torque them to 13-18 ft.-lb. (18-24 N•m).

14. Tighten the upper fork bolts and torque them to 7-9 ft.-lb. (9-12 N•m).

15. Install the steering stem nut and torque to 65-90 ft.-lb. (88-122 N•m).

16. Install the handlebar and headlight nacelle.

> NOTE: *Torque the 4 bolts securing the handlebar to 13-18 ft.-lb. (18-24 N•m).*

17. Install the brake caliper assembly, torque attachment bolts to 22-29 ft.-lb. (29-39 N•m).

18. Install the front wheel as described under *Front Wheel Installation* in this chapter.

19. Bleed the brake as described under *Bleeding the System* in Chapter Eleven.

Steering Stem Adjustment

If play develops in the steering system, it may only require adjustment. However, don't take a chance on it. Disassemble the stem and look for possible damage. Then reassemble and adjust as described in Steps 9-11, *Steering Head Assembly* in this chapter.

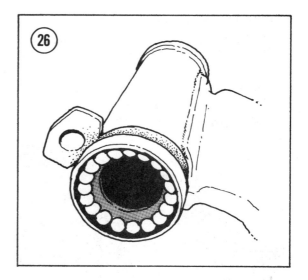

FRONT FORKS

The Honda front suspension consists of a spring-controlled, hydraulically dampened telescopic fork. Before suspecting major trouble, drain the fork oil and refill with the proper type and quantity. If you still have trouble, such as poor dampening, tendency to bottom out or top out, or leakage around rubber seals, then follow the service procedures in this section.

To simplify forks service and to prevent the mixing of parts, the legs should be removed, serviced, and reinstalled individually.

Removal/Installation

1. Remove the front wheel as described under *Front Wheel Removal* in this chapter.

2. Remove the bolts securing the front fender and remove it.

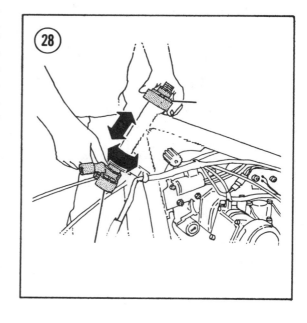

3. Remove the 2 bolts securing the brake caliper assembly to the fork leg (**Figure 29**) and lift the caliper off. Tie it up with wire to keep tension off the brake line.

> NOTE: *Insert a piece of wood in the caliper in place of the disc. That way, if the brake lever is inadvertently squeezed*

the piston will not be forced out of the cylinder. If it does happen the caliper might have to be disassembled to reseat the piston, and the system will have to be bled. By using the wood, bleeding the brake is not necessary when installing the wheel.

4. Loosen the lower fork bridge bolt (**Figure 21**).

5. Loosen the upper fork bolt (**Figure 20**).

6. Remove the fork tube. It may be necessary to slightly rotate the tube while removing it.

7. Install by reversing removal steps. Torque the upper fork bolts (**Figure 20**) to 7-9 ft.- lb. (9-12 N•m), lower fork bridge bolts (**Figure 21**) to 13-18 ft.-lb. (18-24 N•m) and the disc brake caliper assembly bolts (**Figure 29**) to 22-29 ft.-lb. (29-39 N•m).

Disassembly

Refer to **Figure 30** for this procedure.

1. Hold the fork tube in a vise with soft jaws. Keep the slider end lower than the top end.

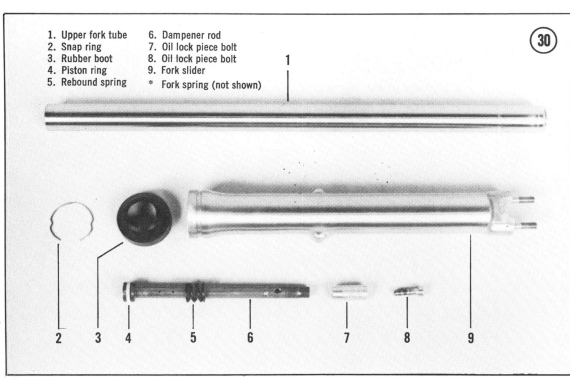

1. Upper fork tube
2. Snap ring
3. Rubber boot
4. Piston ring
5. Rebound spring
6. Dampener rod
7. Oil lock piece bolt
8. Oil lock piece bolt
9. Fork slider
* Fork spring (not shown)

9

WARNING
*Be careful when removing the top bolt
as the spring is under pressure.*

2. Remove the top bolt from the fork. Use a 14mm Allen wrench or insert the head of a 14mm bolt **(Figure 31)** into the socket and turn it with Vise Grips.

3. Remove the washer, spring seat and spring **(Figure 32)**.

4. Remove the fork from vise and pour the oil out and discard. Pump the fork several times by hand to get most of the oil out.

5. Remove the rubber boot **(Figure 33)** out of the notch in the slider and slide it off of the fork tube.

6. Clamp the slider in a vise with soft jaws.

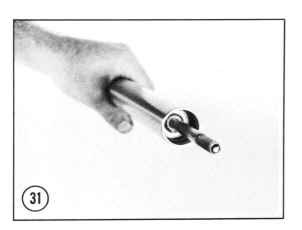

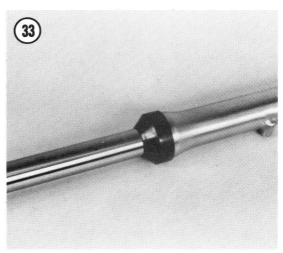

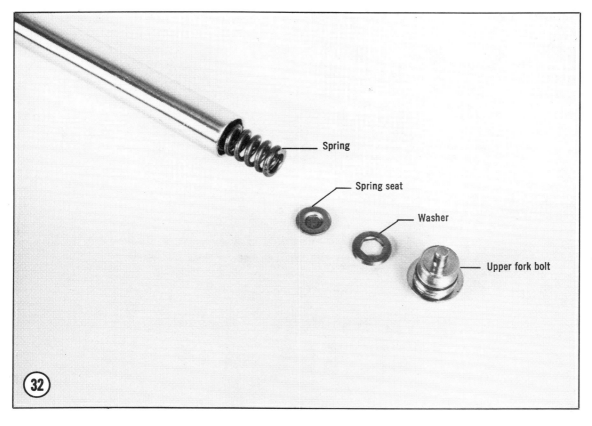

7. Remove the 6mm Allen bolt **(Figure 34)** at the bottom of the slider and pull the fork tube out of the slider.

8. Remove the oil lock piece **(Figure 35)**, the dampener rod and rebound spring **(Figure 36)**.

9. Remove snap ring and oil seal **(Figure 37)**.

CAUTION
Use a dull screwdriver blade to remove oil seal. Do not damage the outer or inner surface of the slider.

Inspection

1. Thoroughly clean all parts in solvent and dry. Check the fork tube for signs of wear or galling.

2. Check the dampener rod for straightness. **Figure 38** shows one method. The rod should be replaced if the runout is 0.008 in. (0.2mm) or greater.

3. Carefully check the dampener valve and the piston ring for wear or damage.

4. Inspect the oil seals for scoring and nicks and loss of resiliency. Replace if its condition is questionable.

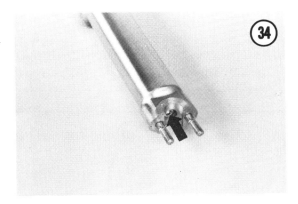

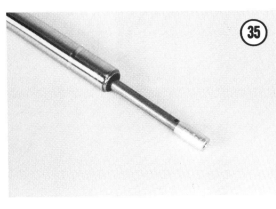

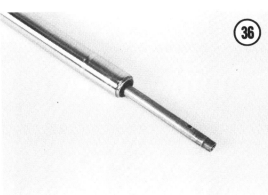

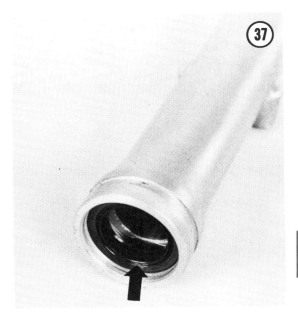

5. Measure uncompressed length of the spring with a square such as shown in **Figure 39**. Replace the spring if it is 17.70 in. (449.5 mm) or shorter.

6. Any parts that are worn or damaged should be replaced; simply cleaning and reinstalling unserviceable components will not improve performance of the front suspension.

Assembly

1. Install the oil seal and snap ring **(Figure 37)**.

> NOTE: *Make sure seal seats squarely and fully in the bore of the slider.*

2. Insert the dampener rod into fork tube **(Figure 36)** and install oil lock piece **(Figure 35)**.

3. Apply a light coat of oil to the outside of the fork tube and install it into the slider. Apply Loctite Lock N' Seal to the threads of the Allen bolt and install it **(Figure 34)**.

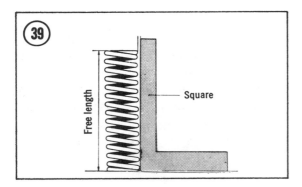

4. Slide the rubber boot into place **(Figure 33)**.

5. Fill the fork tube with 4.5-4.7 oz. (135-140cc) of fresh oil.

> *NOTE*
> *Use DEXRON automatic transmission fluid (ATF).*

> NOTE: *In order to measure the correct amount of fluid, use a plastic baby bottle. These have measurements in fluid ounces (oz.) and cubic centimeters (cc) on the side (Figure 40).*

6. Insert the spring with the tapered end down toward the axle. Install the spring seat, washer, and the top bolt.

7. Install the fork as described under *Front Fork Removal/Installation* in this chapter.

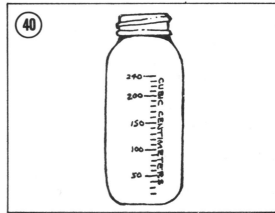

NOTE: If you own a 1980 or later model, first check the Supplement at the back of the book for any new service information.

CHAPTER TEN

REAR SUSPENSION AND FINAL DRIVE

This chapter includes repair and replacement procedures for the rear wheel, final drive unit and rear suspension components.

REAR WHEEL

Refer to **Figure 1** for this procedure.

Removal/Installation

1. Place a support block under the engine crankcase so that the rear wheel clears the ground.

2. Loosen the clamps (A, **Figure 2**) securing the mufflers to the common collector. Remove the bolt securing the rear foot pegs and mufflers (B, **Figure 2**). Slide the mufflers out of the collector and remove them.

3. Remove the brake rod adjusting nut (A, **Figure 3**). Separate the rod from the brake arm.

4. Remove the cotter pin, backing plate stop nut, washer, rubber grommet (B, **Figure 3**) and disconnect the torque arm from the backing plate.

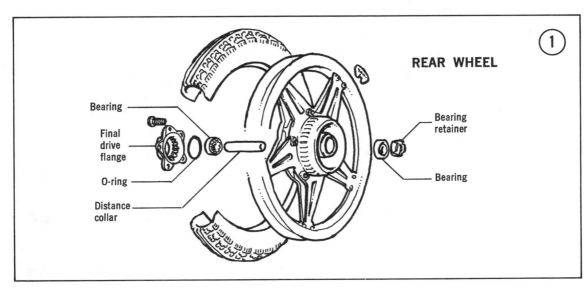

① REAR WHEEL

- Bearing
- Final drive flange
- O-ring
- Distance collar
- Bearing retainer
- Bearing

5. Remove cotter pin and axle nut (**Figure 4**). *Discard the cotter pin.* Loosen the axle holder bolt (A, **Figure 5**).

6. Withdraw the axle bolt from the left side. Catch the axle spacer (B, **Figure 5**) as the axle bolt is withdrawn.

7. Slide the wheel to the left to disengage it from the hub drive spline and remove the wheel.

8. Install by reversing the removal steps. Apply molybdenum disulfide grease to the final drive flange splines on the wheel (**Figure 6**) and the ring gear (**Figure 7**).

9. Make sure that the wheel hub splines engage with the final drive.

10. Torque the axle nut to 40-47 ft.-lb. (54-64 N•m), the brake torque arm bolt and nut to 11-17 ft.-lb. (15-23 N•m) and the axle holder bolt to 15-22 ft.-lb. (20-30 N•m). Install a new cotter pin on the axle nut.

CAUTION
Never reuse a cotter pin. Always install a new one.

Inspection

Measure the wobble and runout of the wheel rim with a dial indicator as shown in **Figure 8**. The standard value for both wobble and runout is 0.02 in. (0.5mm). The maximum permissible limit is 0.08 in. (2mm). If the runout exceeds the limit it will have to be replaced as the Com-Star wheel cannot be serviced.

10

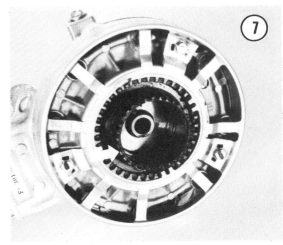

REAR HUB

Disassembly

1. Remove rear wheel as described under *Rear Wheel Removal/Installation* in this chapter.

2. Pull the brake assembly straight up and out of the brake drum.

3. Remove the 5 bolts **(Figure 9)** and pull out the final drive flange and O-ring.

4. Remove the right-hand bearing and distance collar.

5. Remove the bearing retainer from the hub **(Figure 10)**.

6. Remove the left-hand bearing.

Inspection

1. Clean bearings thoroughly in solvent and dry with compressed air. Do not let the bearing spin while drying.

2. Clean the inside and outside of the hub with solvent. Dry with compressed air.

3. Turn each bearing by hand **(Figure 11)**. Make sure bearings turn smoothly. Check the balls for evidence of wear, pitting, or excessive heat (bluish tint). Replace if necessary; always replace as a complete set.

4. Check the axle for wear and straightness. Use V-blocks and a dial indicator as shown in **Figure 12**. If the runout is 0.008 in. (0.2mm) or greater, the axle must be replaced.

5. Check the brake drum surface (A, **Figure 10**) for out-of-round, scoring, and excessive wear.

Assembly

1. Pack the bearing thoroughly with multipurpose grease. Work grease in between the balls completely.

2. Install the left-hand bearing.

3. Install the bearing retainer (B, **Figure 10**) and stake it with a centerpunch.

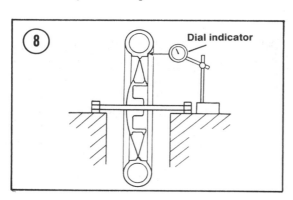

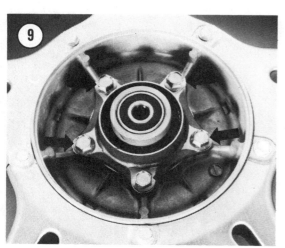

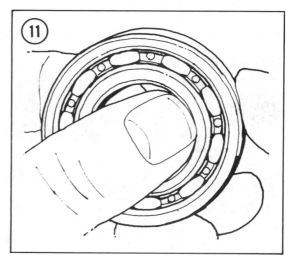

4. Press in the axle spacer.

5. Install the distance collar and drive in the right-hand wheel bearing.

> NOTE: *Install bearings with the sealed side facing outward.*

CAUTION
Tap the bearings squarely into place and tap on the outer race only. Do not tap on the inner race or the bearings might be damaged. Be sure that the bearings are completely seated.

6. Install the O-ring. Apply molybdenum disulfide grease to the O-ring and final drive splines.

7. Install the final drive flange and torque the bolts to 29-36 ft.-lb. (39-48 N•m).

8. Install the brake assembly into the drum.

9. Install the wheel as described under *Rear Wheel Removal/Installation* in this chapter.

WHEEL BALANCING

For complete information refer to *Wheel Balancing* in Chapter Nine.

TIRE CHANGE

Refer to *Tire Changing* in Chapter Nine.

FINAL DRIVE

Removal/Installation

1. Remove rear wheel as described under *Rear Wheel Removal/Installation* in this chapter.

2. Loosen the clamps securing the mufflers (A, **Figure 13**) to the collector and remove the bolts securing the rear foot pegs and mufflers (B, **Figure 13**). Remove the mufflers.

3. Remove the 3 nuts (**Figure 14**) securing the final drive unit to the swing arm.

4. Remove the right-hand lower shock absorber acorn nut (**Figure 15**).

5. Pull the final drive unit straight back until it is free.

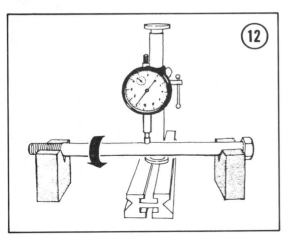

10

6. Wipe the grease from the pinion joint (on the end of the final drive) and drive shaft joint splines.

7. Check the splines (**Figure 16**) on both joints carefully for signs of wear. Replace the joints if necessary.

8. Pack the drive joint with multipurpose molybdenum disulfide grease. Also grease the pinion joint splines.

9. Install the final drive unit onto the swing arm. Install the 3 nuts but *do not* tighten them at this time.

10. Insert the rear axle through the swing arm and final drive to align the final drive unit. Tighten the 3 nuts to 33-44 ft.-lb. (45-59 N•m). Remove the rear axle.

11. Install the lower shock absorber acorn nut and tighten to 22-29 ft.-lb. (30-39 N•m).

12. Install the axle spacer with the small end toward the right-hand side.

13. Check the locking tabs on the 3 bolts (**Figure 17**) securing the dust cover in place. Make sure all are snug up against the bolts to prevent them from working loose during travel.

14. Install the rear wheel and mufflers.

Disassembly and Inspection

Although it may be practical for you to disassemble the final drive for inspection, you cannot replace the bearings or seals (which require bearing removal) without special tools. If there is trouble in the final drive unit, it may be best to remove the unit, take it to your Honda dealer, and let them overhaul it.

1. Remove the final drive unit as described under *Final Drive Removal/Installation* in this chapter.

2. Remove the drain plug, drain the oil from the unit, and reinstall the plug.

3. Straighten the locking tabs (**Figure 17**) against the 3 bolts. Remove the bolts and the dust cover.

4. Remove the 8 bolts securing the case cover.

5. Remove the case cover along with the ring gear and bearing.

6. Remove the ring gear spacer from the case.

7. Separate the left-hand case cover from the ring gear and bearing.

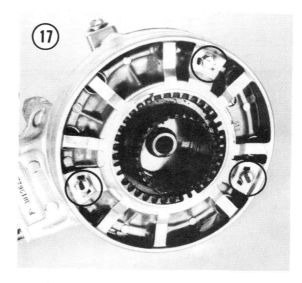

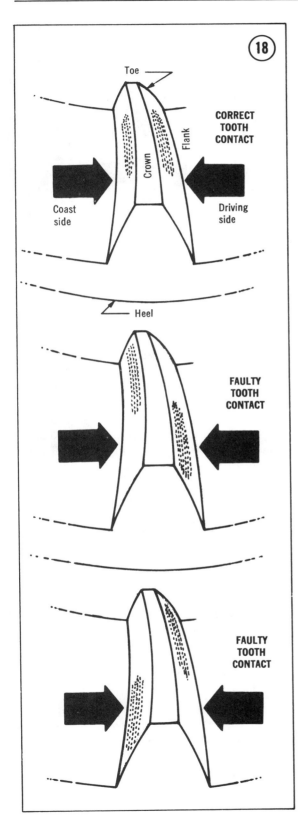

NOTE: *Tap lightly with a plastic or rubber mallet to separate the case cover from the ring gear and bearing.*

8. Inspect the ring gear oil seal for leakage. Replace it if the lip is damaged or if the spring band is distorted.

NOTE: *In order to replace the seal, it is necessary to remove the bearing. This must be done by a Honda dealer or qualified machine shop.*

CAUTION
The bearings are easily damaged if removed. The following inspection procedures do not require bearing removal. Remove the bearings only if they are defective.

9. Make sure that all bearings are clean.

10. Turn each bearing by hand. Make sure that bearings turn smoothly. Check rollers for evidence of wear, pitting, or excessive heat (bluish tint).

11. If any bearing is questionable, take it to your dealer. He will verify if the bearing is defective and replace it for a small bench fee. Special pullers are required to remove the bearings, and a press must be used to install them.

CAUTION
The final drive case is very easily damaged by trying to use improvised bearing replacement tools. Take the job to your dealer to avoid costly and unnecessary damage.

12. Check the wear pattern on the ring and pinion teeth (**Figure 18**). Check for the following characteristics:

   a. Some clearance between top of teeth and top of pattern

   b. No distinct lines indicating high pressure areas

   c. Marks on adjoining teeth should be directly opposite each other

   d. Both drive and coast patterns should be fairly well centered on teeth.

14. Check teeth on ring and pinion gears. Look for visible wear or damage. Check for chipped or missing teeth.

Assembly

This procedure assumes that all seals and bearings are in good condition and properly installed.

1. Clean off all old liquid gasket material from the mating surfaces of the gear case and cover.

> NOTE: *Make sure the entire assembly is clean and free of foreign matter prior to assembly.*

2. Clean the cover mating surface of the gear case; remove any burrs with an oilstone.

3. Apply a liquid gasket sealant like Loctite Fit-All, or equivalent, to the mating surfaces of the gear case and the cover.

> NOTE: *The following steps adjust the gear preload. These steps must be followed exactly or the gears will wear prematurely. If the inspection in Step 12 of* **Final Drive, Disassembly and Inspection** *showed satisfactory gear wear patterns, and nothing has been replaced, use the original ring gear control spacer (shim) and skip Steps 4-13; continue on with Steps 15-18 only.*

4. Apply a thin even coat of Prussian Blue or lead oxide to the teeth of the ring gear and check the tooth contact pattern.

5. Install the original ring gear control spacer (shim) onto the ring gear. A small coating of grease will hold it in place.

6. Install the ring gear into the case and install the gear case cover.

CAUTION

> *Do not allow the gear case cover to become tilted while installing it.*

7. Partially install the 8 case cover bolts. Tighten the 3 indicated 8mm bolts in the sequence shown in **Figure 19** in two or more steps until the gear case cover comes in contact with the gear case. Torque the six 8mm bolts to 17-20 ft.-lb. (23-27 N•m) and the two 10mm bolts to 25-33 ft.-lb. (34-45 N•m) in a crisscross pattern in two or more steps.

8. Turn the pinion shaft several turns in both directions so that the contact pattern on the teeth is pressed into the coating of Prussian Blue or lead oxide.

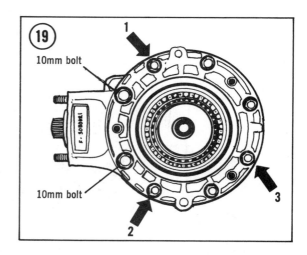

9. Remove the 8 case bolts, remove the case cover, and carefully lift out the ring gear assembly.

10. Examine the contact pattern on the teeth and check for the characteristics listed under Step 12 of the *Disassembly/Inspection* procedure. **Figure 18** shows typical patterns. Your pattern need not be exactly like the illustration to be acceptable.

11. If pattern is not acceptable, purchase different size shims and repeat Steps 4-10 to determine which size shim should be used. Do not use more than one at a time.

12. When you have found a shim which produces an acceptable pattern, clean all traces of Prussian Blue or lead oxide from the gears.

13. Install the proper shim on the ring gear. Hold it in place with a small amount of heavy grease.

14. Apply a liquid gasket sealant like Loctite Fit-All or equivalent, to the mating surfaces of the gear case and the cover.

15. Install the ring gear into the case and install the gear case cover.

CAUTION

> *Do not allow the gear case cover to become tilted while installing it.*

16. Install the 8 cover bolts and tighten in sequence shown in **Figure 19** in 2 or more steps until the gear case comes in contact with the gear case. Tighten two 10mm bolts to 25-33 ft.-lb. (34-45 N•m) and six 8mm bolts to 17-20 ft.-lb. (23-27 N•m).

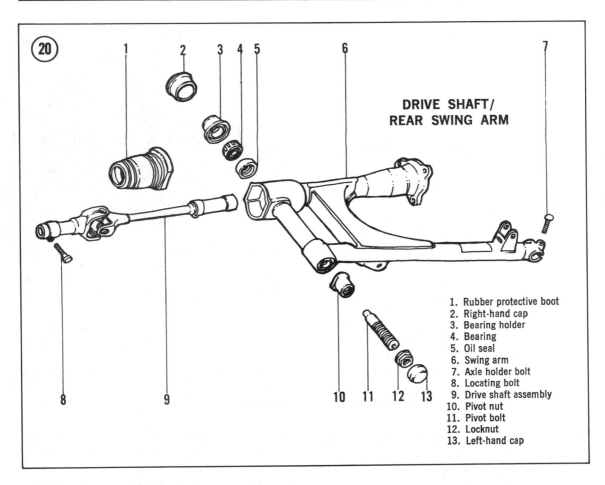

DRIVE SHAFT/
REAR SWING ARM

1. Rubber protective boot
2. Right-hand cap
3. Bearing holder
4. Bearing
5. Oil seal
6. Swing arm
7. Axle holder bolt
8. Locating bolt
9. Drive shaft assembly
10. Pivot nut
11. Pivot bolt
12. Locknut
13. Left-hand cap

17. Install the dust cover and 3 bolts. Tighten the bolts and bend up the locking tabs to secure the bolts in place.

WARNING
If any of the locking tabs are broken or cracked, the dust cover must be replaced. If the bolts work loose during travel, they will cause severe damage to the final drive unit and brake shoe assembly. They may even lock up the rear wheel causing an accident.

18. Install the final drive unit as described under *Final Drive Removal/Installation* in this chapter.

DRIVE SHAFT/REAR SWING ARM

Refer to **Figure 20** for this procedure.

Removal/Installation

1. Remove rear wheel as described under *Rear Wheel Removal/Installation* in this chapter.

2. Remove the final drive unit as described under *Final Drive Removal/Installation* in this chapter.

3. Slide back the rubber protective boot and remove the locating bolt (**Figure 21**).

10

4. Disengage the drive shaft from the engine final shaft.

5. Remove the left-hand shock absorber lower acorn nut.

6. Remove the drain tubes from the clamp (**Figure 22**).

7. Remove the protective cap and remove the locknut (A, **Figure 23**) from the pivot bolt on the left-hand side.

8. Remove the pivot bolt (B, **Figure 23**) from the left-hand side.

9. Remove the right-hand pivot and bearing.

10. Remove the swing arm and the drive shaft assembly.

Inspection

1. Remove rubber boot from swing arm.

2. Withdraw the drive shaft from the swing arm and thoroughly wash the splines in cleaning solvent. Dry them with compressed air.

3. Inspect the splines for wear and damage.

4. Inspect the universal joint for play. Rotate the shaft in both directions. If there is noticeable side play the shaft must be replaced.

5. If the splines in the drive shaft joint (A, **Figure 24**) are damaged, this joint may be replaced. Drive out the spring pin (B, **Figure 24**) with a small drift punch and separate it from the drive shaft.

6. Apply molybdenum disulfide grease to the splines prior to assembly. Assemble new joint onto drive shaft and drive in spring pin.

> CAUTION
> *The spring pin must be driven in so it is below the surface of the joint. It must not stick up or it will interfere with the swing arm housing.*

Installation

1. Installation is the reverse of the removal steps noting the following information. Coat the surfaces of the splines with molybdenum disulfide grease.

2. Make sure the right-hand oil seal bearing and pivot are properly installed.

3. Install the swing arm onto the right-hand side and insert the pivot bolt.

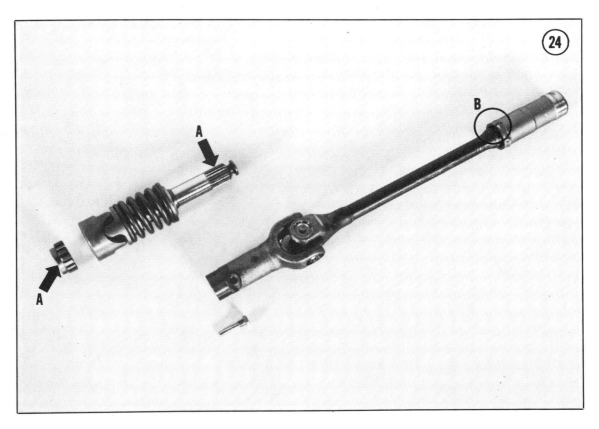

4. Tighten pivot bolt slowly to a torque of 6-9 ft.-lb. (8-12 N•m).

5. Install the locknut and tighten to 58-87 ft.-lb. (79-118 N•m).

6. After installation is completed, fill the final drive Zerk fitting (**Figure 25**) with molybdenum disulfide grease, approximately 1.5 oz. (45cc). Check the fluid level in the final drive unit as described under *Final Drive* in Chapter Three.

REAR SHOCKS

The rear shocks are spring controlled and hydraulically dampened. Spring preload can be adjusted by rotating the cam ring at the base of the spring (**Figure 26**) — *clockwise to increase* preload and *counterclockwise to decrease it*.

> NOTE: *Use spanner wrench furnished in CX500 tool kit for this adjustment.*

Both cams must be indexed on the same detent. The shocks are sealed and cannot be rebuilt. Service is limited to removal and replacement of the hydraulic unit.

10

Removal/Installation

Removal and installation of the rear shocks is easier if they are done separately. The remaining unit will support the rear of the bike and maintain the correct relationship between the top and bottom mounts.

1. Block up the engine or support it on the centerstand.

2. Adjust both shocks to their softest setting, *completely counterclockwise*. Remove the seat.

3. Loosen the clamps securing the mufflers (A, **Figure 27**) to the collector and remove the bolts securing the rear footpegs and mufflers (B, **Figure 27**). Slide the mufflers out of the collector and remove them.

4. Remove upper and lower bolt (**Figure 28**).

5. Pull the shock off.

6. Install by reversing removal steps. Torque the footpeg bolts and shock bolts to 22-29 ft.-lb. (30-39 N•m).

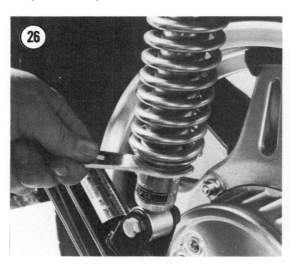

NOTE: If you own a 1980 or later model, first check the Supplement at the back of the book for any new service information.

CHAPTER ELEVEN

BRAKES

The CX500 has a single-disc front brake operated by a hand lever and drum-type rear brake operated by a foot lever. This chapter describes repair and replacement procedures for all brake components.

FRONT DISC BRAKE

The front disc brake is actuated by hydraulic fluid and is controlled by a hand lever like the drum-type brake. As the brake pads wear, the brake fluid level drops in the reservoir and automatically adjusts for wear.

When working on hydraulic brake systems, it is necessary that the work area and all tools be absolutely clean. Any tiny particles of foreign matter and grit in the caliper assembly or the master cylinder can damage the components. Also, sharp tools must not be used inside the caliper or on the piston. If there is any doubt about your ability to correctly and safely carry out major service on the brake components, take the job to a Honda dealer or brake specialist.

Master Cylinder
Removal/Installation

1. Remove the rear view mirror.

CAUTION
Cover the fuel tank and headlight nacelle with a heavy cloth or plastic tarp to protect it from accidental spilling of brake fluid. Wash any brake fluid off of any painted or plated surface immediately, as it will destroy the finish. Use soapy water and rinse completely.

2. Remove bolt (A, **Figure 1**) securing brake hose to master cylinder and remove it.

3. Remove the electrical leads from the brake light switch (A, **Figure 2**).

4. Remove the bolt and nut (B, **Figure 2**) securing the brake lever and remove it.

5. Remove the 2 clamping bolts (B, **Figure 1**) securing the master cylinder to the handlebar, and remove it.

6. Install by reversing the removal steps.

7. Bleed the brake as described under *Bleeding the System* in this chapter.

Master Cylinder Disassembly

Refer to **Figure 3** for this procedure.

1. Remove the master cylinder as described under *Master Cylinder Removal/Installation* in this chapter.

11

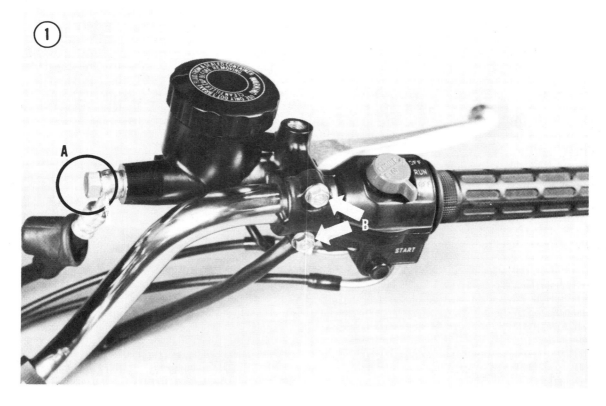

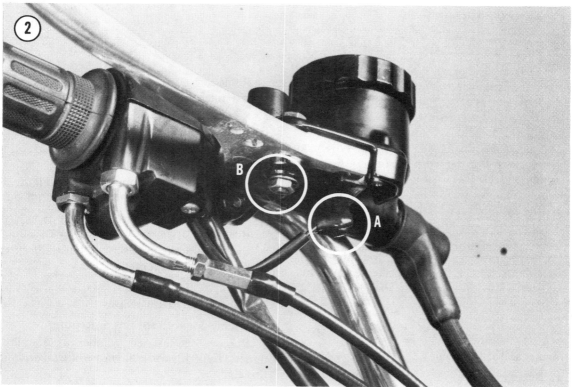

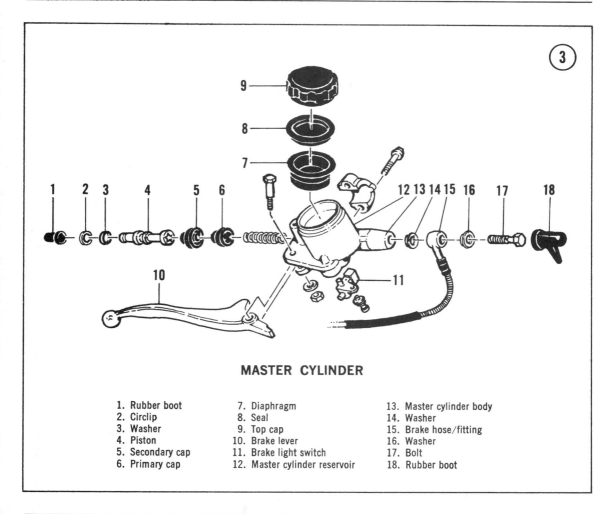

MASTER CYLINDER

1. Rubber boot	7. Diaphragm	13. Master cylinder body
2. Circlip	8. Seal	14. Washer
3. Washer	9. Top cap	15. Brake hose/fitting
4. Piston	10. Brake lever	16. Washer
5. Secondary cap	11. Brake light switch	17. Bolt
6. Primary cap	12. Master cylinder reservoir	18. Rubber boot

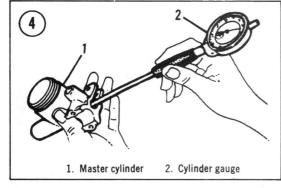

1. Master cylinder   2. Cylinder gauge

2. Remove the top cap and diaphragm; pour out the brake fluid and discard it. *Never* reuse brake fluid.

3. Remove the boot and snap ring.

4. Remove the washer, piston, secondary and primary caps and the spring.

Master Cylinder Inspection

1. Clean all parts in denatured alcohol or fresh brake fluid. Inspect the cylinder bore and piston contact surfaces for signs of wear and damage. If either part is less than perfect, replace it.

2. Check the end of the piston for wear caused by the lever and check the pivot bore in the lever. Discard the caps.

3. Make sure the passages in the bottom of the brake fluid reservoir are clear. Check the reservoir cap and diaphragm for damage and deterioration and replace as necessary.

4. Inspect the condition of the threads in the bores for the brake line and the switch.

5. Check the lever pivot lug for cracks.

6. Measure the cylinder bore (**Figure 4**) and the piston. Cylinder bore must not exceed 0.553 in.

11

(14.053mm) and the piston must not be smaller than 0.549 in. (13.940mm). Replace both parts if they exceed these m asurements.

Master Cylinder Assembly

1. Soak the new caps in fresh brake fluid for at least 15 minutes to make them pliable.

2. Install the spring.

3. Install the primary and secondary caps into the cylinder.

4. Install the piston and washer and install the snap ring and boot.

5. Install the diaphragm and top cap.

6. Install the master cylinder on the handlebar and connect the brake hose and brake light switch electrical leads.

Brake Pad Replacement

There is no recommended mileage interval for changing the friction pads in the disc brake. Pad wear depends greatly on riding habits and conditions. The disc pads should be checked for wear every 1,000 miles and replaced when the red line on the pad (**Figure 5**) reaches the edges of the brake disc. Always replace both pads at the same time.

1. Unscrew the caliper cover (**Figure 6**) and remove it.

2. Pull up and remove the clip (**Figure 7**).

3. Remove the 2 pins securing the pads in place (**Figure 8**), remove the pads (**Figure 9**) and discard them.

4. Clean the pad recess and end of the piston with a soft brush. Do not use solvent, wire brush, or any hard tool which would damage the cylinder or the piston.

5. Lightly coat the end of the piston and the backs of the new pads (*not the friction material*) with disc brake lubricant.

> NOTE: *Check with your dealer to make sure the friction compound of the new pads is compatible with the disc material. Remove any roughness from backs of new pads with a fine cut file; blow them clean with compressed air.*

6. Remove the cap from the master cylinder and slowly push the piston into the caliper while checking the reservoir to make sure the brake

fluid does not overflow. Remove fluid, if necessary, prior to it overflowing. The piston should move freely. If it does not and there is any evidence of it sticking in the cylinder, the caliper should be removed and serviced as described under *Caliper Rebuilding* in this chapter.

7. Push the caliper to the right and push the piston in to allow the new pads to be installed.

8. Install the new pads with the anti-rattle shim on outboard pad next to the piston (**Figure 9**).

9. Insert the 2 pins with the holes (**Figure 8**) facing upward to enable the insertion of the clip. Install the clip (**Figure 7**).

10. Screw the caliper cover into place (**Figure 6**) and snap inspection cover (**Figure 10**) closed.

11. Carefully remove any rust or corrosion from the disc.

12. Block the motorcycle up so that the front wheel is off the ground. Spin the front wheel and activate the brake lever for as many times as it takes to refill the cylinder in the caliper and correctly locate the pads.

13. Refill the fluid in the reservoir if necessary and replace the top cap.

WARNING
Use brake fluid clearly marked DOT 3. Others may vaporize and cause brake failure. Always use the same brand name; do not intermix as many are not compatible.

WARNING
*Do not ride the motorcycle until you are sure the brake is operating correctly with full hydraulic advantage. If necessary, bleed the brakes as described under **Bleeding the System** in this chapter.*

14. Bed the pads in gradually for the first 50 miles by using only light pressure as much as possible. Immediate hard application will glaze the new friction pads and greatly reduce the effectiveness of the brake.

Caliper Removal/Installation

It is not necessary to remove the front wheel to perform this procedure.

11

1. Disconnect the speedometer cable clip (A, **Figure 11**).

2. Remove the bolt (**Figure 12**) securing the brake hose to the caliper and remove it. Drain the fluid from the line and discard it.

3. Remove the 2 caliper mounting bolts (B, **Figure 11**) and slide the caliper off the disc.

4. Install the caliper by reversing the removal steps; carefully insert the caliper onto the disc avoiding damage to the pads. Torque the caliper mounting bolts to 22-29 ft.-lb. (29-39 N•m).

5. Bleed the brakes as described under *Bleeding the System* in this chapter.

> WARNING
> *Do not ride the motorcycle until you are sure the brake is operating correctly.*

Caliper Rebuilding

If the caliper leaks, the caliper should be rebuilt. If the piston sticks in the cylinder, indicating severe wear or galling the entire unit should be replaced. Rebuilding a leaky caliper requires special tools and experience.

Caliper service should be entrusted to your Honda dealer or brake specialist. Considerable money can be saved by removing the caliper yourself and taking it in for repair.

Bleeding the System

1. Remove the dust cap (**Figure 13**) from the brake caliper bleed valve.

2. Connect a length of clear tubing to the bleed valve on the brake caliper (**Figure 14**) and place the other end of the tube into a clean container. Fill the container with enough fresh brake fluid to keep the end submerged. The tube should be long enough so that a loop can be made higher than the bleed valve to prevent air from being drawn into the caliper during bleeding.

> CAUTION
> *Cover the fuel tank and headlight nacelle with a heavy cloth or plastic tarp to protect it from the accidental spilling of brake fluid. Wash any brake fluid off of any painted or plated surface immediately, as it will destroy the finish. Use soapy water and rinse completely.*

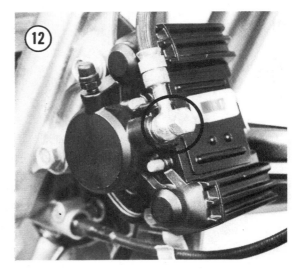

3. Remove the cap of the master cylinder **(Figure 15)**. Fill the fluid reservoir almost to the top lip, insert the diaphragm and *leave in place* during this procedure. Screw the cap on loosely to prevent the entry of dirt.

WARNING
Use brake fluid clearly marked DOT 3. Others may vaporize and cause brake failure. Always use the same brand name, do not intermix, as many are not compatible.

4. Pump the lever several times with the bleed valve closed until you feel pressure building up.

5. Hold the lever down tight and open the bleed valve about one-half turn. Squeeze the lever all the way in. As the fluid enters the system, the level will drop in the reservoir. Maintain the level at about ½ inch from the top of the reservoir to prevent air from being drawn into the system.

6. Continue to pump the lever and fill the reservoir until the fluid emerging from the hose is completely free of bubbles.

NOTE: *Do not allow the reservoir to empty during the bleeding operation or more air will enter the system. If this occurs, the entire procedure must be repeated.*

7. Hold the lever down, tighten the bleed valve, remove the bleed tube and install the bleed valve dust cap.

8. If necessary, add fluid to correct the level in the reservoir. It should be to the UPPER level line **(Figure 16)**.

9. Install the reservoir cap tightly.

10. Test the feel of the brake lever. It should be firm and should offer the same resistance each time it's pulled. If it feels spongy, it's likely that there is still air in the system and it must be bled again. When all air has been bled from the system, and the fluid level is correct in the reservoir, double check for leaks and tighten all the fittings and connections.

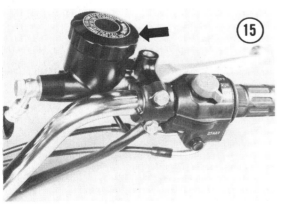

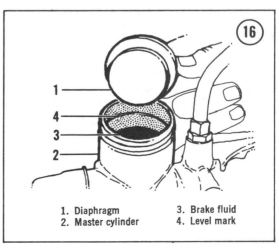

1. Diaphragm
2. Master cylinder
3. Brake fluid
4. Level mark

WARNING
Before riding the motorcycle, make certain that the front brake is operative by compressing the lever several times.

Brake Disc Removal/Installation

1. Remove the front wheel as described under *Front Wheel Removal/Installation* in Chapter Nine.

> NOTE: *Insert a piece of wood in the caliper in place of the disc. That way, if the brake lever is inadvertently squeezed the piston will not be forced out of the cylinder. If this does happen, the caliper might have to be disassembled to reseat the piston, and the system will have to be bled. By using the wood, bleeding the brake is not necessary when installing the wheel.*

2. Remove the 5 bolts securing the disc to the wheel and remove the disc.

3. Install by reversing these removal steps. Torque the 5 bolts to 20-24 ft.-lb. (27-32.5 N•m).

Brake Disc Inspection

It is not necessary to remove the disc from the wheel to inspect it. Small marks on the disc are not important, but deep radial scratches reduce braking effectiveness and increase pad wear. The disc should be replaced.

1. Measure the thickness at several points around the disc with a vernier caliper or micrometer (**Figure 17**). The disc must be replaced if thickness at any point is less than 0.24 in. (6 mm).

2. Measure runout with a dial indicator. Use a procedure similar to that used on wheel wobble (**Figure 18**) in this chapter. If the runout exceeds 0.012 in. (0.3mm) disc must be replaced.

3. Clean the disc of any rust or corrosion with a non-petroleum solvent.

REAR DRUM BRAKE

Disassembly

1. Remove the rear wheel as described under *Rear Wheel Removal* in Chapter Ten.

2. Pull the brake assembly straight up and out of the brake drum.

3. Remove the cotter pins and dual washer from the brake shoe pivot pins (**Figure 19**).

4. Remove the return springs by lightly gripping the coil section with a pair of pipe pliers and extend one of the spring ends with needle nose pliers. Remove the brake shoes.

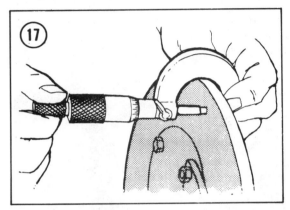

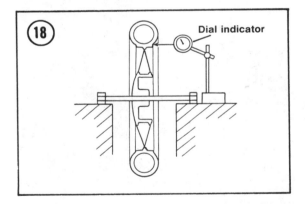

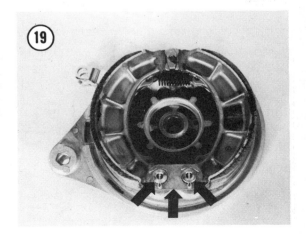

5. Remove the bolt and nut (**Figure 20**) on the brake arm.

6. Remove the arm from the camshaft and pull the cam out of the backing plate.

Inspection

1. Thoroughly clean and dry all the parts except the linings.

2. Check the contact surface of the drum (**Figure 21**) for scoring. If there are deep grooves, deep enough to snag a fingernail, the drum should be reground.

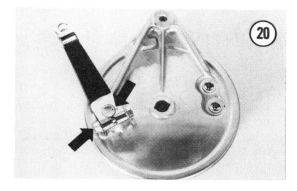

3. Measure the inside diameter of the brake drum with vernier calipers (**Figure 22**). Standard size is 6.29 in. (160.0 mm). If this measurement is 6.34 in. (161.0 mm) or greater, the drum must be replaced.

4. If the brake drum is turned, the linings will have to be replaced and the new ones arced to the new drum contour.

5. Check the brake linings. They should be replaced if worn within 0.08 in. (2.0mm) of the metal shoe table (**Figure 23**).

6. Inspect the linings for imbedded foreign material. Dirt can be removed with a stiff wire brush. Check for any traces of oil or grease; if they are contaminated they must be replaced.

7. Inspect the cam lobe and the pivot pin area of the shaft for wear and corrosion. Minor roughness can be removed with fine emery cloth.

8. Inspect the brake shoe return springs for wear. If they are stretched, they will not fully retract the brake shoes and they will drag and wear out prematurely. Replace if necessary.

Assembly

1. Assemble the brake by reversing the disassembly steps.

2. Grease the shaft, cam, and pivot post with a light coat of a molybdenum disulfide grease; avoid getting any grease on the brake plate where the linings may come in contact with it.

3. When installing the brake arm onto the camshaft, be sure to align the dimples on the two parts (**Figure 20**).

4. Install the wheel as described under *Rear Wheel Installation* in Chapter Ten.

11

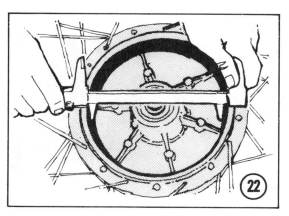

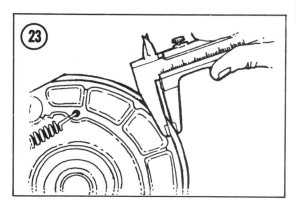

NOTE: If you own a 1980 or later model, first check the Supplement at the back of the book for any new service information.

CHAPTER TWELVE

FRAME AND REPAINTING

The frame does not require periodic maintenance. However, all welds should be inspected immediately after any accident, even a slight one.

This chapter describes procedures for completely stripping the frame. In addition, recommendations are provided for repainting the stripped frame.

This chapter also includes procedures for the kickstand, centerstand, and footpegs.

KICKSTAND (SIDE STAND)

Removal/Installation

1. Block up the engine or support the bike on the centerstand.

2. Raise the kickstand and disconnect the return spring (A, **Figure 1**) from the frame with Vise Grips.

3. Unbolt the kickstand from the frame (B, **Figure 1**).

4. Install by reversing these removal steps. Apply a light coat of multipurpose grease to the pivot surfaces of the frame tab and the kickstand yoke prior to installation.

CENTERSTAND

Removal/Installation

1. Block up the engine or support it on the centerstand.

2. Loosen the clamps securing the mufflers (A, **Figure 2**) to the collector and remove the bolts securing the rear footpegs and mufflers (B, **Figure 2**). Slide the mufflers out of the collector and remove them.

3. Remove the rear wheel as described under *Rear Wheel Removal* in Chapter Ten.

4. Place the centerstand in the raised position and disconnect the return spring (A, **Figure 3**) from the frame peg with Vise Grips.

5. Loosen the bolts and nuts on the clamps (B, **Figure 3**) securing the pivot tube.

6. Withdraw the tube from the right-hand side and lower the centerstand.

7. Install by reversing these removal steps. Apply a light coat of multipurpose grease to all

pivoting points of the centerstand prior to installation.

FOOTPEGS

Replacement

Remove the bolts (**Figure 4**) securing the front and rear footpegs to the frame. The rear bolt also holds the muffler in place.

Replace the footpegs and torque the bolts to 22-29 ft.-lb. (30-39 N•m).

When installing the front footpegs, make sure the alignment tab is correctly positioned.

FRAME

The frame does not require periodic maintenance. However, all welds should be examined immediately after any accident, even a slight one.

Component Removal/Installation

1. Disconnect the negative battery cable. Remove the fuel tank, seat, and battery.

2. Remove the engine as described in Chapter Four.

3. Remove the front wheel, steering, and suspension components as described in Chapter Nine.

4. Remove the rear wheel and suspension components. See Chapter Ten.

5. Remove the lighting and other electrical equipment. Remove the wiring harness; see Chapter Seven.

6. Remove the kickstand and centerstand as described in this chapter.

7. Remove the bearing races from the steering head tube as described in Chapter Nine.

8. Check the frame for bends, cracks, or other damage, especially around welded joints and areas which are rusted.

9. Assemble by reversing the removal steps.

Stripping and Painting

Remove all components from the frame. Thoroughly strip off all old paint. The best way is to have it sandblasted down to bare metal. If this is not possible, you can use a liquid paint remover like Strypeeze, or equivalent, and steel wool and a fine hard wire brush.

12

NOTE: *The headlight nacelle, radiator shroud, side panels, rear fender and taillight housing (Figure 5) are plastic. If you wish to change the color of these parts, consult an automotive paint supplier for the proper procedure.*

CAUTION
Do not use any liquid paint remover on these components as it will damage the surface. The color is an integral part of the component and cannot be removed.

When the frame is down to bare metal, have it inspected for hairline and internal cracks. Magnafluxing is the most common process.

Make sure that the primer is compatible with the type of paint you are going to use for the final coat. Spray one or two coats of primer on as smoothly as possible. Let it dry thoroughly and use a fine grade of wet sandpaper (400-600 grit) to remove any flaws. Carefully wipe clean the surface and then spray the final coat. Use either lacquer or enamel and follow the manufacturer's instructions.

A shop specializing in painting will probably do the best job. However, you can do a surprisingly good job with a good grade of spray paint. Spend a few extra bucks and get a good grade of paint as it will make a difference in how well it looks and how long it will stand up. One trick in using spray paints is to first shake the can thoroughly — make sure the ball inside the can is loose; if not, return it and get a good one. Shake the can as long as is stated on the can. Then immerse the can *upright* in a pot or bucket of *warm water (not hot — not over 120°F).*

WARNING
Higher temperatures could cause the can to burst. Do not place the can in direct contact with any flame or heat source.

Leave the can in for several minutes. When thoroughly warmed, shake the can again and spray the frame. Several light mist coats are better than one heavy coat. Spray painting is best done in temperatures of 70°-80°F, any temperature above and below this will give you problems.

After the final coat has dried completely, at least 48 hours, any overspray or orange peel may be removed with *a light application* of rubbing compound and finished with polishing compound. Be careful not to rub too hard and go through the finish.

Finish off with a couple of good coats of wax prior to reassembling all the components.

SUPPLEMENT

1980-1983 SERVICE INFORMATION

The following supplement provides procedures that are unique to the 1980 and later CX500, GL500, GL650 and CX650C models. All other service procedures are identical to earlier models.

The chapter headings in this supplement correspond to those in the main body of this book. If a change is not included in the supplement, there are no changes affecting 1980 and later models.

CHAPTER ONE

GENERAL INFORMATION

MANUAL ORGANIZATION

Table 1 provides general information and specifications for the GL500, GL500 Interstate, GL650, GL650 Interstate and the CX650C Custom. Specifications that have changed for 1980-on CX500 models are also listed in this table.

Table 1 GENERAL SPECIFICATIONS

Engine type	Water-cooled, 4-stroke, OHC, 80° V-twin
Bore and stroke	
500 cc	78.0 x 52.0 mm (3.071 x 2.047 in.)
650 cc	82.5 x 63.0 mm (3.25 x 2.48 in.)
Displacement	
500 cc	497 cm² (30.3 cu. in.)
650 cc	674 cm² (41.1 cu. in.)
Compression ratio	
500 cc	10.0 to 1
650 cc	9.8 to 1
Carburetion	2 Keihin carburetors
Ignition	Capacitor discharge ignition (CDI)
Lubrication	Wet-sump, filter, oil pump
Clutch	Wet, multi-plate (7)
Transmission	5-speed, constant mesh
Transmission ratios	
1st	2.500
2nd	1.714
3rd	1.280
4th	1.036
5th	0.839
Final reduction ratio	3.091
Starting system	Electric starter only
Battery	12 volt, 14 amp/hour
Alternator	Three phase, AC, 252 W @ 5,000 rpm
Wheelbase	
CX500	
1980-1981	1,455 mm (57.5 in.)
1982	1,465 mm (57.7 in.)
GL models	1,495 mm (58.8 in.)
CX650C	1,515 mm (59.7 in.)
(continued)	

Table 1 GENERAL SPECIFICATIONS (continued)

Steering head angle	
CX500	
1980	63° 15'
1981 Deluxe	63° 15'
1981-1982 Custom	62° 30'
GL models	62°
CX650C	58°
Trail	
CX500	
1980	105 mm (4.1 in.)
1981 Deluxe	105 mm (4.1 in.)
1981-1982 Custom	110 mm (4.3 in.)
GL models	117 mm (4.6 in.)
CX650C	126 mm (5.0 in.)
Front suspension	**Telescopic forks**
Travel	
CX500	
1980	139.5 mm (5.49 in.)
1981-1982	140 mm (5.5 in.)
CX650C	160 mm (6.3 in.)
Rear suspension	**Swing arm and shock absorber(s)**
Travel	
CX500	85 mm (3.3 in.)
GL500 & Interstate	120 mm (4.7 in.)
GL650 & Interstate	110 mm (4.3 in.)
CX650C	120 mm (4.7 in.)
Front tire	
500cc models	350 S-19 4PR tubeless
GL650 & Interstate	3.50 H-19 4PR tubeless
CX650C	100/90-19 57H tubeless
Rear tire	
500 cc models	130/90-16 67S tubeless
GL650 & Interstate	120/90-16 67H tubeless
CX650C	140/90-15 70H tubeless
Ground clearance	
CX500	145 mm (5.7 in.)
GL500	132 mm (5.2 in.)
GL500 Interstate	127 mm (5.0 in.)
GL650	150 mm (5.9 in.)
GL650 Interstate	145 mm (5.7 in.)
CX650C	155 mm (6.1 in.)
Overall height	
CX500	
1980-1981 Deluxe	1,165 mm (45.9 in.)
1980-1981 Custom	1,170 mm (46.1 in.)
1982	1,195 mm (47.0 in.)
GL500	1,178 mm (46.4 in.)
GL500 Interstate	1,505 mm (59.2 in.)
GL650	1,184 mm (46.6 in.)
GL650 Interstate	1,480 mm (58.3 in.)
CX650C	1,165 mm (45.9 in.)
Overall width (handlebar)	
CX500	
1980-1981 Deluxe	865 mm (34.1 in.)
1980 Custom	875 mm (34.4 in.)
1981	885 mm (34.8 in.)
1982	855 mm (33.7 in.)

(continued)

13

Table 1 GENERAL SPECIFICATIONS (continued)

Overall width (handlebar) (cont.)	
GL500 & Interstate	875 mm (34.4 in.)
GL650	890 mm (35.0 in.)
GL650 Interstate	885 mm (34.8 in.)
CX650C	790 mm (31.1 in.)
Overall length	
CX500	
1980-1981 Deluxe	2,185 mm (86.0 in.)
1980 Custom	2,150 mm (84.6 in.)
1981-1982 Custom	2,160 mm (85.0 in.)
GL500	2,207 mm (86.9 in.)
GL500 Interstate	2,305 mm (90.7 in.)
GL650	2,215 mm (87.2 in.)
GL650 Interstate	2,305 mm (90.7 in.)
CX650C	2,180 mm (85.8 in.)
Weight (dry)	
CX500	
1980-1981 Deluxe	205 kg (452 lb.)
1980-1982 Custom	202 kg (445 lb.)
GL500, GL650	224 kg (494 lb.)
Interstate models	247 kg (547 lb.)
CX650C	196 kg (432 lb.)
Fuel capacity (total)	
CX500	
Deluxe	17.0 liters (4.5 U.S. gal., 3.7 Imp. gal.)
Custom	11.0 liters (2.9 U.S. gal., 2.4 Imp. gal.)
GL500 & Interstate,	17.6 liters (4.6 U.S. gal., 3.9 Imp. gal.)
GL650 & Interstate	
CX650C	12.4 liters (3.28 U.S. gal., 2.73 Imp. gal.)
Oil capacity	2.5 liters (2.6 U.S. qt., 2.2 Imp. qt.)
Oil and filter change	3.0 liters (3.2 U.S. qt., 2.6 Imp. qt.)
At overhaul	
Front fork oil capacity*	
CX500	
1980	135 cc (4.7 oz.)
1981 Deluxe	185 cc (6.3 oz.)
1981-1982 Custom	220 cc (7.5 oz.)
GL500 & Interstate	210 cc (7.1 oz.)
GL650 & Interstate	275 cc (9.3 oz.)**
CX650C	480 cc (16.2 oz.)**

* Capacity for each fork leg.
** Capacity after disassembly. Honda does not provide information for fork draining procedure.

CHAPTER THREE

PERIODIC MAINTENANCE AND LUBRICATION

ROUTINE CHECKS

Tire Pressure

Tire pressure must be checked with the tires cold. Refer to **Table 2** for correct pressures.

PERIODIC LUBRICATION

Front Fork Oil Change
(Air Assist Models)

There is no factory-recommended fork oil change interval but it's a good practice to change the oil every 6,000 miles (10,000 km) or once a year. If it becomes contaminated with dirt or water, change it immediately.

Some models are equipped with air assist front forks.

1. Place the bike on the centerstand and place wood block(s) under the engine to support the bike so there is no weight on the front wheel.
2. Unscrew the dust cap (A, **Figure 1**) and *bleed off all fork air pressure* by depressing the valve stem.

> *NOTE*
> *Release air pressure gradually. If it is released too fast, oil will spurt out with the air. Protect your eyes and clothing accordingly.*

3. Disconnect the air hose from the fittings on both the right- and left-hand top fork cap/air valve assemblies (B, **Figure 1**).
4. Unscrew the fitting from the top fork cap/air valve assembly (C, **Figure 1**). Unscrew the top fork cap/air valve assembly (D, **Figure 1**) slowly as it is under spring pressure from the fork spring.
5. Place a drain pan under the drain screw (**Figure 2**) and remove the drain screw. Allow the oil to drain for at least 5 minutes. *Never reuse the oil.*

> *CAUTION*
> *Do not allow the fork oil to come in contact with any of the brake components.*

13

6. Inspect the condition of the gasket on the drain screw; replace it if necessary. Install the drain screw.

7. Repeat Steps 5 and 6 for the other fork.

NOTE
In order to keep the inside of the fairing clean on Interstate models, place a shop cloth around the top of the fork tube to catch any remaining oil on the upper fork spring as it is removed.

8. Withdraw the upper short fork spring from each fork tube.

NOTE
The spring spacer may stick to the bottom of the upper fork spring when the spring is removed; don't lose it if it does come out with the spring.

9. Refill each fork leg with the following standard quantity of DEXRON ATF (automatic transmission fluid) or fork oil:

    a. CX500 Deluxe (1981-on): 6.3 oz. (185 cc).

    b. CX500 Custom (1981-on): 7.5 oz. (220 cc).

    c. GL500 and GL500 Interstate (1981-on): 7.1 oz. (210 cc).

    d. GL650 and GL650 Interstate (1983): 9.3 oz. (275 cc).

    e. CX650C: 16.2 oz. (480 cc).

NOTE
*In order to measure the correct amount of fluid, use a plastic baby bottle. These have measurements in fluid ounces (oz.) and cubic centimeters (cc) on the side (**Figure 3**).*

10. Inspect the condition of the O-ring seal (**Figure 4**) on the top fork cap bolt; replace if necessary.

11. If removed, install the fork spring spacer.

12. Install the upper short fork spring. Install the fork top cap bolt while pushing down on the spring. Start the fork cap bolt slowly, don't cross thread it. Tighten fork top cap bolt to 11-22 ft.-lb. (15-30 N•m).

13. Apply a light coat of grease to all new O-ring seals (**Figure 5**) on the air hose and fitting.

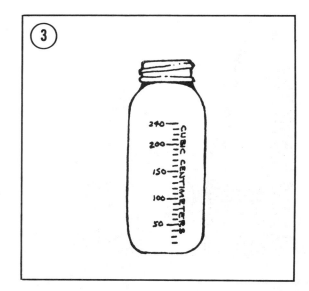

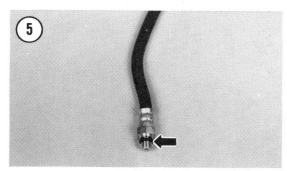

14. Install the air connector and tighten to 3-5 ft.-lb. (4-7 N•m).

15. Install the air hose first to the top fork cap (without the connector) and tighten to 3-5 ft.-lb. (4-7 N•m). Then install the air hose to the connector and tighten to 11-14 ft.-lb. (15-20 N•m).

NOTE
Hold onto the air connector (attached to the fork top cap/air valve assembly)

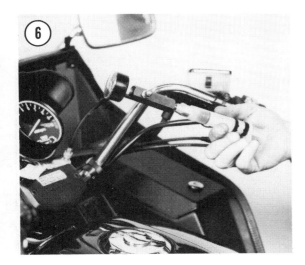

with a wrench while tightening the air hose fitting.

16. Inflate the forks. Do not use compressed air; use only a small hand-operated air pump as shown in **Figure 6** or equivalent. Inflate the forks to the following air pressure:

   a. GL500, GL500 Interstate: 10-17 psi (0.7-1.2 kg/cm²).

   b. GL650, GL650 Interstate: 5.5-17 psi (0.4-1.2 kg/cm²).

   c. CX650C: 0-6 psi (0-0.4 kg/cm²).

WARNING
Never use any type of compressed gas as an explosion may be lethal. Never heat the fork assembly with a torch or place it near an open flame or extreme heat as this will also result in an explosion. **Never** *exceed the maximum specified air pressure.*

17. Road test the bike and check for leaks.

Oil Strainer Cleaning (1983 Models) (GL650, GL650 Interstate, CX650C)

An oil pan has been added to the crankcase to allow easy access to the oil strainer.

1. Drain the engine oil as described in Chapter Three in the main body of this book.
2. Loosen the bolts securing the oil pan in a crisscross pattern in 2-3 steps.
3. Remove the bolts, oil pan and gasket. Discard the old gasket.
4. Remove the oil strainer from the oil pan.
5. Thoroughly clean the oil pan and the oil strainer in solvent and dry with compressed air.
6. Inspect the oil strainer screen for damage; replace if necessary.
7. Inspect the O-ring seal on the strainer neck; replace if necessary.
8. Align the tabs of the oil strainer with the raised lugs on the oil pan and install the oil strainer into the oil pan.
9. Make sure the O-ring seal is in place on the neck of the oil strainer.
10. Install a new gasket onto the oil pan.
11. Insert the neck of the oil strainer into the oil pump inlet while installing the oil pan.
12. Install the oil pan and the bolts securing the oil pan. Tighten the bolts in 2-3 steps in a crisscross pattern.
13. Refill the crankcase with the recommended type and quantity of engine oil. Refer to Chapter Three in the main body of this book.

PERIODIC MAINTENANCE

Disc Brake Fluid Level

The fluid level in the reservoir should be up to the upper line (**Figure 7**). If necessary, correct the level by adding fresh brake fluid. Clean any dirt from the area around the cover

13

prior to removing the cover. Remove the cover, gasket and diaphragm.

> *WARNING*
> *Use brake fluid clearly marked DOT 3 only and specified for disc brakes. Others may vaporize and cause brake failure.*

> *CAUTION*
> *Be careful when handling brake fluid. Do not spill it on painted or plated surfaces as it will destroy the surface. Wash the area immediately with soapy water and thoroughly rinse it off.*

Reinstall the diaphragm, gasket and cover. Tighten the screws securely.

Front Disc Brake Pad Wear

Inspect the brake pads for excessive or uneven wear, scoring, and oil or grease on the friction surface. Look through the slot in the top of the caliper assembly (indicated by an arrow cast into the caliper). If the pads are worn to the red wear line (**Figure 8**), they must be replaced.

> *NOTE*
> *Always replace both pads at the same time.*

If any of these conditions exist, replace the pads as described under *Brake Pad Replacement* in the Chapter Eleven section of this supplement.

Air Cleaner Servicing (GL500 and GL500 Interstate)

The air cleaner element should be removed and cleaned every 3,750 miles (6,000 km) and replaced every 7,500 miles (12,000 km).

The air cleaner removes dust and abrasive particles from the air before the air enters the carburetors and engine. Without the air cleaner, very fine particles could enter into the engine and cause rapid wear of the piston rings, cylinder and bearings or clog small passages in the carburetors. Never run the bike without the air cleaner element installed.

Proper air cleaner servicing can do more to ensure long service from your engine than any other single item.

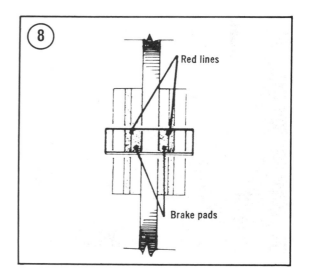

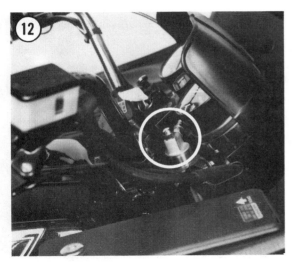

1. Remove the right-hand side cover.

2. Turn the air cleaner cover (**Figure 9**) counterclockwise until the cover is free from the tabs on the air box. Remove the cover.

3. Pull the air cleaner element out of the air box (**Figure 10**).

4. Gently tap the air cleaner element to loosen the dust and dirt. Apply compressed air to the *outside* of the element to remove all loosened dirt and dust from inside the element. Tap the element again and repeat this step until all loose dirt and dust are removed.

5. Inspect the element; if it is torn or broken in any area it should be replaced. Do not run

with a damaged element as it may allow dirt to enter the engine.

6. Wipe out the interior of the air box with a shop rag dampened with cleaning solvent. Remove any foreign matter that may have passed through a broken element.

7. Slide in the element and install the cover with the arrow on the cover aligned with the arrow on the air box (**Figure 11**).

8. Install the right-hand side cover.

**Air Cleaner Servicing
(CX650C)**

1. Remove the right-hand side cover.

2. Remove the screws securing the air cleaner cover and remove the cover.

3. Pull the air cleaner element out of the air box.

4. Gently tap the air cleaner element to loosen the dust and dirt. Apply compressed air to the *outside* of the element to remove all loosened dirt and dust from inside the element. Tap the element again and repeat this step until all loose dirt and dust are removed.

5. Inspect the element; if it is torn or broken in any area it should be replaced. Do not run with a damaged element as it may allow dirt to enter the engine.

6. Wipe out the interior of the air box with a shop rag dampened with cleaning solvent. Remove any foreign matter that may have passed through a broken element.

7. Slide in the element and install the cover. Install the screws and tighten securely.

8. Install the right-hand side cover.

**Front Fork Air Pressure Check
(Air Assist Forks)**

Check the front fork air pressure when the forks are cold.

1. Place the bike on the centerstand with the front wheel off the ground.

2. Remove the air valve cap (**Figure 12**).

3. Measure the air pressure with the air gauge furnished with the factory tool kit (or equivalent gauge). The correct air pressure is as follows:

13

a. GL500, GL500 Interstate: 10-17 psi (0.7-1.2 kg/cm²).

b. GL650, GL650 Interstate: 5.5-17 psi (0.4-1.2 kg/cm²).

c. CX650C: 0-6 psi (0-0.4 kg/cm²).

4. Adjust if necessary. Do not use compressed air; use only a small hand-operated air pump as shown in **Figure 13** or equivalent.

> *WARNING*
> *Never use any type of compressed gas as an explosion may be lethal. Never heat the fork assembly with a torch or place it near an open flame, or extreme heat as this will also result in an explosion.* **Never** *exceed the maximum specified air pressure.*

5. Remove the hand-operated air pump and install the air valve cap.

Rear Shock Air Pressure Check
(Pro-Link Models)

Check the rear shock air pressure when the shock is cold.

1. Place the bike on the centerstand with the rear wheel off the ground.

2. Remove the right-hand side cover.

3. Remove the air valve cap (**Figure 14**).

4. Measure the air pressure with the air gauge furnished with the factory tool kit (or equivalent gauge). The correct air pressure is as follows:

a. GL500 and GL650: 0-70 psi (0-5.0 kg/cm²).

b. GL500 Interstate and GL650 Interstate: 14-70 psi (1.0-5.0 kg/cm²).

5. Adjust if necessary. Do not use compressed air; use only a small hand-operated air pump as shown in **Figure 15** or equivalent.

> *WARNING*
> *Never use any type of compressed gas as an explosion may be lethal. Never heat the fork assembly with a torch or place it near an open flame, or extreme heat as this will also result in an explosion.* **Never** *exceed the maximum specified air pressure.*

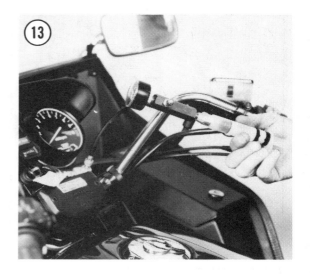

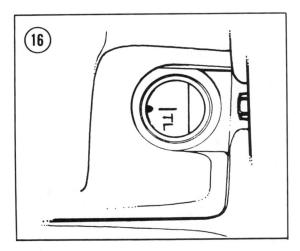

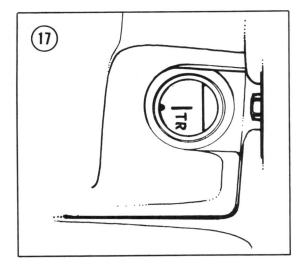

described in Chapter Three in the main body of this book). However, the timing marks on the alternator rotor are slightly different in appearance and the clearance specification on all 1983 models is different.

The new TL timing mark is shown in **Figure 16** and the new TR timing mark is shown in **Figure 17**.

The correct valve clearance for all 1983 models is as follows:

    a. Intake valves: 0.004 in. (0.10 mm).
    b. Exhaust valves: 0.005 in. (0.12 mm).

Correct Spark Plug Heat Range

Spark plug service is the same as described in Chapter Three in the main body of this book. Refer to **Table 3** for the correct spark plug heat range for 1981-on.

Capacitor Discharge Ignition Timing Check and Adjustment (1982-on CX500, All Other Models 1981-on)

These models are equipped with a capacitor discharge ignition (CDI) system that is slightly different from the system used on previous years. This system also uses no breaker points, but ignition timing does have to be checked as the base plate may move and alter timing.

Incorrect ignition timing can cause a drastic loss of engine performance and efficiency. It may also cause overheating.

Before starting on this procedure, check all electrical connections related to the ignition system. Make sure all connections are tight and free of corrosion and that all ground connections are tight.

1. Start the engine and let it reach normal operating temperature, then shut it off.
2. Place the bike on the centerstand.
3. Remove the timing inspection hole cover cap (**Figure 18**).
4. Connect a portable tachometer following the manufacturer's instructions. The bike's tachometer is not accurate enough in the low rpm range for this adjustment.
5. Connect a timing light to the right-hand cylinder spark plug lead following the manufacturer's instructions.

6. Remove the hand-operated air pump and install the air valve cap.

Camshaft Chain Adjustment

On 1983 models there is no provision for cam chain adjustment. The cam chain tensioner works automatically and requires no routine adjustment to maintain the correct amount of pressure on the cam chain.

TUNE-UP

Valve Clearance Adjustment (1982-on CX500, All Other Models 1981-on)

The valve clearance adjustment procedure is the same as on previous models (as

13

6. Start the engine and let it idle (1,000 ±100 rpm); aim the timing light at the timing window and pull the trigger. If the FI/TR timing mark aligns with the fixed pointer (**Figure 19**) the timing is correct.

7. Also check the ignition advance alignment. Increase engine speed to slightly above 3,100 rpm; check alignment of the full advance marks and the fixed pointer (**Figure 20**). If the idle speed alignment is correct but the full advance is incorrect, refer to *Ignition Advance Mechanism Inspection* in the Chapter Four section of this supplement.

8. Repeat Steps 5-7 for the left-hand cylinder. In Step 6 the timing is correct if the FI/TL timing mark aligns with the fixed pointer (**Figure 21**).

9. If the timing is incorrect, shut the engine off and remove the pulse generator cover; refer to the Chapter Four section of this supplement.

10. To adjust the timing, rotate the crankshaft until the FS/TR timing mark aligns with the fixed pointer. To turn the crankshaft, use a socket on the bolt on the front of the crankshaft (**Figure 22**). Loosen the base plate screws (A, **Figure 23**) and slightly rotate the base plate in either direction until the tooth on the center rotor aligns with the tooth on the right pulse coil (left-hand coil on the pulse coil assembly). Tighten the base plate screws. Rotate the crankshaft clockwise until the FS/TL timing mark aligns with the fixed pointer. At this point the tooth on the center rotor should align with the tooth on the left pulse coil (bottom coil on the pulse coil assembly). This second alignment is usually automatic but a slight adjustment may be made by loosening the screws securing the pulse coil to the base plate and moving the coil.

11. After timing is correct the air gap must be checked. Insert a non-metallic flat feeler gauge (B, **Figure 23**) between the tooth on the pulse coil and the tooth on the center rotor. The gap should be 0.018-0.026 in. (0.45-0.65 mm); refer to **Figure 24**. To adjust the clearance, loosen the pulse coil screws (C,

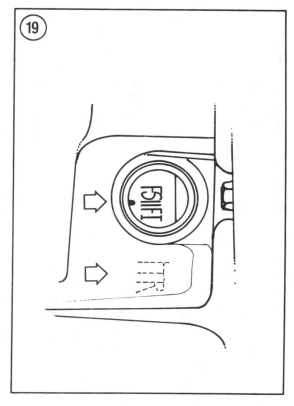

Figure 23) and move the coil to achieve the correct gap. Tighten the screws securely.
12. Restart the engine and verify that ignition timing is correct. Shut the engine off.
13. Disconnect the timing light and portable tachometer. Install the timing inspection hole cover cap.

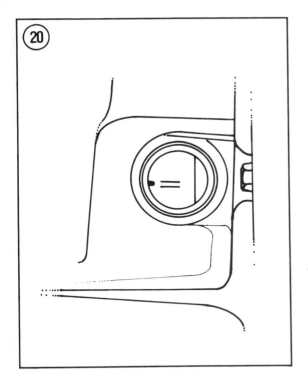

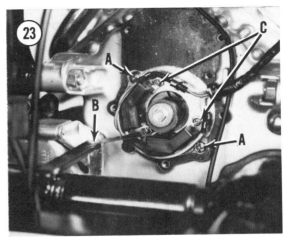

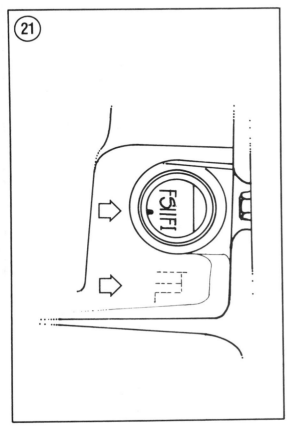

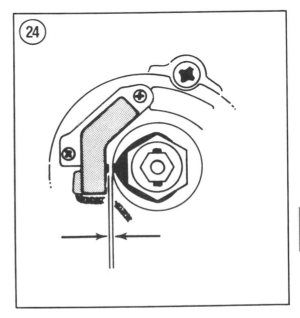

13

Table 2 TIRE INFLATION PRESSURE (COLD)

Load/Model	Air Pressure Front	Rear
Up to 200 lb. (90 kg)		
500cc models	28 psi (2.0 kg/cm²)	28 psi 2.0 kg/cm²
650cc models	32 psi (2.25 kg/cm²)	32 psi (2.25 kg/cm²)
Maximum load limit*		
CX500 Custom, Deluxe	28 psi (2.0 kg/cm²)	32 psi (2.25 kg/cm²)
GL500 & Interstate	28 psi (2.0 kg/cm²)	36 psi (2.5 kg/cm²)
650cc models	32 psi (2.25 kg/cm²)	40 psi (2.80 kg/cm²)

* Maximum load limit includes total weight of motorcycle with accessories, rider(s) and luggage.

Table 3 SPARK PLUG HEAT RANGE

Spark plug type (1981)	
Standard heat range	
U.S.	ND X24ES-U or NGK D8EA
Canadian	ND X24ESR-U or NGK DR8ES-L
Cold weather*	
U.S.	ND X22ES-U or NGK D7EA
Canadian	ND X22ESR-U or NGK DR7ES
Extended high-speed riding	
U.S.	ND X27ES-U or NGK D9EA
Canadian	ND X27ESR-U or NGK DR9ES
Spark plug type (1982)	
Standard heat range	
U.S. and Canadian	ND X24ESR-U or NGK DR8ES-L
Cold weather*	
U.S. and Canadian	ND X22ESR-U or NGK DR7ES
Extended high-speed riding	
U.S. and Canadian	ND X27ESR-U or NGK DR8EA
Spark plug type (1983)	
Standard heat range	
U.S. and Canadian	ND X24EPR-U9 or NGK DPR8EA-9
Extended high-speed riding	
U.S. and Canadian	ND X27EPR-U9 or NGK DPR9EA-9
Spark plug gap	
1980-1982	0.6-0.7 mm (0.024-0.028 in.)
1983	0.8-0.9 mm (0.031-0.035 in.)

* Cold weather climate—below 41° F (5° C).
** Honda does not provide Canadian specifications for 1983.

CHAPTER FOUR

ENGINE

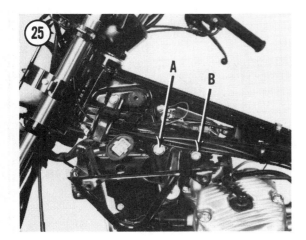

500 CC ENGINE

The V-twin engine in the CX500, GL500 and GL500 Interstate is the same as in previous years except for the size and specifications of the upper rocker arm shafts and rocker arm bore. These specifications are covered in this section of the supplement.

650 CC ENGINE

The V-twin engine used in the GL650, GL650 Interstate and the CX650C is basically the same as the 500 cc engine with an increase in displacement. Refer to **Table 4** for 650 cc engine specifications and wear limits.

ENGINE

Removal/Installation (Except CX500)

The frame on the GL500, GL500 Interstate, GL650, GL650 Interstate and CX650C is different than the CX500. With the different frame the upper rear engine mounting brackets have been deleted.

Removal and installation are the same as for the CX500 with the exception of the previously described mounting brackets and different torque specifications for the mounting bolts and nuts:

a. Tighten the front mounting bolt and nut (A, **Figure 25**) to 43-58 ft.-lb. (60-80 N•m).
b. Tighten the front mounting bolt (B, **Figure 25**) to 33-51 ft.-lb. (45-70 N•m).
c. Tighten the rear mounting bolt (A, **Figure 26**) to 33-51 ft.-lb. (45-70 N•m).
d. Tighten the rear mounting bolt (B, **Figure 26**) to 43-58 ft.-lb. (60-80 N•m).

UPPER ROCKER ARM ASSEMBLIES (GL500 AND GL500 INTERSTATE)

On GL500 and GL500 Interstate models the upper rocker arm shaft and rocker arm bore are slightly larger in diameter.

Removal, installation, disassembly and assembly are the same as on previous models;

13

refer to Chapter Four in the main body of this book.

Inspection

1. Measure the inside diameter of the rocker arm bore (A, **Figure 27**) with a micrometer. If worn to 0.592 in (15.03 mm) or greater the rocker arm must be replaced.
2. Measure the outside diameter of the rocker arm shaft (B, **Figure 27**) with a micrometer. If worn to 0.589 in. (14.95 mm) or less the rocker arm shaft must be replaced.
3. Measure the inside diameter of the rocker arm shaft bore in the rocker arm holder. If worn to 0.592 in. (15.03 mm) or greater the rocker arm holder must be replaced.

CAMSHAFT
(1982-ON CX500, ALL OTHER MODELS 1981-ON)

Camshaft removal and installation are the same as for previous models with the exception of removing the engine rear cover. On these models the pulse generator mechanism and ignition advance mechanism must be removed prior to removing the engine rear cover. Refer to *Ignition Advance and Pulse Generator* in this section of the supplement.

CAMSHAFT
(1983 MODELS)

The camshaft is driven by a Hy-Vo chain off of the timing sprocket on the crankshaft.

The main difference from previous models is that there is a new cam chain tensioner assembly (**Figure 28**). Also, the cooling fan is

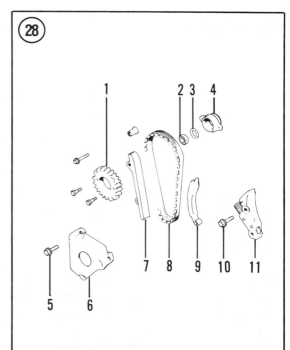

CAM CHAIN TENSIONER (1983)

1. Cam chain sprocket
2. 27 mm nut
3. Lockwasher
4. Cam sprocket boss
5. Bolt
6. Set plate
7. Cam chain guide
8. Cam chain
9. Cam chain tensioner slipper
10. Bolt (special threads)
11. Cam chain tensioner

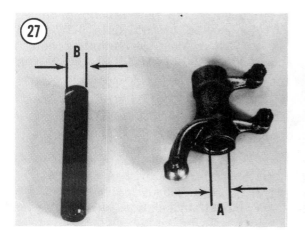

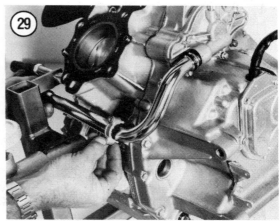

no longer attached to the front end of the camshaft. The cooling fan is now driven by an electric motor.

Removal

1. On Interstate models, remove the front fairing as described in this supplement.
2. Remove the engine as described in Chapter Four in the main body of this book and in the supplement.
3. Remove cylinder heads as described in Chapter Four in the main body of this book.
4. Remove the clamps securing the water pipe to the cylinder block (**Figure 29**) and remove the water pipe.
5. Remove the bolts (**Figure 30**) securing the water pump housing and remove the housing. Don't lose the locating dowels (A, **Figure 31**).
6. Remove the cap nut and copper washer (B, **Figure 31**) securing the water pump impeller and remove the impeller.

7. Remove the bolts securing the engine rear cover. Hold the shift lever shaft in position and remove the cover. Don't lose the locating dowels (**Figure 32**).

NOTE
*In the next step, to prevent the rotor from turning, secure the rotor with a strap wrench as shown in **Figure 33**.*

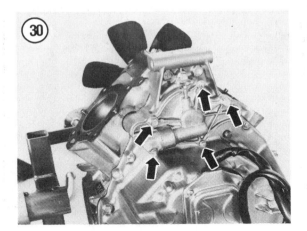

13

8. Remove the bolt (**Figure 34**) securing the alternator rotor to the crankshaft.

9. Screw a flywheel puller in all the way until it stops (**Figure 35**).

10. Hold the rotor with the strap wrench and turn the puller clockwise until the rotor disengages from the crankshaft. Remove the rotor, starter gear (**Figure 36**) and the needle bearing.

CAUTION
Be careful not to damage the pulser pickup on the outer surface of the flywheel.

11. Remove the bolts (**Figure 37**) securing the cam chain guide set plate and remove the set plate.

12. Remove the bolt (**Figure 38**) securing the cam chain tensioner.

13. Using a narrow-blade screwdriver, depress the steel ball (A, **Figure 39**) and push in to compress the pushrod (B, **Figure 39**).

14. Pull the cam chain tensioner off the pivot pin on the cylinder block and remove the tensioner assembly.

15. Remove the cam chain slipper (right-hand side) and the cam chain guide (left-hand side).

16. Remove the bolts (**Figure 40**) securing the cam sprocket to the camshaft.

17. Remove the cam sprocket and chain (**Figure 41**).

18. Using a deep socket, remove the 27 mm nut (**Figure 42**) securing the cam sprocket boss. Remove the nut, washer and sprocket boss.

19. Remove the bolts (**Figure 43**) securing the camshaft holder and tachometer drive. Remove the holder.

CAUTION
Using pieces of wire, raise all lower rocker arms and tie them up and off the

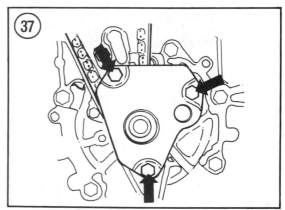

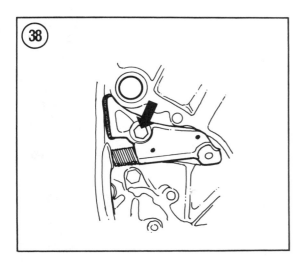

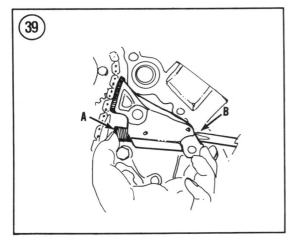

13

cam during removal. This is to prevent them from damage during camshaft removal.

20. Withdraw the camshaft and thrust washer from the front of the engine.

Inspection

Inspect the camshaft as described in Chapter Four in the main body of this book. For specifications, refer to **Table 4** located in this section of the supplement.

Installation

1. Lubricate the camshaft journals with molybdenum disulfide grease and apply assembly oil to the cam lobes.
2. Install the thrust washer to the front end of the camshaft.
3. Insert the camshaft into the cylinder block from the front of the engine.
4. Install the O-ring and collar (**Figure 44**). Install a new gasket on the camshaft holder.
5. Lubricate the camshaft holder oil seal with fresh engine oil.
6. Align the cutout on the backside of the camshaft holder with the dowel pin on the camshaft and install the holder (**Figure 45**).
7. Install the lockwasher with the "OUTSIDE" mark facing out.
8. Install the 27 mm locknut and tighten it as tight as possible for now.
9. Using the bolt on the front of the crankshaft (**Figure 46**), rotate the crankshaft until the left-hand piston is at top dead center (TDC).

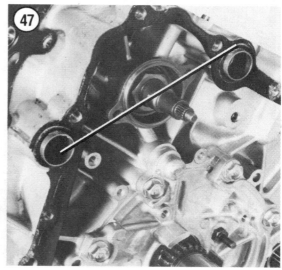

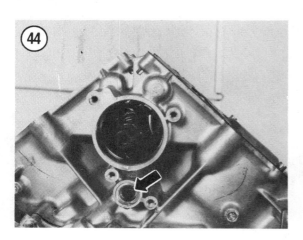

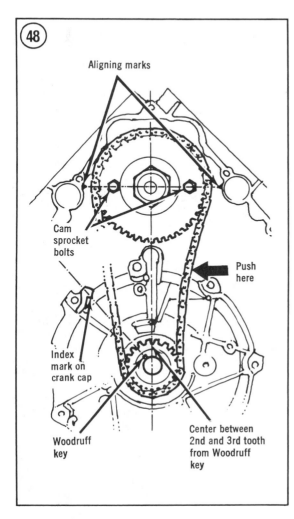

Aligning marks

Cam sprocket bolts

Push here

Index mark on crank cap

Woodruff key

Center between 2nd and 3rd tooth from Woodruff key

10. Verify that the piston is at TDC by checking the following:

   a. The holes in the camshaft sprocket boss (**Figure 47**) are horizontal and align with the punch marks on the cylinder block. Also refer to **Figure 48**.

   b. The Woodruff key on the crankshaft is aligned with the index mark on the crankshaft cap (**Figure 48**).

11. Install the camshaft sprocket and chain (**Figure 49**).

12. Install the cam sprocket bolts (**Figure 40**) and tighten to 12-14 ft.-lb. (16-19 N•m).

13. After the cam sprocket and chain have been installed, press on the right-hand side of the cam chain so that the tensioner side of the chain is tight. Check again that all items in **Figure 48** are aligned as shown. Proper valve timing depends on the accurate alignment of all of these parts.

CAUTION
*Very expensive damage to the engine can result from improper camshaft installation. Before proceeding, rotate the crankshaft several revolutions with a wrench on the bolt shown in **Figure 46**. If there is any binding, **stop**. Determine the cause before assembling beyond this point.*

14. Tighten the cam locknut, installed in Step 8, to 58-72 ft.-lb. (80-100 N•m).

15. Install the cam chain guide on the left-hand side and the cam chain slipper on the right-hand side.

16. Push the pushrod (B, **Figure 39**) of the cam chain tensioner into the body. Place a small pin into the shaft (**Figure 50**) to hold the tensioner in the relaxed position.

CAUTION
In the next step, be sure to use the correct set bolt as the threads are unique. If an incorrect bolt is used by mistake you will destroy the threads in the cylinder block.

17. Install the tensioner onto the pivot pin on the cylinder block and install the set bolt. Tighten the set bolt to 13-18 ft.-lb. (18-25 N•m).

13

18. Remove the pin from the end of the tensioner pushrod. Make sure the pushrod moves smoothly by pushing in on the steel ball on the left-hand end of the tensioner. The tensioner will automatically adjust to apply the correct amount of tension to the cam chain.

19. Install the cam chain set plate and tighten the bolts securely.

20. Install the needle bearing, starter gear and the alternator rotor.

21. Use the same tool set-up as Step 10 of *Removal* and install the rotor bolt. Tighten to 65-76 ft.-lb. (90-105 N•m).

22. Align the pulser rotor locating tab with the notch in the alternator rotor and install the pulser rotor.

23. Install the locating dowels and O-rings.

24. Install a new gasket on the engine rear cover and install the rear cover. Tighten the 6 mm bolts to 6-9 ft.-lb. (8-12 N•m) and the 8 mm bolts to 13-18 ft.-lb. (18-25 N•m).

25. Install the water pump impeller, copper washer and cap nut. Make sure the locating dowels are in place on the engine rear cover.

26. Inspect the seal (**Figure 51**) on the water pump housing. If it is cracked or deteriorated it must be replaced. Make sure the seal is properly seated in the groove in the housing. Install the housing.

27. Pour about 3 1/4 oz. (100 cc) of fresh engine oil into the oil pockets (**Figure 52**) in the lower rocker arm area.

NOTE
*Make sure the O-ring seal is properly seated between the 2 ribs on the water pipe (**Figure 53**).*

28. Install the water pipe and clamps to the cylinder block.

29. Install the cylinder heads as described in Chapter Four in the main body of this book and in this supplement.

30. Install the engine as described in Chapter Four in the main body of this book.

31. Adjust the valve clearances as described in Chapter Three in the main body of this book.

32. Refill the engine with the correct amount and type of engine oil as described in Chapter Three in the main body of this book.

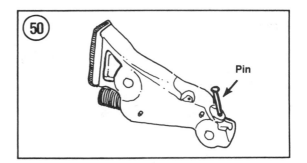

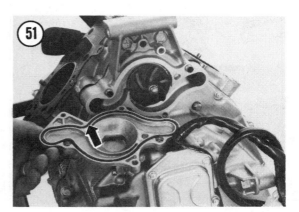

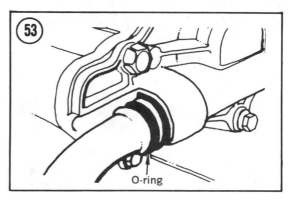

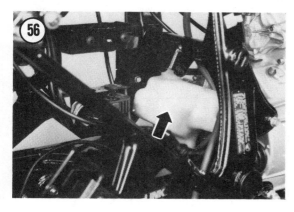

33. On Interstate models, install the front fairing as described in this supplement.

ALTERNATOR
(1982-ON CX500, ALL OTHER
MODELS 1981-ON)

Alternator removal and installation are the same as for previous models with the exception of removing the engine rear cover

and the torque specifications for the rotor bolt.

On these models the pulse generator mechanism and ignition advance mechanism must be removed prior to removing the engine rear cover. Refer to *Ignition Advance and Pulse Generator* in this section of the supplement.

Tighten the rotor bolt to 65-76 ft.-lb. (90-105 N•m).

IGNITION ADVANCE AND
PULSE GENERATOR
(1982-ON CX500, ALL OTHER
MODELS 1981-ON)

The ignition advance and pulse generator can be removed with the engine in the frame.

Removal/Installation

1. Place the bike on the centerstand.
2. Remove the side covers, the seat and the fuel tank.
3. On Interstate models, remove the saddlebags.
4. Remove the rear wheel. On dual shock CX500 models, refer to *Rear Wheel Removal/Installation* in Chapter Eleven in the main body of this book. For Pro-link models, refer to *Rear Wheel (Pro-Link Models) Removal/Installation* in the Chapter Eleven section of this supplement.
5. Disconnect the battery positive and negative leads and remove the battery from the frame.
6. Remove the bolts securing the air box (**Figure 54**) and remove the air box assembly.
7. Disconnect the breather hose from the pulse generator cover (**Figure 55**).
8. On Pro-Link models, remove the shock absorber unit as described under *Shock Absorber (Pro-Link Models) Removal* in the Chapter Eleven section of this supplement.
9. Remove the radiator coolant recovery tank (**Figure 56**).
10. Disconnect the 4-pin pulse generator electrical connector adjacent to the battery.
11. Remove the bolts (**Figure 57**) securing the pulse generator cover and remove the cover.

13

12. Prior to removing the pulse generator assembly, make a mark on the base plate that lines up with one of the attachment screws. This will assure correct ignition timing (providing it was correct prior to removal).

13. Remove the screws (**Figure 58**) securing the pulse generator assembly and remove the assembly.

14. To remove the ignition advance mechanism, remove the 6 mm bolt (**Figure 59**) securing the ignition advance mechanism and remove the mechanism.

15. Inspect the ignition advance mechanism as described under of the supplement.

16. Install by reversing these removal steps, noting the following.

17. Apply gasket sealer to the area indicated in **Figure 60** and install a new gasket (A, **Figure 61**).

18. When installing the ignition advance mechanism, index the pin on the backside of the mechanism (**Figure 62**) into the *small cutout* in the end of the crankshaft (B, **Figure 61**).

> *NOTE*
> *There are 2 cutouts in the end of the crankshaft. Do not index the pin into the large slot or ignition timing will be incorrect.*

19. Install the 6 mm bolt and tighten to 6-9 ft.-lb. (8-12 N•m).

20. When installing the pulse generator assembly, align the mark made in Step 12 for preliminary ignition timing.

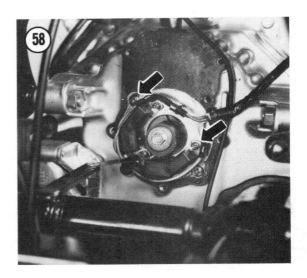

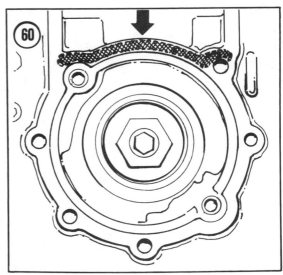

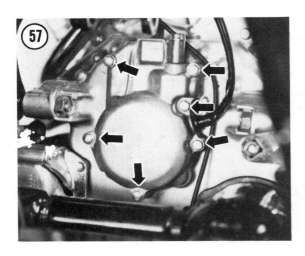

21. Check and adjust ignition timing as described in the Chapter Three section of this supplement.

Inspection

1. Inspect the condition of the pivot points (A, **Figure 63**) of each centrifugal weight. It must pivot freely to maintain proper ignition advance. Apply lightweight grease to the pivot pins and all sliding surfaces.

2. Inspect the pivot cam (B, **Figure 63**) operation on the shaft. It must operate freely.

3. Make sure the centrifugal advance weight return springs (**Figure 64**) completely retract the weights. If not, replace the ignition advance unit.

OIL PUMP
(1983 MODELS)

Removal/Installation

Oil pump removal and installation are the same as on previous models except that the oil pickup screen assembly will not come out of the cylinder block along with the oil pump. It must be removed as described under *Oil Strainer Cleaning* in the Chapter Three section of this supplement.

CRANKSHAFT
(1983 MODELS)

Removal/Installation

Crankshaft removal and installation are the same as on previous models except the cooling fan is no longer attached to the front of the camshaft. The cooling fan was removed during engine removal and installation.

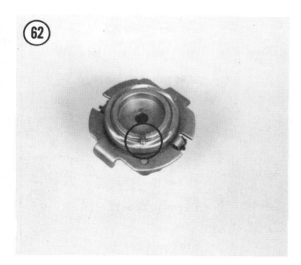

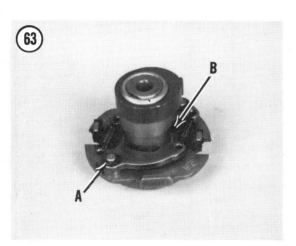

13

Table 4 ENGINE SPECIFICATIONS (650 CC)

Item	Specifications	Wear Limit
General		
Engine type	Water-cooled, 4-stroke, OHC, 80° V-twin	
Bore and stroke	82.5 x 63.0 mm (3.25 x 2.48 in.)	
Displacement	674 cm² (41.1 cu. in.)	
Compression ratio	9.8 to 1	
Valve train	Hi-Vo multi-link drive chain, OHC and rocker arms	
Lubrication	Wet sump	
Air filtration	Replaceable paper element type	
Engine weight (dry)	74.5 kg (164 lb.)	
Cylinders		
Bore	82.50-82.51 mm (3.248-3.248 in.)	82.60 mm (3.25 in.)
Out of round	-	0.10 mm (0.004 in.)
Piston/cylinder clearance	-	0.10 mm (0.004 in.)
Pistons	82.46-82.48 mm (2.754-2.755 in.)	82.38 mm (3.243 in.
Diameter	-	0.10 mm (0.004 in.)
Clearance in bore		21.0 mm (0.84 in.)
Piston pin bore	21.002-21.008 mm (0.8268-0.8271 in.)	
Piston pin outer diameter	20.994-21.000 mm (0.8265-0.8268 in.)	20.98 mm (0.83 in.)
Piston rings		
Number per piston		
Compression	2	-
Oil control	1	-
Ring end gap		
Top and second	0.10-0.25 mm (0.004-0.010 in.)	0.6 mm (0.024 in.)
Oil (side rail)	0.30-0.90 mm (0.012-0.035 in.)	1.1 mm (0.04 in.)
Ring side clearance		
Top and second	0.015-0.050 mm (0.0006-0.0020 in.)	0.10 mm (0.004 in.)
Crankshaft		
Runout	-	0.03 mm (0.001 in.)
Main bearing oil clearance	0.020-0.060 mm (0.0008-0.0024 in.)	0.08 mm (0.003 in.)
Connecting rod oil clearance	0.028-0.052 mm (0.0011-0.0020 in.)	0.08 mm (0.003 in.)
Connecting rod big end side clearance	0.15-0.35 mm (0.0059-0.014 in.)	0.5 mm (0.020 in.)
Camshaft		
Cam lobe height		
Intake	37.988 mm (1.4956 in.)	37.0 mm (1.456 in.)
Exhaust	38.143 mm (1.5017 in.)	37.1 mm (1.463 in.)

(continued)

Table 4 ENGINE SPECIFICATIONS (650 CC) (continued)

Item	Specifications	Wear Limit
Runout	-	0.1 mm (0.004 in.)
Journal diameter		
Front	21.959-21.980 mm (0.8645-0.8654 in.)	21.910 mm (0.8526 in.)
Rear	25.959-26.980 mm (1.022-1.062 in.)	25.91 mm (1.020 in.)
Valves		
Valve stem outer diameter		
Intake	6.580-6.590 mm (0.2591-0.2594 in.)	6.54 mm (0.258 in.)
Exhaust	6.550-6.560 mm (0.2579-0.2583 in.)	6.54 mm (0.258 in.)
Valve guide inner diameter		
Intake and exhaust	6.600-6.620 mm (0.2598-0.2506 in.)	6.70 mm (0.264 in.)
Stem to guide clearance		
Intake and exhaust	-	0.10 mm (0.040 in.)
Valve seat width		
Intake and exhaust	1.1-1.3 mm (0.04-0.05 in.)	2.0 mm (0.08 in.)
Valve springs free length (intake and exhaust)		
Outer	50.4 mm (1.984 in)	48.50 mm (1.91 in.)
Inner	50.3 mm (1.98 in.)	48.40 mm (1.91 in.)
Oil pump		
Inner rotor tip to outer clearance	-	0.15 mm (0.006 in.)
Outer rotor to body clearance	-	0.35 mm (0.014 in.)
Oil pump pressure relief	5.0-6.0 kg/cm² (71-85 psi)	

CHAPTER FIVE

CLUTCH AND TRANSMISSION

CLUTCH (1983 MODELS)

The clutch is basically the same as on previous models except that the clutch outer housing bushing has been replaced with an outer guide and needle bearing for longer service life.

Inspection

Measure the outside diameter of the outer guide. If the dimension is 1.256 in. (31.90 mm) or less, the guide must be replaced.

Inspect the needle bearing within the clutch outer housing. It must rotate freely with no signs of wear; replace the bearing if necessary.

TRANSMISSION (1983 MODELS)

The transmission is a 5-speed constant mesh type. To increase transmission gear service life, bushings have been added between gears and the shafts at some points.

13

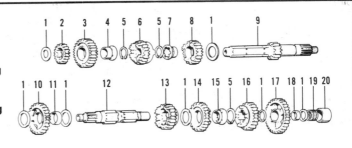

TRANSMISSION (1983)
1. Thrust washer
2. Main shaft 2nd gear
3. Main shaft 5th gear
4. Main shaft 5th gear splined bushing
5. Circlip
6. Main shaft 3rd gear
7. Main shaft 3rd gear splined bushing
8. Main shaft 4th gear
9. Main shaft/1st gear
10. Countershaft 2nd gear
11. Countershaft 2nd gear bushing
12. Countershaft
13. Countershaft 5th gear
14. Countershaft 3rd gear
15. Countershaft 3rd gear

16. Countershaft 4th gear
17. Countershaft 1st gear
18. Countershaft 1st gear bushing
19. Needle bearing
20. Needle bearing outer race

Disassembly/Assembly

The disassembly and assembly of the transmission shaft assemblies from the cylinder block and transmission cover/holder are the same as on previous models (as described in Chapter Five in the main body of this book).

Main Shaft Disassembly/Inspection/Assembly

Refer to **Figure 65** for this procedure.

1. Place the assembled shaft into a large can or plastic bucket and thoroughly clean with solvent and a stiff brush. Dry with compressed air or let it sit on rags to drip dry.
2. Slide off the thrust washer and the 2nd gear.
3. Slide off the 5th gear and 5th gear splined bushing.
4. Remove the circlip and slide off the 3rd gear.
5. Remove the circlip and slide off the 4th gear, 4th gear splined bushing and thrust washer.
6. Check each gear for excessive wear, burrs, pitting, or chipped or missing teeth. Make sure the lugs on the gears are in good condition.

CAUTION
Defective gears should be replaced. It is a good idea to replace the mating gear on the countershaft even though it may not show as much wear or damage.

NOTE
The 1st gear is part of the shaft; therefore, if the gear is defective the shaft must be replaced.

7. Make sure that all gears slide smoothly on the main shaft splines.

8A. On GL650 and GL650 Interstate models, measure the outside diameter of the transmission shaft at locations "A," "B" and "C" as shown in **Figure 66**. Refer to dimensions listed in **Table 5** for this specific model. If the shaft is worn to less than the service limit, the shaft must be replaced.

8B. On CX650C models, measure the outside diameter of the transmission shaft at locations "A" and "C" only as shown in **Figure 66**. Refer to dimensions listed in **Table 5** for your specific model. If the shaft is worn to less than the the service limit, the shaft must be replaced.

9. Measure the inside and outside diameter of the gear bushings (not the splined bushings). Refer to dimensions listed in **Table 5** for your specific model. If the bushing(s) are worn to less than the service limit, the bushing(s) must be replaced.

10. On all models, measure the inside diameter of the 4th and 5th gears. Refer to dimensions listed in **Table 5** for your specific

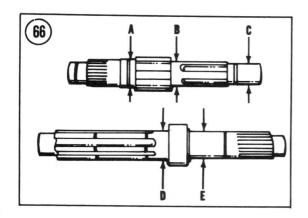

model. If the gear(s) are worn to less than the service limit, the gear(s) must be replaced.

NOTE
It is a good idea to replace all circlips every other time the transmission is assembled to ensure proper gear alignment.

11. Apply fresh engine oil to all sliding surfaces of all gears and bushings prior to assembly.
12. Slide on the thrust washer, the 4th gear and the 4th gear splined bushing.
13. Install the circlip.
14. Slide on the 3rd gear and install the circlip.
15. Slide on the 5th gear splined bushing.
15. Install the 5th gear, the 2nd gear and the thrust washer.
16. Make sure all circlips are seated correctly in the main shaft grooves.

Countershaft Disassembly/ Inspection/Assembly

Refer to **Figure 65** for this procedure.
1. Place the assembled shaft into a large can or plastic bucket and thoroughly clean with solvent and a stiff brush. Dry with compressed air or let it sit on rags to drip dry.
2. Slide off the thrust washer, the 2nd gear, 2nd gear bushing and thrust washer.
3. From the other end of the shaft, slide off the thrust washer, the 1st gear, 1st gear bushing and thrust washer.
4. Slide off the 4th gear.
5. Remove the circlip and slide off the 3rd gear and 3rd gear splined bushing.

6. Remove the thrust washer and slide off the 5th gear.
7. Check each gear for excessive wear, burrs, pitting or chipped or missing teeth. Make sure the lugs on the gears are in good condition.

CAUTION
Defective gears should be replaced. It is a good idea to replace the mating gear on the main shaft even though it may not show as much wear or damage.

8. Make sure that all gears slide smoothly on the countershaft splines.
9. On GL650 and GL650 Interstate models only, measure the outside diameter of the countershaft at locations "D" and "E" as shown in **Figure 66**. Refer to dimensions listed in **Table 5**. If the shaft is worn to less than the service limit, the shaft must be replaced.
10A. On GL650 and GL650 Interstate models, measure the inside and outside diameter of the 1st gear bushing. Refer to dimensions listed in **Table 5** for your specific model. If the bushing is worn to less than the service limit, the bushing must be replaced.
10B. On CX650C models, measure the inside and outside diameter of the 1st and 2nd gear bushings. Refer to dimensions listed in **Table 5** for your specific model. If the bushing(s) are worn to less than the service limit, the bushing(s) must be replaced.
11. Measure the inside diameter of the 1st, 2nd, 3rd and (on CX650C models) the 4th gears. Refer to dimensions listed in **Table 5** for your specific model. If the gear(s) are worn to less than the service limit, the gear(s) must be replaced.

NOTE
It is a good idea to replace the circlip every other time the transmission is assembled to ensure proper gear alignment.

12. Apply fresh engine oil to all sliding surfaces of all gears and bushings prior to assembly.
13. Slide on the 5th gear and thrust washer.

13

14. Slide on the 3rd gear and the 3rd gear splined bushing.

15. Install the circlip.

16. Slide the 4th gear, thrust washer and the 1st gear bushing.

17. Slide on the 1st gear (flush side on last) and thrust washer.

18. Onto the other side of the shaft, slide on the thrust washer, the 2nd gear bushing.

19. Slide on the 2nd gear (flush side on last) and thrust washer.

20. Make sure the circlip is seated correctly in the countershaft groove.

FINAL DRIVE (1982-ON CX500, ALL OTHER MODELS 1981-ON)

Final drive removal and installation are the same as for previous models with the exception of removing the engine rear cover. On these models the pulse generator mechanism and ignition advance mechanism must be removed prior to removing the engine rear cover. Refer to *Ignition Advance and Pulse Generator* in this section of the supplement.

Table 5 TRANSMISSION SPECIFICATIONS

Item	Wear limit
GL650, Interstate	
Gear ID main shaft (4th and 5th)	29.10 mm (1.1457 in.)
Gear ID countershaft	
1st	24.10 mm (0.949 in.)
2nd	31.109 mm (1.2248 in.)
3rd	29.10 mm (1.1457 in.)
Countershaft 1st gear bushing	
ID	25.025 mm (0.9825 in.)
OD	28.945 mm (1.1396 in.)
Main shaft OD	
At location A	27.43 mm (1.080 in.)
At location B	24.93 mm (0.981 in.)
At location C	19.96 mm (0.786 in.)
Countershaft OD	
At location D	24.93 mm (0.981 in.)
At location E	24.96 mm (0.983 in.)
Gear-to-bushing clearance	0.15 mm (0.006 in.)
CX650C	
Gear ID main shaft (4th and 5th)	29.10 mm (1.1457 in.)
Gear ID countershaft	
1st	24.10 mm (0.949 in.)
2nd	31.109 mm (1.2248 in.)
3rd	29.10 mm (1.1457 in.)
Main shaft 4th and 5th gear bushing OD	28.95 mm (81.140 in.)
Countershaft bushing	
1st gear	
ID	20.06 mm (0.790 in.)
OD	23.95 mm (0.943 in.)
2nd gear	
ID	27.54 mm (1.084 in.)
OD	30.95 mm (1.219 in.)
3d gear	
OD	28.95 mm (1.140 in.)
Countershaft OD	
At location A	27.44 mm (1.080 in.)
At location C	19.96 mm (0.786 in.)
Gear-to-bushing clearance	0.15 mm (0.006 in.)
Bushing-to-shaft clearance	0.10 mm (0.004 in.)

CHAPTER SIX

FUEL AND EXHAUST SYSTEMS

CARBURETORS

An accelerator pump circuit has been added to the carburetors on 1980-on models to aid performance when accelerating (**Figure 67**). The accelerator pump assembly is part of the left-hand carburetor and the fuel is delivered to the right-hand carburetor via the accelerator pump joint pipe.

Removal, installation, disassembly and assembly are the same as on previous models with the exception of the accelerator pump assembly and a limiter cap on the pilot screw. Both of these service procedures are included in this section of this supplement.

Accelerator Pump
Disassembly/Inspection/Assembly

1. Remove the carburetor assembly as described under *Carburetors, Removal/Installation* in the main body of this book.
2. On the left-hand carburetor remove the screws (**Figure 68**) securing the accelerator pump cover.
3. Remove the cover and spring (**Figure 69**).
4. Carefully hold onto the small rubber boot on the diaphragm rod (**Figure 70**) and withdraw the diaphragm.
5. Inspect the diaphragm rod for bending or scratches; replace if necessary.
6. Inspect the rubber diaphragm for signs of deterioration and cracks; replace if necessary.
7. Install the diaphragm and rod into the carburetor. Make sure that the locating tabs (**Figure 71**) are indexed properly into the cutouts in the carburetor.
8. Install the small rubber boot onto the diaphragm rod (**Figure 70**) and push the boot up against the base of the carburetor.

9. Install the spring and the accelerator pump cover. Tighten the screws securely.
10. Adjust the accelerator pump as described under *Accelerator Pump Adjustment* in this section of the supplement.
11. Install the carburetor assembly as described under *Carburetors, Removal/Installation* in the main body of this book.

Refilling Dry Float Bowls
(1981-on)

> *WARNING*
> ***Do not*** *attempt this procedure with a warm engine as this presents a real fire danger.* ***Do not*** *allow anyone to smoke and do not work in an area with an open flame (i.e., water heater or clothes drier gas pilots). Have a fire extinguisher rated for gasoline or chemical fires within reach.*

After the carburetors have been disassembled both float bowls are empty. On 1981-on models, the engine must be running in order for fuel to flow from the fuel tank, through the vacuum controlled fuel shutoff valve diaphragm and into the carburetors. To avoid prolonged cranking while the dry carburetors fill, use the following method to refill the carburetor. After the carburetor assembly is reinstalled, install a funnel in the fuel line going to the carburetors (A, **Figure 72**). *Slowly and carefully* pour fuel into the funnel and into the float bowls. The float bowls should fill up within 30 seconds. To check if there is fuel in the carburetor, open one of the drain screws (B, **Figure 72**); if fuel flows out, the bowl has fuel in it.

Remove the funnel and install the fuel tank.

13

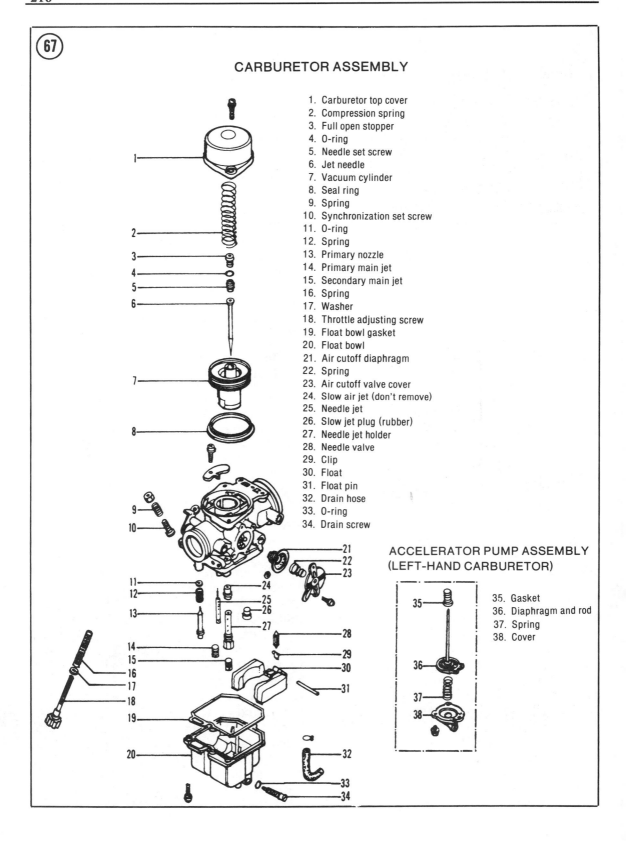

67

CARBURETOR ASSEMBLY

1. Carburetor top cover
2. Compression spring
3. Full open stopper
4. O-ring
5. Needle set screw
6. Jet needle
7. Vacuum cylinder
8. Seal ring
9. Spring
10. Synchronization set screw
11. O-ring
12. Spring
13. Primary nozzle
14. Primary main jet
15. Secondary main jet
16. Spring
17. Washer
18. Throttle adjusting screw
19. Float bowl gasket
20. Float bowl
21. Air cutoff diaphragm
22. Spring
23. Air cutoff valve cover
24. Slow air jet (don't remove)
25. Needle jet
26. Slow jet plug (rubber)
27. Needle jet holder
28. Needle valve
29. Clip
30. Float
31. Float pin
32. Drain hose
33. O-ring
34. Drain screw

ACCELERATOR PUMP ASSEMBLY (LEFT-HAND CARBURETOR)

35. Gasket
36. Diaphragm and rod
37. Spring
38. Cover

CARBURETOR ADJUSTMENTS

Needle Jet Adjustment

The needle jet is *non-adjustable* on all models.

Accelerator Pump Adjustment
(Left-hand Carburetor Only)

1. Remove the carburetor assembly as described under *Carburetors, Removal/ Installation* in Chapter Six in the main body of this book.

> *NOTE*
> *For the following step the throttle valve must be in the closed position.*

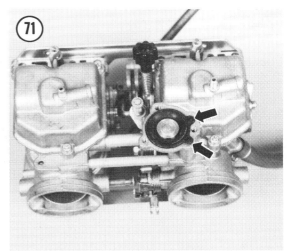

2. Measure the distance between the accelerator pump rod and the choke link arm (**Figure 73**). The correct clearance is 0.004-0.012 in. (0.1-0.3 mm); refer to **Figure 74**.

3. If adjustment is necessary, carefully bend the choke link arm and repeat Step 2 until correct clearance is obtained.

4. Measure the distance between the choke link arm and the stopper on the carburetor. The correct clearance is 0.12-0.13 in. (3.1-3.3 mm); refer to **Figure 74**.

5. If adjustment is necessary, carefully bend the choke link arm and repeat Step 4 until correct clearance is obtained.

6. Install the carburetor assembly as described under *Carburetors, Removal/Installation* in Chapter Six in the main body of this book.

Choke Adjustment

1. Remove the side covers, seat and fuel tank.

2. Operate the choke knob and check for smooth operation of the cable and choke mechanism.

3. Pull the knob all the way *up* to the closed position.

NOTE
Figure 75 and Figure 76 are shown with the carburetor assembly partially removed from the engine for clarity.

4. At the carburetor assembly, pull up on the choke lever (**Figure 75**) to make sure it is at the end of its travel thus closing the choke valves. If you can move the choke lever an additional amount it must be adjusted.

5. To adjust, loosen the cable clamping screw (**Figure 76**) and move the cable sheath *up* until the choke lever is fully closed. Hold the choke lever in this position and tighten the cable clamping screw securely.

6. Push the choke knob all the way *down* to the fully open position.

7. At the carburetor assembly, check that the choke lever is fully open by checking for free play between the cable and the choke lever. The cable should move slightly as there should be no tension on it.

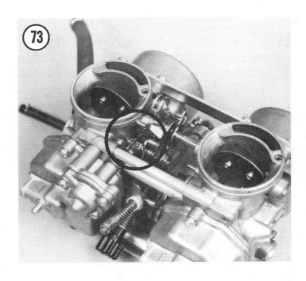

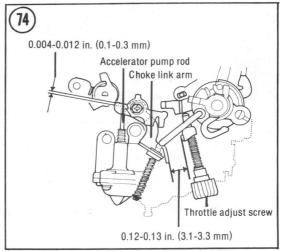

0.004-0.012 in. (0.1-0.3 mm)
Accelerator pump rod
Choke link arm
Throttle adjust screw
0.12-0.13 in. (3.1-3.3 mm)

8. If proper adjustment cannot be achieved using this procedure the cable has stretched and must be replaced. Refer to *Choke Cable Replacement* in Chapter Six of the basic book.

9. The choke knob should remain in whatever position it is placed from fully closed to fully open. If it does not, pull up on the rubber cover and turn the adjuster. Look down onto the knob and turn it either clockwise to increase resistance or counterclockwise to decrease resistance.

10. Reinstall the fuel tank, seat and side covers.

Fast Idle Adjustment

The engine must be *cold* to perform this inspection and adjustment procedure.

1. Connect a portable tachometer following the manufacturer's instructions. The bike's tachometer is not accurate enough at this rpm range.

2. Pull the choke knob all the way *up* to the closed position.

3. Start the engine and *immediately* check the fast idle speed. The idle speed should be between 1,500-2,500 rpm.

4. Turn the engine off.

5. If the engine speed is not within specifications, remove the carburetor assembly as described under *Carburetors, Removal/Installation* in Chapter Six in the main body of this book.

6. Close the throttle valve and open the choke valve. Measure the clearance between the choke link arm and the throttle drum (**Figure 77**). The specified clearance is 0.047 in. (0.8 mm).

7. If the clearance is incorrect, adjust by opening or closing the fork end of the fast idle adjusting arm.

8. Install the carburetor assembly and repeat Step 2 and Step 3.

Pilot Screw Adjustment (1981-on Models) And New Limiter Cap Installation (U.S. Only)

To comply with U.S. emission control standards, a limiter cap is attached to each pilot screw. This is to prevent the owner from readjusting the factory setting. The limiter cap will allow a maximum of 7/8 of a turn of the pilot screw *to a leaner mixture only*. The pilot screw is preset at the factory and should

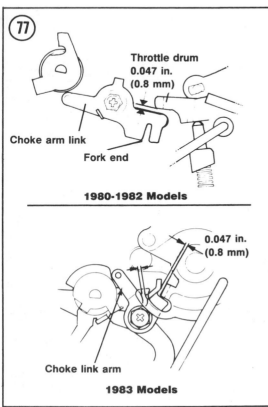

13

not be reset unless the carburetor has been overhauled.

CAUTION
Do not try to remove the limiter cap from the pilot screw as it is bonded in place and will break off and damage the pilot screw if removal is attempted.

NOTE
*Perform Steps 1, 2 and 3 only if new pilot screws have been installed or the carburetors have been overhauled. **Do not install** the new limiter caps onto the pilot screws until this procedure is completed.*

1. Remove the carburetor asssembly as described in Chapter Six in the main body of this book.
2. Remove the screws securing the float bowls and remove the float bowls.
3. For a preliminary adjustment, carefully turn the pilot screw on each carburetor in until it *lightly* seats and then back it out the following number of turns:
   a. CX500, GL500, GL500 Interstate: 1 5/8 turns out.
   b. GL650, GL650 Interstate: 2 turns out.
   c. CX650C: 2 3/8 turns out.

NOTE
Remember, do not install the limiter caps at this time.

4. Install the float bowls and install the carburetor assembly.
5. Start the engine and let it reach normal operating temperature. Stop-and-go riding for approximately 10 minutes is sufficient.
6. Connect a portable tachometer following the manufacturer's instructions. The bike's tachometer is not accurate enough at a low rpm.
7. Start the engine and turn the large idle adjust screw (**Figure 78**) in or out to achieve the idle speed of 1,100 ±100 rpm.
8. On the right-hand carburetor, turn the pilot screw in or out to obtain the highest engine speed.
9. Readjust the idle adjust screw (**Figure 78**) in or out to again achieve the idle speed of 1,100 ±100 rpm.

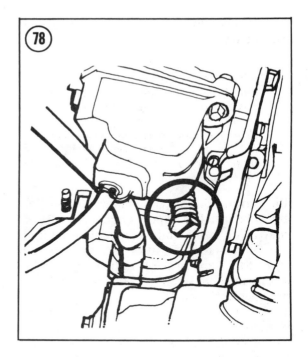

NOTE
In the next step, if the pilot screw seats before the idle speed drops by 100 rpm, continue to Step 11.

10. Turn the pilot screw in *gradually* until the engine idle speed drops by 100 rpm.
11. Turn the pilot screw out one turn from the position obtained in Step 10.
12. Turn the idle adjust screw in or out *again* to achieve the desired idle speed of 1,100 ±100 rpm.

13. Perform Steps 8-12 for the left-hand carburetor.

WARNING
With the engine idling, move the handlebar from side to side. If idle speed increases during this movement, the throttle cables need adjustment or they may be incorrectly routed through the frame. Correct this problem immediately. Do not ride the bike in this unsafe condition.

14. Perform this step only if new limiter caps are to be installed. Apply Loctite No. 601, or equivalent, to the limiter cap and install it on the pilot screw. Position the limiter cap against the stop on the float bowl (**Figure 79**) so that the pilot screw can *only turn clockwise*, not counterclockwise.
15. Turn the engine off and disconnect the portable tachometer.
16. After this adjustment is completed, test ride the bike. Throttle response from idle should be rapid and without any hesitation.

High Altitude Adjustment
(1982-on U.S. Models Only)

If the bike is going to be operated above 6,500 ft. (2,000 m) for any sustained period, the carburetors must be readjusted to improve performance and decrease exhaust emissions.
1. Start the engine and let it reach normal operating temperature. Stop-and-go riding for approximately 10 minutes is usually sufficient. Turn off the engine.
2. Connect a portable tachometer following the manufacturer's instructions. The bike's tachometer is not accurate enough at low rpm.
3A. On 1982 models, turn each pilot screw 1/2 turn *clockwise* (as viewed from the bottom of the carburetor).
3B. On 1983 models, turn each pilot screw 1/4 turn *clockwise* (as viewed from the bottom of the carburetor).
4. Restart the engine and turn the black idle adjust screw (**Figure 78**) to achieve an idle speed of 1,100 ±100 rpm.
5. Turn the engine off and disconnect the portable tachometer.

6. When the bike is returned to lower elevations (near sea level), the pilots screws must be returned to their orignal positions and the idle speed readjusted to 1,100 ±100 rpm.

THROTTLE CABLE

On Interstate models, the front fairing must be removed as described in the Chapter Twelve section of this supplement before the throttle cables can be replaced.

CHOKE CABLE
REPLACEMENT
(INTERSTATE MODELS)

On Interstate models, the front fairing must be removed as described in the Chapter Twelve section of this supplement before the choke cable can be replaced.

CHOKE CABLE
REPLACEMENT
(CX650C)

1. Remove the seat and fuel tank.
2. Partially remove the carburetor assembly as described in Chapter Six of the main book.

NOTE
It may not look like it, but it is practically impossible to remove the choke cable from the carburetors with the carburetor assembly in place. There is just not enough room for 2 hands within the area.

3. Loosen the choke cable clamp screw (**Figure 80**) and remove the cable end from the choke linkage (**Figure 81**).
4. Remove the clutch switch wires at the clutch lever.
5. Remove the screws (A, **Figure 82**) securing the clutch lever bracket holder and bracket and remove the switch assembly from the handlebar.
6. Remove the choke cable (B, **Figure 82**) from the clutch and choke lever assembly on the handlebar.

NOTE
The piece of string attached in the next step will be used to pull the new choke

13

cable back through the frame so it will be routed in the same position as the old cable.

7. Tie a piece of heavy string or cord (approximately 6-8 ft./1.8-2.4 m long) to the carburetor end of the choke cable. Wrap this end with masking or duct tape. Do not use an excessive amount of tape as it must be pulled through the frame loop during removal. Tie the other end of the string to the frame or air box.

8. At the choke lever end of the cable, carefully pull the cable (and attached string) out through the frame and from behind the headlight housing. Make sure the attached string follows the same path that the cable does through the frame.

9. Remove the tape and untie the string from the old cable.

10. Lubricate the new cable as described under *Control Cables* in Chapter Three in the main body of this book.

11. Tie the string to the new choke cable and wrap it with tape.

12. Carefully pull the string back through the frame routing the new cable through the same path as the old cable.

13. Remove the tape and untie the string from the cable and the frame.

14. Install the choke cable onto the choke lever assembly.

15. Attach the choke cable to the carburetor choke linkage and tighten the clamping screw.

16. Install the clutch lever bracket holder and bracket onto the handlebar and install the screws (A, **Figure 82**) securing the halves together.

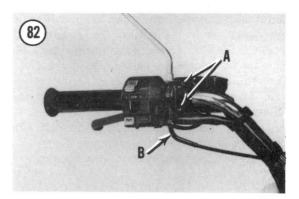

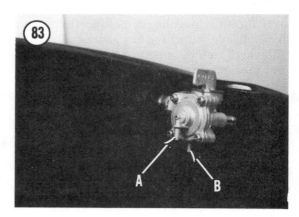

17. Attach the clutch switch wires to the clutch lever.

18. Operate the choke lever and make sure the carburetor choke linkage is operating correctly, with no binding. If operation is incorrect or there is binding carefully check that the cable is attached correctly and there are no tight bends in the cable.

19. Install the carburetor assembly, fuel tank and seat.

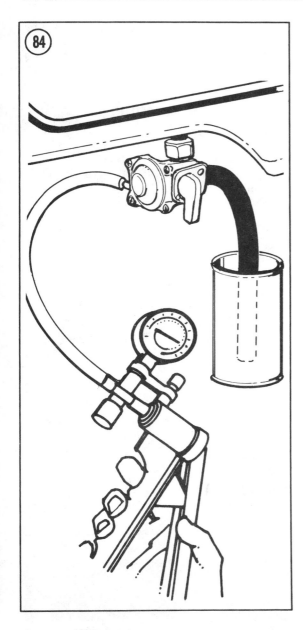

FUEL SHUTOFF VALVE (1981-ON MODELS)

On 1981-on models the fuel shutoff valve can be left in the ON or RES position at all times. Vacuum from the engine opens the valve only when the engine is running and automatically closes the valve to stop the flow of fuel when the engine is shut off. The fuel shutoff valve OFF position is used only when the motorcycle is to be stored for any length of time or when servicing the fuel system.

Testing

1. Remove the fuel tank as described in this section of the supplement.
2. Leave the carburetor fuel hose attached to the fuel shutoff valve (the one that normally leads to the carburetor assembly).
3. Place the fuel tank up on a box so it is higher than the work surface of your workbench. Position the loose end of the fuel line into a clean container.

> *NOTE*
> *If this fuel is kept clean it can be reused. If it becomes contaminated during this procedure dispose of it properly. Check with local regulations for proper disposal of gasoline.*

4. Connect a portable hand vacuum pump to the vacuum side (diaphragm cover) of the fuel shutoff valve (A, **Figure 83**).

> *NOTE*
> **Figure 83** *is shown with the fuel tank positioned on its side for clarity only.*

5. Turn the fuel shutoff valve to the ON position. Fuel should *not* flow from the carburetor fuel hose.
6. Apply vacuum to the diaphragm with the hand pump (**Figure 84**). Fuel *should* flow out when 0.4-0.8 in. Hg (10-20 mm Hg) of vacuum is applied.
7. If fuel does not flow turn the fuel shutoff valve to the RES position and repeat Step 6.
8. If fuel will not flow in either the ON or RES position, disassemble the fuel shutoff valve as described under *Removal/ Cleaning/ Installation* in this section of the supplement.
9. Disconnect the portable hand vacuum pump.
10. Turn the fuel shutoff valve to the OFF position.
11. Install the fuel tank as described in this section of the supplement.

Removal/Cleaning/Installation

Refer to **Figure 85** for this procedure.
1. Remove the fuel tank as described in this section of the supplement.

13

2. Hold onto the fuel shutoff valve assembly, unscrew the locknut from the tank (A, **Figure 86**) and remove the valve.

3. Remove the screws securing the cover (B, **Figure 86**).

4. Remove the cover, spring and spring seat. Remove the spacer and both diaphragms.

5. Remove the fuel strainer and O-ring. Clean the strainer with a medium soft toothbrush and compressed air.

6. Clean all diaphragm parts in cleaning solvent and thoroughly dry.

7. Inspect both diaphragms for deterioration. Replace both diaphragms even though only one may be faulty.

8. Turn the shutoff valve to both the ON and the RES positions and blow out all passages with compressed air.

9. Reassemble the shutoff valve. Make sure that neither diaphragm is pinched in the valve body during reassembly.

10. Install the fuel shutoff valve onto the fuel tank. Hold onto the valve assembly and tighten the locknut securely.

11. Install the fuel tank as described in this section of the supplement.

12. After installation is complete, thoroughly check for fuel leaks.

FUEL STRAINER (1982-ON MODELS)

1. Turn the fuel shutoff valve to the OFF position.

2. Remove the fuel cup, O-ring seal and filter screen (**Figure 87**) from the bottom of the fuel shutoff valve. Properly dispose of fuel remaining in the fuel cup.

3. Clean the filter screen with a medium soft toothbrush and blow out with compressed air. Replace the filter screen if it is broken in any area.

4. Wash the fuel cup in kerosene to remove any residue or foreign matter. Thoroughly dry with compressed air.

5. Align the index marks on the filter screen and the fuel shutoff valve body.

6. Install the O-ring seal and screw on the fuel cup.

7. Hand-tighten the fuel cup and then tighten to a final torque of 2-4 ft.-lb. (3-5 N•m). Do

not overtighten the fuel cup as it may be damaged.

8. Turn the fuel shutoff valve to the ON position and check for leaks.

FUEL TANK (1981-ON MODELS)

Removal/Installation

1. Place the bike on the centerstand.

2. Turn the fuel shutoff valve to the OFF position.

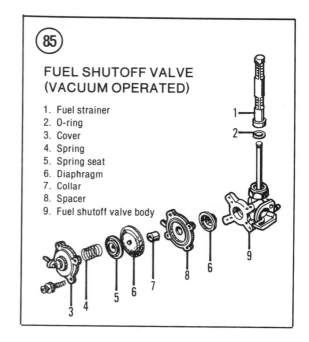

85

FUEL SHUTOFF VALVE (VACUUM OPERATED)

1. Fuel strainer
2. O-ring
3. Cover
4. Spring
5. Spring seat
6. Diaphragm
7. Collar
8. Spacer
9. Fuel shutoff valve body

86

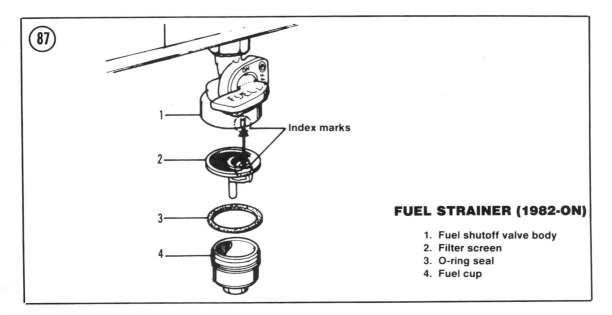

FUEL STRAINER (1982-ON)

1. Fuel shutoff valve body
2. Filter screen
3. O-ring seal
4. Fuel cup

3. Remove the side panels and the seat.

4. Disconnect the battery negative lead.

5. Remove the bolt securing the rear of the fuel tank.

6. Partially lift up on the rear of the tank and disconnect the fuel line to the carburetors, the vacuum line and the air vent tube from the fuel shutoff valve.

7. Lift the fuel tank the rest of the way up, pull the tank to the rear and remove it.

8. Install by reversing these removal steps, noting the following.

9. Attach the vacuum line to the vacuum side (diaphragm cover—A, **Figure 83**) and the air vent tube to the center fitting (spacer—B, **Figure 83**) of the fuel shutoff valve.

CHAPTER SEVEN

ELECTRICAL SYSTEM

ALTERNATOR (1982-ON CX500, ALL OTHER MODELS 1981-ON)

Alternator removal and installation are the same as for previous models with the exception of removing the engine rear cover and the torque specifications for the rotor bolt.

On these models the pulse generator mechanism and ignition advance mechanism must be removed prior to removing the engine rear cover. Refer to *Ignition Advance and Pulse Generator* in this section of the supplement.

Tighten the rotor bolt to 65-76 ft.-lb. (90-105 N•m).

IGNITION SYSTEM (1982-ON CX500, ALL OTHER MODELS 1981-ON)

The updated CDI ignition system used on these models differs from previous models. The system consists of 2 ignition coils, 2 spark units, an ignition pulse generator assembly and 2 spark plugs. Refer to **Figure 88** for a diagram of the ignition circuit.

CDI Precautions

Certain measures must be taken to protect the capacitor discharge system. Instantaneous damage to the semiconductors in the system

13

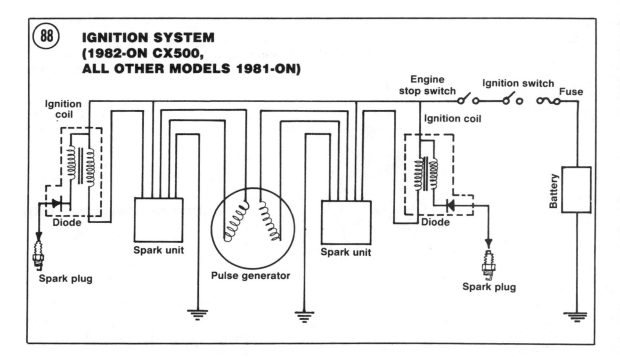

(88) **IGNITION SYSTEM (1982-ON CX500, ALL OTHER MODELS 1981-ON)**

will occur if the following precautions are not observed.

1. Never connect the battery backwards. If the connected battery polarity is wrong, damage will occur to the voltage regulator/rectifier, the alternator and the spark unit.

2. Do not disconnect the battery when the engine is running. A voltage surge will occur which will damage the voltage regulator/ rectifier and possibly burn out the lights.

3. Keep all connections between the various units clean and tight. Be sure that the wiring connections are pushed together firmly to help keep out moisture.

4. Do not substitute another type of ignition coil.

5. Each component is mounted within a rubber vibration isolator. Always be sure that the isolator is in place when installing any units of the system.

CDI Troubleshooting

Problems with the capacitor discharge system are usually the production of a weak spark or no spark at all.

1. Check all connections to make sure they are tight and free of corrosion.

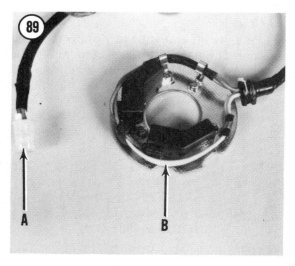

2. Check the ignition coils as described under *Ignition Coil Testing* in this section of the supplement.

3. Check the pickup coils in the ignition pulse generator with an ohmmeter. Remove the left-hand side cover and disconnect the ignition pulse generator electrical connector containing 4 wires (2 yellow and 2 blue). Connect the ohmmeter leads between both blue leads (right-hand cylinder) and then between both yellow leads (left-hand

3. Disconnect the electrical connectors going to each spark unit (A, **Figure 90**).

4. Remove the bolt (B, **Figure 90**) securing the spark unit to the frame and remove the spark unit(s).

5. Install by reversing these removal steps. Make sure all electrical connections are tight and free of corrosion.

Spark Unit Testing

Tests may be performed on the units but a good one may be damaged by someone unfamiliar with the test equipment. To be safe, have the test made by a dealer or substitute a known good unit for a suspected one.

IGNITION COIL

There are 2 ignition coils; the one on the left-hand side fires the left-hand spark plug and the one on the right-hand side fires the right-hand spark plug.

Removal/Installation

1. Remove the side covers and seat.
2. Remove the fuel tank.
3. Disconnect the battery negative lead.
4. Disconnect the spark plug leads (A, **Figure 91**) from the spark plugs.
5. Disconnect the primary wire connectors (B, **Figure 91**) for both coils (blue and black/white—left-hand coil; yellow and black/white—right-hand coil).

NOTE
The connector for the right-hand coil is red; for the left-hand coil it is white.

6. Remove the bolts (C, **Figure 91**) securing the ignition coils to the frame and remove both coils.
7. Install by reversing these removal steps, noting the following.
8. Make sure all electrical connections are tight and free of corrosion.
9. Make sure that the ground wire is attached to the front bolt and nut (D, **Figure 91**).

cylinder); refer to A, **Figure 89**. Each coil resistance should be 530 ± 50 ohms at 68° F (20° C). If the pickup coils do not meet these specifications, the ignition pulse generator assembly (B, **Figure 89**) must be replaced. It cannot be serviced; refer to *Ignition Advance and Pulse Generator Removal/Installation* in the Chapter Four section of this supplement.

4. If the ignition coils and ignition pulse generator assembly check out okay, one of the spark units is at fault and must be replaced.

Spark Unit Replacement

1. Remove both side covers and the seat.
2. Disconnect the battery negative lead.

Testing

The ignition coil is a form of transformer which develops the high voltage required to

13

jump the spark plug gap. The only maintenance required is that of keeping the electrical connections clean and tight and occasionally checking to see that the coils are mounted securely.

As a quick check of coil condition, disconnect the high voltage lead from the spark plug. Remove the spark plug from the cylinder head. Connect a new or known good spark plug to the high voltage lead and place the spark plug base on a good ground like the engine cylinder. Position the spark plug so you can see the electrode.

WARNING
If it is necessary to hold the high voltage lead, do so with an insulated pair of pliers. The high voltage generated could produce serious or fatal shocks.

Push the starter button to turn the engine over a couple of times. If a fat blue spark occurs the coil is in good condition; if not it must be replaced. Make sure that you are using a known good spark plug for this test. If the spark plug used is defective the test results will be incorrect.

Reinstall the spark plug in the cylinder head.

LIGHTING SYSTEM

Headlight Replacement
(1981-on, Except Interstate)

These models are equipped with a quartz halogen headlight. Special handling of the bulb is required as specified in this procedure.

Refer to **Figure 92** for this procedure.
1. Remove the mounting screws securing the headlight assembly.
2. Pull the headlight/rim assembly out of the headlight case.
3. Disconnect the electrical connector from the headlight lens unit.
4. Remove the bulb cover.
5. Unhook the set spring and remove the bulb assembly. Replace with a new bulb assembly—do not touch the bulb with your fingers.

CAUTION
Carefully read all instructions shipped with the replacement bulb. Do not touch the bulb glass with your fingers. Any traces of oil on the quartz halogen bulb will drastically reduce the life of the bulb. Clean any traces of oil from the bulb with a cloth moistened in alcohol or lacquer thinner.

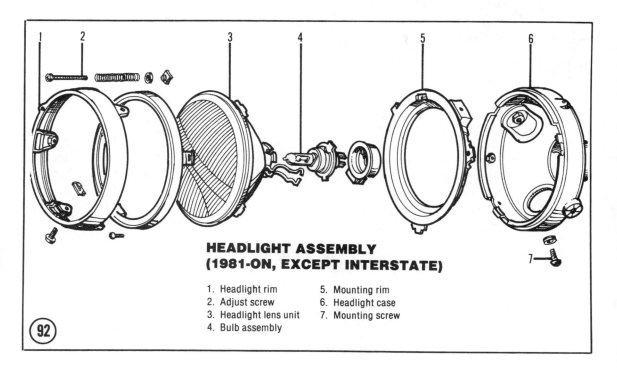

HEADLIGHT ASSEMBLY (1981-ON, EXCEPT INTERSTATE)
1. Headlight rim
2. Adjust screw
3. Headlight lens unit
4. Bulb assembly
5. Mounting rim
6. Headlight case
7. Mounting screw

92

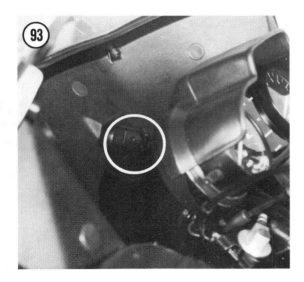

6. Install by reversing these removal steps.
7. Adjust the headlight as described under *Headlight Adjustment* in Chapter Seven in the main body of this book.

**Headlight Replacement
(Interstate Models)**

All models are equipped with a quartz halogen headlight. Special handling of the bulb is required as specified in this procedure.
1. Remove the small set screw in the adjusting knob (**Figure 93**).
2. Unscrew the nut, lockwasher and flat washer (**Figure 94**) on the post of the mounting bracket. Carefully tap on the end of this post to help push the headlight assembly forward and out of the fairing.
3. From the front of the fairing pull the headlight assembly out the rest of the way.
4. Disconnect the electrical connector (A, **Figure 95**) from the headlight lens unit.
5. Remove the bulb cover (B, **Figure 95**).
6. Remove the set spring and bulb assembly (**Figure 96**). Replace with a new bulb assembly—do not touch the bulb with your fingers.

> *CAUTION*
> *Carefully read all instructions shipped with the replacement bulb. Do not touch the bulb glass with your fingers. Any traces of oil on the quartz halogen bulb will drastically reduce the life of the bulb. Clean any traces of oil from the bulb with a cloth moistened in alcohol or lacquer thinner.*

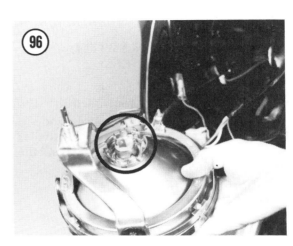

13

7. Install by reversing these removal steps. Do not overtighten the set screw on the adjusting knob as the threads are very fine and are easily stripped.

8. Adjust the headlight as described under *Headlight Adjustment (Interstate Models)* in this section of the supplement.

Headlight Adjustment (Interstate Models)

Adjust the headlight horizontally and vertically according to Department of Motor Vehicle regulations in your area.

To adjust the headlight horizontally, turn the screw (**Figure 97**) on the right-hand side of the headlight trim bezel. Screwing in turns the light toward the right-hand side of the rider and loosening the screw will direct the light to the left-hand side of the rider.

To adjust the headlight vertically, turn the adjusting knob (**Figure 98**) inside the fairing. Turn it in the direction indicated on the knob.

Front Directional Signal Light Replacement (Interstate Models)

Remove the screws (**Figure 99**) securing the lens and remove the lens. Wash the inside and outside of the lens with a mild detergent and wipe dry.

Inspect the condition of the lens gasket and replace if it is damaged or deteriorated.

Replace the bulb (**Figure 100**) and install the lens; do not overtighten the screws as the lens may crack.

COOLING FAN SWITCH (1983 MODELS)

The radiator cooling fan is run by an electric motor and is controlled by the thermostatic switch which senses coolant temperature. The thermostatic switch is located on the base of the radiator on the right-hand side.

Testing

If the cooling fan does not operate under any circumstances check the following:

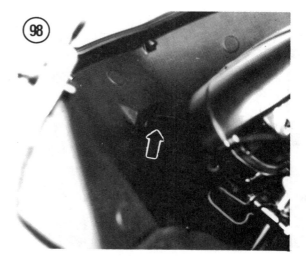

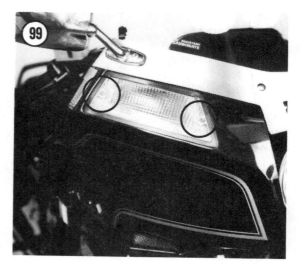

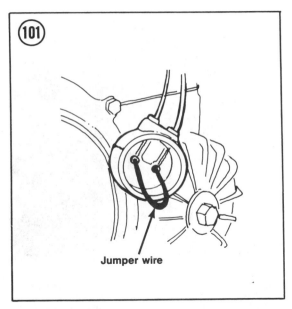

Jumper wire

making. Do not use a medical type thermometer as it is rated for much lower temperatures.

3. Start the engine and let it reach normal operating temperature.

4. The cooling fan should start running when the coolant temperature reaches the following temperatures:

   a. GL650, GL650 Interstate: 191-197° F (88-92° C).

   b. CX650C: 208-216° F (98-102° C).

5. The cooling fan should stop running when the coolant temperature reaches the following temperatures:

   a. GL650, GL650 Interstate: 182-188° F (83-87° C).

   b. CX650C: 200-207° F (93-97° C).

6. If the switch turns the fan on and off at the wrong temperatures, replace the switch.

7. If the cooling fan does not start at all, turn the engine off.

8. Disconnect the 2-pin electrical connector from the thermostatic switch at the right-hand rear side of the radiator.

9. Place a jumper wire across the 2 wire terminals in the connector (**Figure 101**)—not at the switch terminals.

10. Turn the ignition switch to the ON position. If the cooling fan runs, the thermostatic switch is faulty and must be replaced.

11. If the cooling fan still does not run, check the following:

   a. With the ignition switch in the ON position, check for battery voltage to the cooling fan. At the fan motor coupler, use a voltmeter and check between the black lead (battery positive voltage) and the green lead of the fan motor. Voltage should be present.

   b. If voltage is present, check for a blown or faulty fuse, loose or corroded electrical connectors within the circuit or an open circuit.

12. Remove the thermometer and install the radiator cap.

Removal/Installation

1. Remove the radiator as described in the Chapter Eight section of this supplement.

   a. Make sure that a fuse has not blown. There is no specific fuse for the fan, so check all fuses.

   b. Make sure the battery is fully charged.

If these items are okay, perform the following.

1. With the engine cold, place the bike on the centerstand and remove the radiator cap.

2. Place a thermometer into the filler neck of the radiator.

NOTE

Use a kitchen type thermometer designed for deep fat frying or candy

13

2. Unscrew the thermostatic switch and washer from the base of the radiator.

3. Apply a non-hardening sealer to the theads of the new switch.

4. Install the washer onto the new switch and install the new switch onto the radiator. Tighten the switch securely but do not overtighten as you may damage the radiator.

5. Install the radiator as described in the Chapter Eight section of this supplement.

6. Start the engine and make sure there is no coolant leaking from around the switch. Retighten if necessary.

FUSES

There are 4 fuses used on the 1981-on non-Interstate models plus a main fuse (fusible link). On Interstate models, there are 4 fuses, the main fuse (fusible link) plus 3 accessory fuses located within the fairing adjacent to the left-hand front turn signal (**Figure 102**). The main fuse (fusible link) on all models is located next to the starter solenoid.

If the main fusible link blows, disconnect the electrical connector (**Figure 103**) and open the fuse door. Remove the Phillips screws securing the fusible link and replace it (**Figure 104**). There is a spare link inside the panel.

The remaining fuses are accessible by removing the cover at the base of the handlebar. There is a spare fuse attached to the fuse panel also; always carry spares.

Whenever a fuse blows, find out the reason for the failure before replacing the fuse. Usually the trouble is a short circuit in the wiring. This may be caused by worn-through insulation or a disconnected wire shorted to ground.

> *CAUTION*
> *Never substitute aluminum foil or wire for a fuse. Never use a higher amperage fuse than specified. An overload could cause a fire and complete loss of the motorcycle.*

WIRING DIAGRAMS

Full color wiring diagrams are located at the end of this book.

CHAPTER EIGHT

COOLING SYSTEM

Figure 105 shows the major components of the 1983 cooling system.

RADIATOR
(1983 MODELS)

Removal/Installation

1. On Interstate models, remove the front fairing as described in the Chapter Twelve section of this supplement.
2. Remove the seat and the fuel tank.
3. Remove the exhaust system as described in Chapter Six in the main body of this book.
4. Remove the bolts securing the radiator grill and remove the grill.
5. Place a drain pan under the radiator and remove the drain plug (**Figure 106**) at the base of the radiator. Remove the radiator cap; this will speed up the draining process. Completely drain the radiator; reinstall the drain plug and radiator cap.
6. On Interstate models, perform the following:
   a. Disconnect the electrical wires to the horn.
   b. Remove the bolts securing the horns and remove the horns.
   c. Remove the nut securing the left-hand side of the main bracket.
   d. Unhook the wire band securing the clutch and tachometer cable.
   e. Remove the nut securing the right-hand side of the main bracket.
   f. Remove the main bracket.
7. Disconnect the overflow tube at the radiator cap (A, **Figure 107**).
8. Disconnect the electrical connectors to the fan motor and the thermostatic switch.
9. Disconnect the electrical wires to the right-hand ignition coil. Remove the bolts securing the right-hand ignition coil and remove the coil.
10. Loosen the clamps on the upper (**Figure 108**) and lower (**Figure 109**) radiator hoses. Do not remove the hoses at this time.
11. Remove the upper and lower radiator mounting bolt assemblies. See **Figure 110** and B, **Figure 107**.

CAUTION
Care must be taken when handling the radiator to avoid damaging the cooling fins and tubes.

12. Pull the radiator out at the bottom, slide it down and pull it out of the bike frame. The radiator hoses may stay either with the radiator or the engine.
13. Install by reversing these removal steps, noting the following.
14. Fill the radiator with the recommended type and quantity of coolant; refer to Chapter Three in the main body of this book.
15. Start the engine and check for leaks.

COOLING FAN
(1983 MODELS)

Removal/Installation

1. Remove the radiator as described in this section of the supplement.
2. Bend down the wire clips securing the electrical wires for the fan motor and thermostatic switch. Remove the wires from the clips.
3. Remove the bolts securing the fan shroud. Remove the fan shroud and fan from the radiator.
4. Remove the nut, lockwasher and washer in the center of the fan. Remove the fan from the fan motor.

13

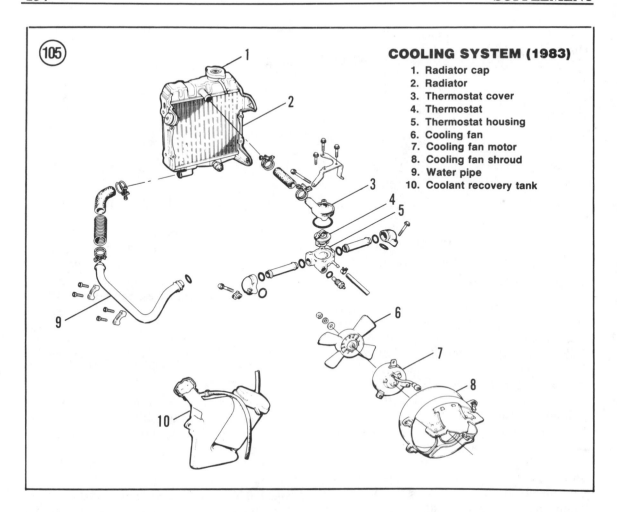

COOLING SYSTEM (1983)

1. Radiator cap
2. Radiator
3. Thermostat cover
4. Thermostat
5. Thermostat housing
6. Cooling fan
7. Cooling fan motor
8. Cooling fan shroud
9. Water pipe
10. Coolant recovery tank

5. Turn the fan shroud over and remove the screws securing the fan motor to the shroud. Remove the fan motor.

6. Install by reversing these removal steps, noting the following.

7. Position the fan motor with the "TOP" mark facing up toward the top of the fan shroud.

8. Apply Loctite Lock N' Seal to the threads on the fan motor shaft prior to installing the fan motor nut, lockwasher and washer. Tighten the nut securely.

WATER PUMP
(1982-ON CX500, ALL OTHER
MODELS 1981-ON)

Water pump removal and installation are the same as for previous models with the

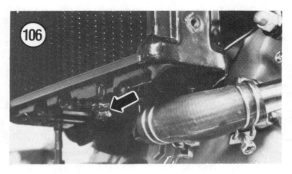

exception of removing the engine rear cover. On these models the pulse generator mechanism and ignition advance mechanism must be removed prior to removing the engine rear cover. Refer to *Ignition Advance and Pulse Generator* in this section of the supplement.

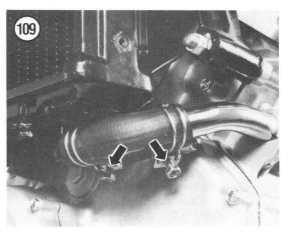

WATER PUMP MECHANICAL SEAL (1983 MODELS)

Replacement

1. Remove the water pump as described in this section of the supplement.

2. Remove the oil seal from the inside surface of the rear cover.

3. Set the engine rear cover on soft wood blocks with the inner surface facing up.

4. Using a suitable size socket, drive out the mechanical seal from the inside. Be careful not to damage the cover.

13

5. Install the mechanical seal using the mechanical seal installer (Honda part No. GN-AH-065-415):

a. Install the mechanical seal onto the special tool as shown in **Figure 111**.

NOTE
Some mechanical seals are pre-coated with a sealant at the factory.

b. If not pre-coated, apply a thin coat of liquid sealer to the outer surface of the mechanical seal.

c. Position the seal and tool in the engine rear cover.

d. Attach the guide plate and nut as shown in **Figure 111**.

e. Slowly tighten the nut and draw the mechanical seal into the engine rear case. Tighten the nut to a final torque of 31-33 ft.-lb. (42-45 N•m).

f. Remove the nut, guide plate and special tool from the engine rear cover.

6. Visually inspect the mechanical seal, make sure it is completely seated.

7. Install the oil seal in from the backside until it is flush with the raised boss surrounding the oil seal as shown in **Figure 112**. Do not install the oil seal any farther in or it will block the drain hole.

8. Install the engine rear cover as described in Chapter Four in the main body of this book.

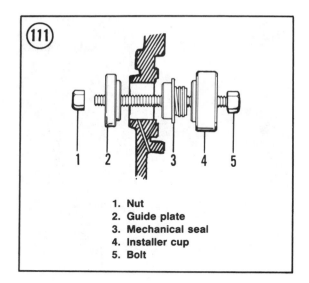

1. Nut
2. Guide plate
3. Mechanical seal
4. Installer cup
5. Bolt

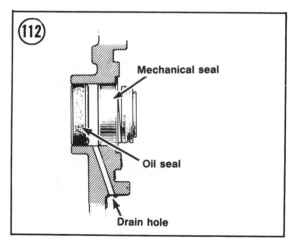

Mechanical seal
Oil seal
Drain hole

CHAPTER NINE

FRONT SUSPENSION AND STEERING

FRONT WHEEL

Removal (Standard Axle Fork Models)

1. Place the bike on the centerstand or place wooden blocks under the engine to lift the front wheel off the ground.

2A. On 1981-1982 dual disc brake models, remove the bolts (**Figure 113**) securing one of the caliper assemblies to the front fork.

Remove either the right- or left-hand caliper assembly; it is necessary to remove only one. Tie the caliper up to the front fork to relieve strain on the brake line.

2B. On 1983 dual disc brake models, remove the bolts (**Figure 113**) securing both caliper assemblies to the front fork. Remove both caliper assemblies. Tie the calipers up to the front fork to relieve strain on the brake line.

3. Remove the axle clamp nuts (A, **Figure 114**), washers and lockwashers. There are 2 on each side. Remove both axle clamps.

4. Pull the wheel down and forward, being careful not to damage the studs on the fork end.

5. Unscrew the speedometer cable set screw (**Figure 115**) and pull the speedometer cable free from the hub.

CAUTION
Do not set the wheel down on the disc surface as it may get scratched or warped. Set the wheel on 2 blocks of wood.

NOTE
Insert a piece of wood or vinyl tubing in the calipers in place of the discs. That way, if the brake lever is inadvertently squeezed, the piston will not be forced out of the cylinder. If this does happen, the caliper might have to be disassembled to reseat the piston and the system will have to be bled. By using the wood, bleeding the brake is not necessary when installing the wheel.

Installation

(Standard Axle Fork Models)

1. Make sure the axle bearing surfaces of the fork slider and the lower clamps are free from dirt or small burrs.

2. Remove the vinyl tubing or wood pieces from the calipers.

3. Position the wheel in place, carefully inserting the disc between the pads.

4. Install the axle clamps with the "F" mark and the arrow facing forward. Install the washers, lockwashers and nuts, finger-tight only at this time.

5. Position the speedometer housing so that the cable inlet is at the 3 o'clock position.

6. Tighten the front axle clamp nut first and then the rear nut to 13-18 ft.-lb. (18-25 N•m).

WARNING
The clamp nuts must be tightened in this manner and to this torque value. After installation is complete, there will be a slight gap (B, Figure 114) at the rear, with no gap at the front. If done incorrectly, the studs could fail,

13

resulting in loss of control of the bike when riding.

7. Install the speedometer cable into the speedometer housing. Tighten the cable set screw.

NOTE
Slowly rotate the wheel while inserting the cable so it will engage properly.

8A. On 1981-1982 models, install the caliper assembly that was removed from the disc. Tighten the bolts to 22-33 ft.-lb. (30-45 N•m).
8B. On 1983 models, install both caliper assemblies and tighten the bolts to 22-33 ft.-lb. (30-45 N•m).
9. Measure the distance between the outside surface of the disc and the left-hand caliper holder with a flat feeler gauge. The clearance must be 0.028 in. (0.7 mm) or more. If clearance is insufficient, loosen the axle holder nuts and pull the left-hand fork leg out until this dimension is achieved. Tighten the nuts by repeating Step 6.
10. After the wheel is completely installed, rotate it several times and apply the brakes a couple of times to make sure it rotates freely and that the brake pads are against the discs.

Removal (Leading Axle Fork Models)

1. Place the bike on the centerstand or place wood block(s) under the engine to support it securely with the front wheel off the ground.
2. Expand the speedometer cable set spring. Pull the speedometer cable free from the hub.
3. Remove the axle pinch bolt and nut.
4. Unscrew and withdraw the front axle.
5. Pull the wheel down and forward and remove it.

CAUTION
Do not set the wheel down on the disc surface as it may get scratched or warped. Set the sidewalls on 2 wood blocks.

NOTE
Insert a piece of vinyl tubing or wood in the caliper in place of the brake disc. That way if the brake lever is inadvertently squeezed, the piston will not be forced out of the cylinder. If this

does happen, the caliper may have to be disassembled to reseat the piston and the system will have to be bled. By using the wood, bleeding the brake is not necessary when installing the wheel.

Installation
(Leading Axle Fork Models)

1. Make sure the axle bearing surfaces of the fork slider and axle are free from burrs and nicks.
2. Remove the vinyl tubing or pieces of wood from the brake caliper.
3. Position the wheel into place, carefully inserting the brake disc between the brake pads.
4. Position the speedometer housing so that it is perpendicular to the left-hand fork leg.
5. Insert the front axle from the right-hand side and screw it into the left-hand fork leg.
6. Tighten the front axle to 40-47 ft.-lb. (55-65 N•m).
7. Install the axle pinch bolt and nut and tighten it to 11-18 ft.-lb. (15-25 N•m).
8. Slowly rotate the wheel and install the speedometer cable into the speedometer housing. Install the cable set spring.
9. After the wheel is completely installed, rotate it several times and apply the brakes a couple of times to make sure that it rotates freely and that the brake pads correctly seat against the disc.

FRONT HUB
(GL AND INTERSTATE MODELS)

Removal of the bearing retainers can be accomplished with a small drift and hammer or with the use of special tools. These are available from a Honda dealer and are as follows:
   a. Retainer wrench body: Honda part No. 07710-0010401.
   b. Retainer wrench "B": Honda part No. 07710-0010200.

Disassembly

Refer to **Figure 116** for 1981-1982 models or **Figure 117** for 1983 models.

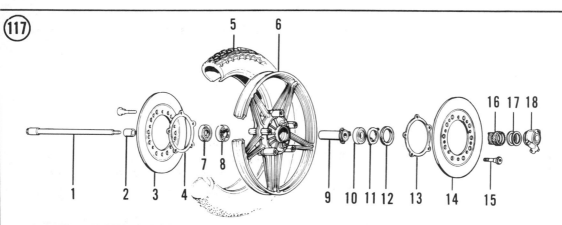

(116)

FRONT WHEEL ASSEMBLY
(1981-1982)

1. Axle nut
2. Spacer
3. Bearing retainer
4. Disc bolt nut
5. Oil seal
6. Brake disc—right-hand side
7. Hub cover—single-disc models
8. Damping shim
9. Bearing
10. Distance collar
11. Tubeless tire

12. Wheel
13. Bearing
14. Damping shim—left-hand side (dual-disc models)
15. Brake disc—left-hand side
16. Speedometer drive dog
17. Oil seal
18. Speedometer housing
19. Disc bolts
20. Front axle
21. Valve stem
22. Balance weight

(117)

FRONT WHEEL (1983)

1. Front axle
2. Spacer
3. Brake disc (right-hand side)
4. Damping shim
5. Tubeless tire
6. Wheel

7. Grease seal
8. Bearing
9. Distance collar
10. Bearing
11. Speedometer drive dog
12. Oil seal

13. Damping shim
14. Brake disc (left-hand side)
15. Disc bolt
16. Speedometer drive gear
17. Washers
18. Speedometer housing

13

1. Remove the front wheel as described under *Front Wheel (Standard Axle Fork Models) Removal* in this section of the supplement.

2. Unscrew the axle nut.

3. Withdraw the axle (A, **Figure 118**) and remove the speedometer housing (B, **Figure 118**).

4. Remove the spacer (**Figure 119**) from the right-hand side.

5. Remove the grease seal and speedometer drive dog (**Figure 120**).

6. Remove the grease seal (A, **Figure 121**) from the right-hand side.

7. Use a small drift and hammer or special tools (Honda part No. 07710-0010200 and 07710-0010401) and unscrew the bearing retainer from the hub (B, **Figure 121**).

8. To remove the right- and left-hand bearings and distance collar, insert a soft aluminum or brass drift into one side of the hub. Push the distance collar over to one side and place the drift on the inner race of the lower bearing. Tap the bearing out of the hub with a hammer, working around the perimeter of the inner race.

9. Remove the other bearing in the same manner.

Inspection

1. Do not clean sealed bearings. If non-sealed bearings are installed, throroughly clean them in solvent and dry with compressed air. Do not let the bearing spin while drying.

2. Clean the inside and the outside of the hub with solvent. Dry with compressed air.

3. Turn each bearing by hand. Make sure the bearings turn smoothly. On non-sealed bearings, check the balls for evidence of wear, pitting or excessive heat (bluish tint). Replace bearings if necessary; always replace as a complete set. When replacing, be sure to take your old bearings along to ensure a perfect matchup.

NOTE
Some axial play is normal, but radial play should be negligible. The bearings should turn smoothly.

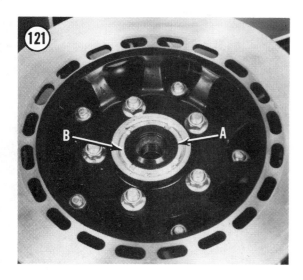

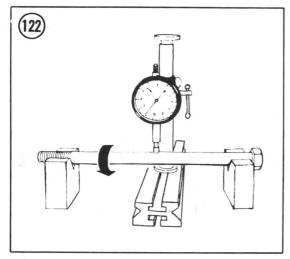

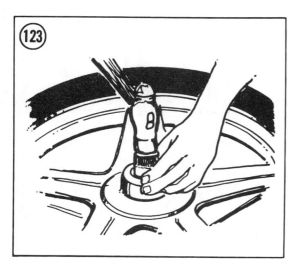

NOTE
Fully sealed bearings are available from many good bearing specialty shops. Fully sealed bearings provide better protection from dirt and moisture that may get into the hub.

4. Check the axle for wear and straightness. Use V-blocks and a dial indicator as shown (**Figure 122**). If the runout is 0.01 in. (0.2 mm) or greater, the axle should be replaced.

Assembly

1. On non-sealed bearings, pack the bearings with a good quality bearing grease. Work the grease in between the balls thoroughly; turn the bearing by hand a couple of times to make sure the grease is distributed evenly inside the bearing.

2. Blow any dirt or foreign matter out of the hub prior to installing the bearings.

CAUTION
*Install the factory bearings with the sealed side facing outward. Tap the bearings squarely into place and tap on the outer race only. Use a socket (**Figure 123**) that matches the outer race diameter. Do not tap on the inner race or the bearing might be damaged. Be sure that the bearings are completely seated.*

3. Install the right-hand bearing and press the distance collar into place.

4. Install the left-hand bearing.

5. Inspect the condition of the threads on the bearing retainer; replace if the threads are damaged. Screw the bearing retainer into the right-hand side securely. Lock it into place by staking it with a center punch and hammer.

6. Install the dust seal.

7. Pack the speedometer drive gear housing with multipurpose grease.

8. Align the tangs of the speedometer drive gear with the drive dog in the hub (**Figure 124**) and install the speedometer housing.

9. Install the spacer (**Figure 119**).

10. Install the axle and axle nut. Tighten the axle nut to 40-47 ft.-lb. (55-65 N•m).

11. Install the front wheel as described under *Front Wheel (Standard Axle Fork Models) Installation* in this section of the supplement.

13

TIRE REPAIRS
(TUBELESS TIRES)

Patching a tubeless tire on the road is very difficult. If both beads are still in place against the rim, a can of pressurized tire sealant (**Figure 125**) may inflate the tire and seal the hole. The beads must be against the wheel for this method to work.

Another solution is to carry a spare inner tube that could be temporarily installed and inflated. This will enable you to get to a service station where the tire can be correctly repaired. Be sure that the tube is designed for use with a tubeless tire.

Honda (and the tire industry) recommends that the tubeless tire be patched from the inside. Therefore do not patch the tire with an external type plug. If you find an external patch on a tire, it is recommended that it be patch-reinforced from the inside.

Due to the variations of material supplied with different tubeless tire repair kits, follow the instructions and recommendations supplied with the repair kit.

Honda recommends that the valve stem be replaced each time the tire is removed from the wheel.

FRONT FORKS
(1981-ON, EXCEPT CX650)

The front suspension uses a spring-controlled, hydraulically-damped, telescopic fork with air assist.

Before suspecting major trouble, drain the front fork oil and refill with the proper type and quantity; refer to *Front Fork Oil Change (Air Assist Models)* in the Chapter Three section of this supplement. If you still have trouble, such as poor damping, a tendency to bottom or top out or leakage around the rubber seals, follow the service procedures in this section.

To simplify fork service and to prevent the mixing of parts, the legs should be removed, serviced and installed individually.

Removal

1. Remove the front wheel as described in this section of the supplement.
2A. On 1981-on CX500 models, remove the brake caliper assembly as described under *Caliper Removal/Installation* in Chapter Eleven in the main body of this book.
2B. On GL500, GL650 and Interstate models, remove the front brake caliper assembly as described under *Caliper Removal/Installation (Dual-piston Caliper Models)* in the Chapter Eleven section of this supplement.
3. Disconnect the speedometer cable and the hydraulic brake line(s) from the clip on the fork leg(s).
4. On Interstate models, remove the front fairing as described in the Chapter Twelve section of this supplement.

5. Remove the air valve cap (A, **Figure 126**) and *bleed off all air pressure* by depressing the valve stem.

> *WARNING*
> *Always bleed off all air pressure; failure to do so may cause personal injury when disassembling the fork assembly.*

> *NOTE*
> *Release the air pressure gradually. If released too fast, fork oil will spurt out with the air. Protect your eyes and clothing accordingly.*

6. Disconnect the air hose from both fork top cap bolts (B, **Figure 126**).
7. Unscrew the connector (C, **Figure 126**) from the fork top cap bolt.
8. Loosen, but do not remove, the fork top cap bolts (D, **Figure 126**).

> *NOTE*
> ***Figure 126*** *shows an Interstate model where the air hose is routed behind the instrument cluster. On other models, the air hose is routed in front of the instruments. Removal and installation of the air hose are the same for both models.*

9. Remove the bolts securing the front fender and remove the fender.
10. On Interstate models, loosen the clamp bolt (**Figure 127**) on the wire harness front electrical connector housing.
11. Loosen the upper and lower fork bridge bolts (**Figure 128**).
12. Remove the fork tube. It may be necessary to slightly rotate the fork tube while pulling it down and out.

Installation

1. Insert the fork tube up through the lower and upper fork bridges.

> *NOTE*
> *On Interstate models, be sure to slip the fork tube through the bracket (**Figure 129**) on the wire harness front electrical connector housing.*

13

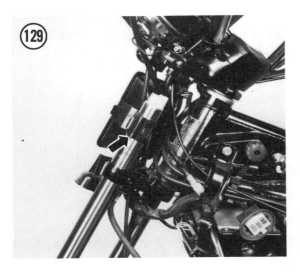

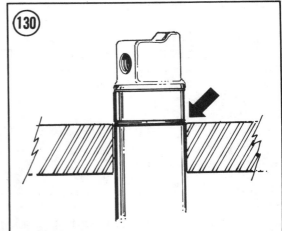

2. Position the fork tube so that the groove on the fork tube aligns with the top surface of the upper fork bridge (**Figure 130**).

3. Tighten the upper and lower fork bridge bolts loosely at this time—just tight enough to hold them in place.

4. Apply a light coat of grease to new O-ring seals (**Figure 131**) and install them onto the air hose fittings and the connector.

5. Install the connector into the top fork cap bolt/air valve assembly and tighten to 3-5 ft.-lb. (4-7 N•m).

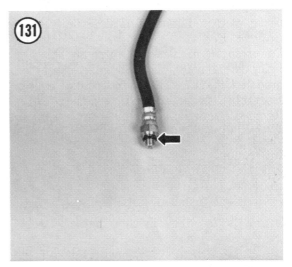

> *NOTE*
> *The connector can be fitted to either the right- or left-hand fork tube.*

6. Loosen the fork bridge bolts and rotate the fork tubes so the air hose will have a natural curve after installation (either behind the instruments on Interstate models or in front of them on all other models).

7. Install the air hose fitting first onto the top fork cap bolt without the connector and tighten to 3-5 ft.-lb. (4-7 N•m).

8. Install the air hose to the connector and tighten the air hose to 11-14 ft.-lb. (15-20 N•m).

> *NOTE*
> *Hold onto the connector (attached to the top fork cap bolt/air valve assembly) with a wrench while tightening the air hose fitting.*

9. If necessary, realign the groove in the fork tube with the top surface of the upper fork bridge (**Figure 130**).

10. Tighten the upper and lower fork bridge bolts to the following torque specifications:

   a. CX500—upper: 7-9 ft.-lb. (9-13 N•m).

   b. CX500—lower: 13-18 ft.-lb. (18-25 N•m).

   c. GL500, GL650—upper: 7-11 ft.-lb. (9-15 N•m).

   d. GL500, GL650—lower: 22-29 ft.-lb. (30-40 N•m).

11. Install the front fender and tighten the bolts securely.

12. Install the front wheel as described in this section of the supplement.

13A. On 1981-on CX500 models, install the brake caliper assembly as described under *Caliper Removal/Installation* in Chapter Eleven in the main body of this book.

13B. On GL500, GL650 and Interstate models, install the front brake caliper assembly as described under *Caliper Removal/Installation (Dual-piston Caliper Models)* in the Chapter Eleven section of this supplement.

14. Attach the speedometer cable and the hydraulic brake line(s) to the clip on the fork leg(s).

15. On Interstate models, install the front fairing as described in the Chapter Twelve section of this supplement.

16. Make sure the front wheel is off the ground and inflate the forks to the standard air pressure. Do not use compressed air; only use a small hand-operated air pump as shown in **Figure 132**. See the Chapter Three section of this supplement.

WARNING
Never use any type of compressed gas as an explosion may be lethal. Never heat the fork assembly with a torch or place it near an open flame or extreme heat as this will also result in an explosion.

CAUTION
Never exceed the maximum specified pressure as damage may occur to internal components of the fork assembly.

17. Take the bike off of the centerstand, apply the front brake and pump the forks several times. Recheck the air pressure and readjust if necessary.

Disassembly

Refer to **Figure 133** during the disassembly and assembly procedures.

1. Clamp the slider in a vise with soft jaws.

2. Remove the Allen head screw and gasket from the bottom of the slider.

NOTE
This screw has been secured with Loctite and is often very difficult to remove because the damper rod will turn inside the slider. It sometimes can be removed with an air impact driver. If you are unable to remove it, take the fork tubes to a dealer and have them remove the screws.

3. Hold the upper fork tube in a vise with soft jaws and loosen the fork top cap bolt/air valve assembly (if it was not loosened during the fork removal sequence).

WARNING
Be careful when removing the fork top cap bolt as the spring is under pressure.

4. Remove the fork top cap bolt from the fork.

5A. On 1981-on CX500 Deluxe models, remove the fork spring.

5B. On all other models, remove the upper short spring A, spring seat and lower long spring B.

6. Remove the fork from the vise, pour the fork oil out and discard it. Pump the fork several times by hand to expel most of the remaining oil.

7. Remove the dust seal (**Figure 134**).

8. Remove the circlip (**Figure 135**) and the backup plate from the slider.

9. Install the fork slider in a vise with soft jaws.

NOTE
On this type of fork, force is needed to remove the fork tube from the slider.

13

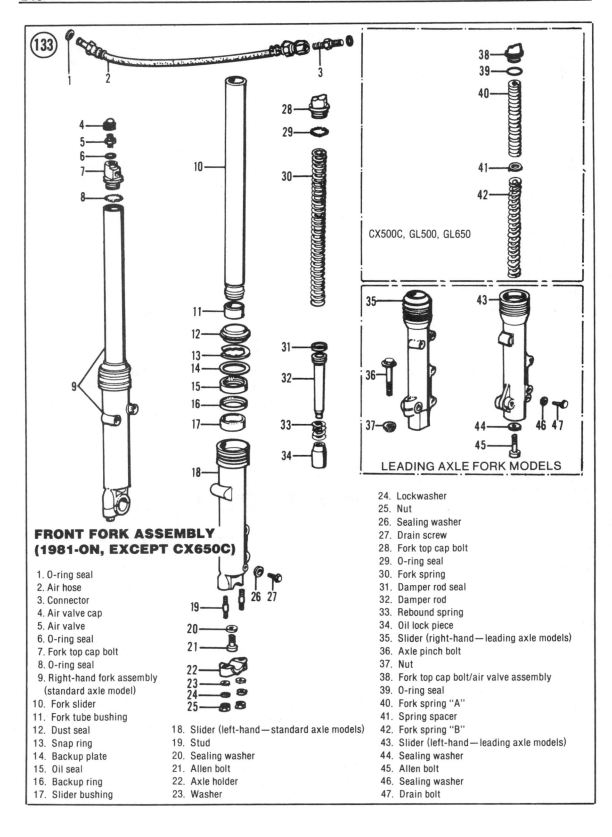

(133)

CX500C, GL500, GL650

LEADING AXLE FORK MODELS

FRONT FORK ASSEMBLY
(1981-ON, EXCEPT CX650C)

1. O-ring seal
2. Air hose
3. Connector
4. Air valve cap
5. Air valve
6. O-ring seal
7. Fork top cap bolt
8. O-ring seal
9. Right-hand fork assembly
   (standard axle model)
10. Fork slider
11. Fork tube bushing
12. Dust seal
13. Snap ring
14. Backup plate
15. Oil seal
16. Backup ring
17. Slider bushing

18. Slider (left-hand—standard axle models)
19. Stud
20. Sealing washer
21. Allen bolt
22. Axle holder
23. Washer

24. Lockwasher
25. Nut
26. Sealing washer
27. Drain screw
28. Fork top cap bolt
29. O-ring seal
30. Fork spring
31. Damper rod seal
32. Damper rod
33. Rebound spring
34. Oil lock piece
35. Slider (right-hand—leading axle models)
36. Axle pinch bolt
37. Nut
38. Fork top cap bolt/air valve assembly
39. O-ring seal
40. Fork spring "A"
41. Spring spacer
42. Fork spring "B"
43. Slider (left-hand—leading axle models)
44. Sealing washer
45. Allen bolt
46. Sealing washer
47. Drain bolt

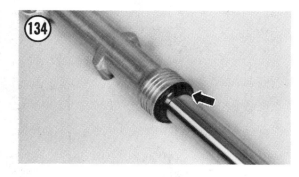

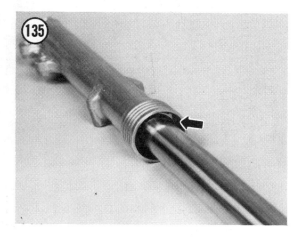

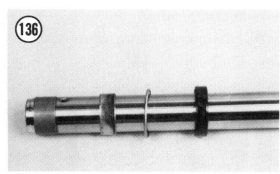

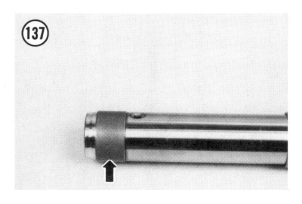

10. There is an interference fit between the bushing in the fork slider and the bushing on the fork tube. In order to remove the fork tube from the slider, pull hard on the fork tube using quick in and out strokes. Doing this will withdraw the bushing, backup ring and oil seal from the slider.

> *NOTE*
> *It may be necessary to slightly heat the area on the slider around the oil seal prior to removal. Use a rag soaked in hot water; do not apply a flame directly to the fork slider.*

11. Withdraw the fork tube from the slider.

> *NOTE*
> *Do not remove the fork tube bushing unless it is going to be replaced. Inspect it as described under **Inspection** in this section of the supplement.*

12. Turn the fork tube upside down and slide off the oil seal, backup ring and slider bushing from the fork tube (**Figure 136**).

> *NOTE*
> *Do not discard the slider bushing at this time. It will be used during the installation procedure.*

13. Remove the oil lock piece, the damper rod and rebound spring.
14. Inspect the components as described under *Inspection* in this section of the supplement.

Assembly

1. Coat all parts with fresh automatic transmission fluid or fork oil prior to installation.
2. If removed, install a new fork tube bushing (**Figure 137**).
3. Install the rebound spring onto the damper rod and insert this assembly into the fork tube (**Figure 138**).
4. Temporarily install the fork spring(s) and fork top cap bolt to hold the damper rod in place.
5. Install the oil lock piece onto the damper rod (**Figure 139**).
6. Install the upper fork assembly into the slider (**Figure 140**).

13

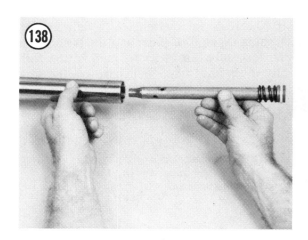

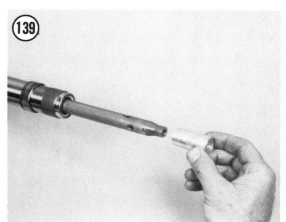

8. Slide the fork slider bushing down the fork tube and rest it on the slider.

9. Slide the fork slider backup ring (flange side up) down the fork tube and rest it on top of the fork slider bushing.

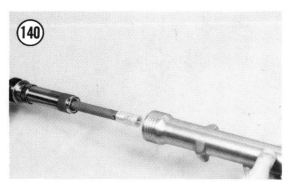

10. Place the old slider bushing on top of the backup ring. Drive the bushing into the fork slider with Honda special tool Fork Seal Driver Body (part No. 07747 - 0010100) and Fork Seal Driver Attachment (part No. 07947 - KA20200); refer to **Figure 141**. Drive the bushing into place until it seats completely in the recess in the slider. Remove the installation tools and the old slider bushing.

NOTE
*The slider bushing can be driven in with a homemade tool (**Figure 142**) as shown in **Figure 143**. This tool can be made at a machine shop from a piece of aluminum. Refer to **Figure 144** for dimensions.*

11. Install the backup ring.

12. To prevent damage to the inside of the new fork seal during installation, wrap the groove in the top of the fork tube with clear tape (something smooth and non-abrasive—do not use duct or masking tape).

13. Coat the new seal with automatic transmission fluid. Position the seal with the marking facing upward and slide it down onto the fork tube. Drive the seal into the slider (**Figure 141**) with Honda special tool Fork Seal Driver Body (part No. 07747-0010100) and Fork Seal Driver Attachment (part No. 07947-KA20200). Drive the oil seal in until

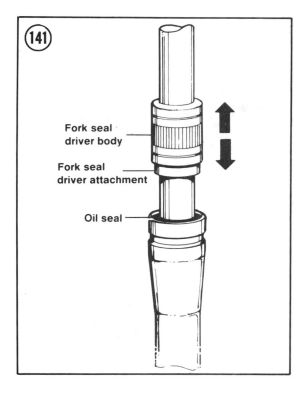

Fork seal driver body

Fork seal driver attachment

Oil seal

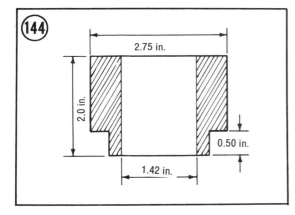

2.75 in.

2.0 in.

0.50 in.

1.42 in.

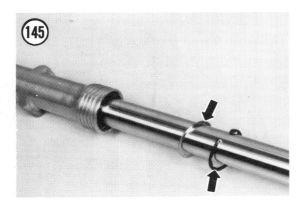

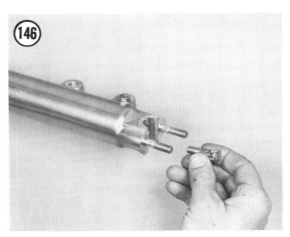

the groove in the slider can be seen above the top surface of the oil seal. Remove the tape from the top of the fork tube.

NOTE
If the seal must be driven further down, remove the special tools and insert the backup plate on top of the seal. Repeat Step 13 until the seal is correctly seated.

NOTE
The slider seal can be driven in with a homemade tool as described in the NOTE following Step 10.

14. Install the backup plate and circlip (**Figure 145**). Make sure the circlip is completely seated in the groove in the fork slider.

15. Install the dust seal (**Figure 134**).

16. Make sure the gasket is on the Allen head screw.

17. Apply Loctite Lock N' Seal to the threads of the Allen head screw prior to installation. Install it in the fork slider (**Figure 146**) and tighten to 11-18 ft.-lb. (15-25 N•m).

18. Remove the fork top cap bolt and fork springs.

19. Fill the fork tube with the following quantity of DEXRON automatic transmission fluid:

  a. CX500 Deluxe (since 1981): 6.3 oz. (185 cc).

  b. CX500 Custom (since 1981): 7.5 oz. (220 cc).

13

c. GL500, GL650 and Interstate: 7.1 oz. (210 cc).

20A. On 1981-on CX500 Deluxe, install the fork spring with the tapered end in first (**Figure 147**).

20B. On all other models, install the lower long fork spring B (**Figure 148**), the spring seat (**Figure 149**) and the upper short fork spring A (**Figure 150**).

21. Inspect the condition of the O-ring seal (**Figure 151**) on the fork top cap bolt/air valve assembly; replace if necessary.

22. Install the fork top cap bolt/air valve assembly (**Figure 152**) while pushing down on the spring(s). Start the bolt slowly; don't cross thread it.

23. Place the slider in a vise with soft jaws and tighten the top fork cap bolt to 11-22 ft.-lb. (15-30 N•m).

24. Repeat for the other fork assembly.

25. Install the fork assembly as described in this section of the supplement.

Inspection

1. Thoroughly clean all parts in solvent and dry them. Check the fork tube for signs of wear or scratches.

2. Check the damper rod for straightness. **Figure 153** shows one method. The rod should be replaced if the runout is 0.008 in. (0.2 mm) or greater.

3. Carefully check the damper rod and piston ring (**Figure 154**) for wear or damage.

4. Check the upper fork tube for straightness. If bent or severely scratched, it should be replaced.

5. Check the lower slider for dents or exterior damage that may cause the upper fork tube to hang up during riding. Replace if necessary.

6. Measure the uncompressed length of the fork spring (not rebound spring) as shown in **Figure 155**. If the spring has sagged to the folowing service limit dimensions or less it must be replaced:

    a. CX500 Deluxe: 21.9 in. (556.6 mm).

    b. CX500 Custom—Spring A: 3.8 in. (96.7 mm).

    c. CX500 Custom—Spring B: 19.5 in. (495.1 mm).

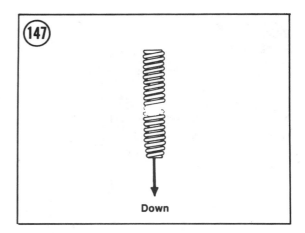

(147)

Down

(148)

(149)

(150)

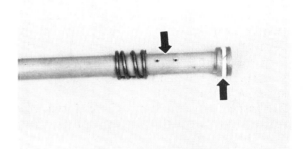

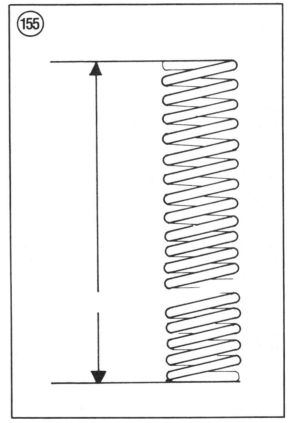

d. GL500, GL650 and Interstate—Spring A: 3.8 in. (97.7 mm).

e. GL500 and GL500 Interstate—Spring B: 19.4 in. (493 mm).

7. Inspect the slider and fork tube bushings. If either is scratched or scored they must be replaced. If the Teflon coating is worn off so that the copper base material is showing on approximately 3/4 of the total surface, the bushing must be replaced. Also check for distortion on the check points of the backup ring; replace as necessary. Refer to **Figure 156**.

8. Any parts that are worn or damaged should be replaced. Simply cleaning and reinstalling unserviceable components will not improve performance of the front suspension.

13

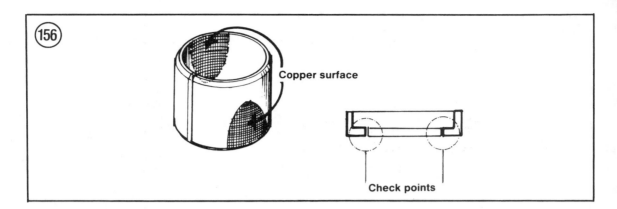

Copper surface

Check points

FRONT FORKS
(CX650C)

To simplify fork service and to prevent the mixing of parts, the legs should be removed, serviced and installed individually.

Removal

1. Remove the front wheel as described in this section of the supplement.
2. Remove the brake caliper as described in the Chapter Eleven section of this supplement.
3. Remove the bolts securing the front fender and remove the front fender.
4. Remove the air valve cap and *bleed off all air pressure* by depressing the valve stem.

WARNING
Always bleed off all air pressure; failure to do so may cause personal injury when disassembling the fork assembly.

NOTE
Release the air pressure gradually. If released too fast, fork oil will spurt out with the air. Protect your eyes and clothing accordingly.

5. Remove the chrome cover caps. Remove the bolts securing the fork brace and remove the fork brace.
6. Loosen, but do not remove, the fork top cap bolts.
7. Loosen the upper and lower fork bridge bolts.
8. Remove the fork tube. It may be necessary to slightly rotate the fork tube while pulling it down and out.

Installation

1. Insert the fork tube up through the lower and upper fork bridges.
2. Align the top of the fork tube with the top surface of the upper fork bridge.
3. Tighten the upper and lower fork bridge bolts to the following torque specifications:
    a. Upper fork bridge: 7-9 ft.-lb. (9-13 N•m).
    b. Lower fork bridge: 33-40 ft.-lb. (45-55 N•m).
4. Install the fork brace and tighten the bolts to 13-20 ft.-lb. (18-28 N•m). Install the trim caps onto the bolts.
5. Install the front fender and tighten the bolts securely.
6. Install the brake caliper as described in the Chapter Eleven section of this supplement.
7. Install the front wheel as described in this section of the supplement.
8. Make sure the front wheel is off the ground and inflate the forks to 0-6 psi (0-0.4 kg/cm²). Do not use compressed air, only use a small hand-operated air pump.

WARNING
Never use any type of compressed gas as an explosion may be lethal. Never heat the fork assembly with a torch or place it near an open flame or extreme heat, as this will also result in an explosion.

CAUTION
Never exceed an air pressure of 43 psi (3.0 kg/cm²) as damage may occur to internal components of the fork assembly.

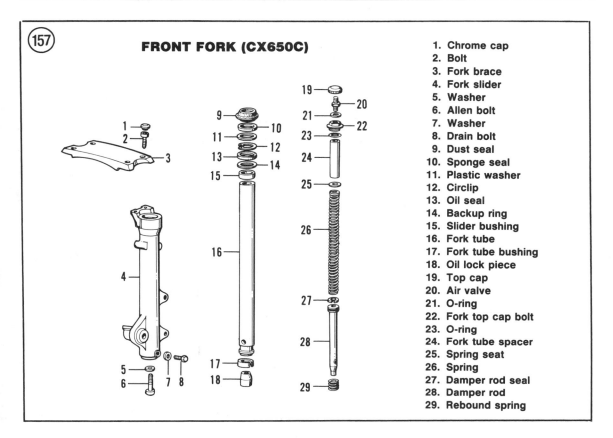

FRONT FORK (CX650C)

1. Chrome cap
2. Bolt
3. Fork brace
4. Fork slider
5. Washer
6. Allen bolt
7. Washer
8. Drain bolt
9. Dust seal
10. Sponge seal
11. Plastic washer
12. Circlip
13. Oil seal
14. Backup ring
15. Slider bushing
16. Fork tube
17. Fork tube bushing
18. Oil lock piece
19. Top cap
20. Air valve
21. O-ring
22. Fork top cap bolt
23. O-ring
24. Fork tube spacer
25. Spring seat
26. Spring
27. Damper rod seal
28. Damper rod
29. Rebound spring

9. Take the bike off of the centerstand, apply the front brake and pump the forks several times. Recheck the air pressure and readjust if necessary.

Disassembly

Refer to **Figure 157** during the disassembly and assembly procedures.
1. Clamp the slider in a vise with soft jaws.
2. Remove the Allen head screw and gasket from the bottom of the slider.

NOTE
This screw has been secured with Loctite and is often very difficult to remove because the damper rod will turn inside the slider. It sometimes can be removed with an air impact driver. If you are unable to remove it, take the fork tubes to a dealer and have the screws removed.

3. Hold the upper fork tube in a vise with soft jaws and loosen the fork top cap bolt/air

valve assembly (if it was not loosened during the fork removal sequence).

WARNING
Be careful when removing the fork top cap bolt as the spring is under pressure. Protect your eyes accordingly.

4. Remove the fork top cap bolt from the fork.
5. Remove the fork tube spacer, the spring seat and the fork spring.
6. Remove the fork from the vise, pour the fork oil out and discard it. Pump the fork several times by hand to expel most of the remaining oil.
7. Remove the dust seal (**Figure 134**).
8. Remove the sponge washer, the plastic washer and the circlip (**Figure 135**).
9. Install the fork slider in a vise with soft jaws.

NOTE
On this type of fork, force is needed to remove the fork tube from the slider.

13

10. There is an interference fit between the bushing in the fork slider and the bushing on the fork tube. In order to remove the fork tube from the slider, pull hard on the fork tube using quick in and out strokes. Doing this will withdraw the bushing, backup ring and oil seal from the slider.

NOTE
It may be necessary to slightly heat the area on the slider around the oil seal prior to removal. Use a rag soaked in hot water; do not apply a flame directly to the fork slider.

11. Withdraw the fork tube from the slider.

NOTE
*Do not remove the fork tube bushing unless it is going to be replaced. Inspect it as described under **Inspection** in this section of the supplement.*

12. Turn the fork tube upside down and slide off the oil seal, backup ring and slider bushing from the fork tube (**Figure 136**).

NOTE
Do not discard the slider bushing at this time. It will be used during the installation procedure.

13. Remove the oil lock piece, the damper rod and rebound spring.
14. Inspect the components as described under *Inspection* in this section of the supplement.

Assembly

1. Coat all parts with fresh automatic transmission fluid (ATF) or fork oil prior to installation.
2. If removed, install a new fork tube bushing (**Figure 137**).
3. Install the rebound spring onto the damper rod and insert this assembly into the fork tube (**Figure 138**).
4. Temporarily install the fork spring, spring seat, the spacer and fork top cap bolt. This will help hold the damper rod in place.
5. Install the oil lock piece onto the damper rod (**Figure 139**).
6. Install the upper fork assembly into the slider (**Figure 140**).

7. Slide the fork slider bushing down the fork tube and rest it on the slider.
8. Slide the fork slider backup ring (flange side up) down the fork tube and rest it on top of the fork slider bushing.
9. Place the old fork slider bushing on top of the backup ring. Drive the bushing into the fork slider with Honda special tool Fork Seal Driver (part No. 07947-4630100). Drive the bushing into place until it seats completely in the recess in the slider. Remove the installation tool and the old fork slider bushing.

NOTE
*The slider bushing can be driven in with a homemade tool (**Figure 142**) as shown in **Figure 143**. This tool can be made at a machine shop from a piece of aluminum.*

10. To prevent damage to the inside of the new fork seal during installation, wrap the groove in the top of the fork tube with clear tape (something smooth and non-abrasive; do not use duct or masking tape).
11. Coat the new seal with ATF. Position the seal with the marking facing upward and slide it down onto the fork tube. Drive the seal into the slider with Honda special tool Fork Seal Driver (part No. 07947-4630100); refer to **Figure 141**. Drive the oil seal in until the groove in the slider can be seen above the top surface of the oil seal. Remove the tape from the top of the fork tube.

NOTE
The slider seal can be driven in with a homemade tool described in the NOTE following Step 9.

12. Install the circlip with the sharp side facing up. Make sure the circlip is completely seated in the groove in the fork slider.

NOTE
***Figure 158** shows the correct placement of all components on 1982 models, installed during Steps 8-12.*

13. Install the plastic seal washer and the sponge washer. Install the dust seal.
14. Make sure the gasket is on the Allen head screw.

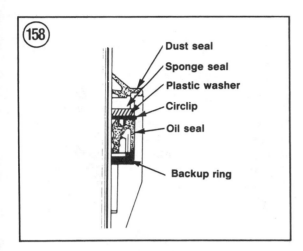

Dust seal
Sponge seal
Plastic washer
Circlip
Oil seal
Backup ring

15. Apply Loctite Lock N' Seal to the threads of the Allen head screw prior to installation. Install it in the fork slider (**Figure 146**) and tighten to 11-18 ft.-lb. (15-25 N•m).

16. Remove the fork top cap bolt, the fork tube spacer, the spring seat and the fork spring.

17. Fill the fork tube with the correct quantity of **DEXRON** automatic transmission fluid. The correct amount for each fork leg is 16.2 oz. (480 cc).

18. Install the fork spring (**Figure 148**) with the closer wound coils and tapered end in first (**Figure 147**).

19. Install the fork seat (**Figure 149**) and the fork tube spacer.

20. Inspect the O-ring seal (**Figure 151**) on the fork top cap bolt/air valve assembly; replace if necessary.

21. Install the fork top cap bolt/air valve assembly while pushing down on the spring. Start the bolt slowly, don't cross thread it.

22. Place the slider in a vise with soft jaws and tighten the top fork cap bolt to 11-22 ft.-lb. (15-30 N•m).

23. Repeat for the other fork assembly.

24. Install the fork assemblies as described in this section of the supplement.

Inspection

Inspect all fork components as described in this section of the supplement under *Front Forks (1981-on, Except CX650C)*.

The service limit on the fork spring is 19.03 in. (483.4 mm). If the spring has sagged to this limit or less, it must be replaced.

CHAPTER TEN

REAR SUSPENSION AND FINAL DRIVE

REAR WHEEL
(PRO-LINK MODELS)

Removal/Installation

NOTE
The mufflers can either be left in place or removed.

1. Place a milk crate or wood block(s) under the engine to support the bike securely so that the rear wheel is off the ground.

2. On Interstate models, remove both saddle bags.

3. Remove both side covers and the seat.

13

4. Loosen the rear axle nut (**Figure 159**).

5. Remove the axle pinch bolt (A, **Figure 160**).

6. Remove the cotter pin (B, **Figure 160**) and unscrew the nut and bolt securing the brake torque link to the brake backing plate. Disconnect the brake torque link from the backing plate. Let the torque link pivot down out of the way.

7. Completely unscrew the brake adjusting nut from the brake rod. Separate the brake rod from the brake lever arm.

8. Remove the 6 mm bolts securing the rear section of the fender.

9. Remove the axle nut and withdraw the axle from the left-hand side. Catch the axle spacer (C, **Figure 160**) as the axle is withdrawn.

10. Slide the wheel to the left to disengage it from the splines on the final drive unit. Pull the wheel toward the rear, hold the rear portion of the rear fender up and remove the wheel.

11. Install by reversing these removal steps, noting the following.

12. Apply molybdenum disulfide grease to the splines of the wheel flange and the final drive unit.

13. Make sure the wheel is completely engaged with the splines of the final drive unit before installing and tightening the rear axle and nut.

14. Tighten the brake torque link bolt and nut to 11-18 ft.-lb. (15-25 N•m). Install a new cotter pin and bend the ends over completely.

15. Install and tighten the axle nut to 36-58 ft.-lb. (50-80 N•m).

16. Install the axle pinch bolt and tighten to 14-22 ft.-lb. (20-30 N•m).

17. After the wheel is completely installed, rotate it several times to make sure it rotates smoothly. Apply the brake several times to make sure it operates correctly.

18. Adjust the rear brake as described under *Rear Brake Adjustment* in Chapter Three in the main body of this book.

19. Install the saddle bags on Interstate models.

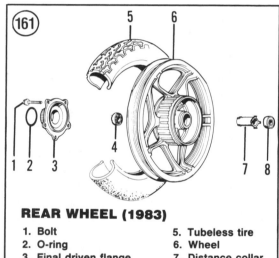

REAR WHEEL (1983)

1. Bolt	5. Tubeless tire
2. O-ring	6. Wheel
3. Final driven flange	7. Distance collar
4. Bearing	8. Bearing

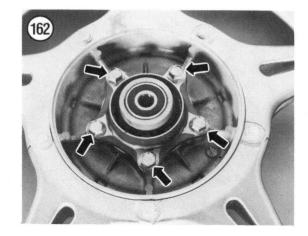

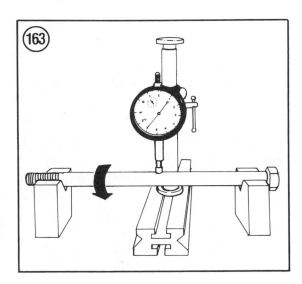

REAR HUB
(1983 MODELS)

Disassembly

Refer to **Figure 161** during this procedure.
1. Remove the rear wheel as described in Chapter Ten in the main body of this book.
2. Pull the brake drum straight up and out of the brake drum.
3. Remove the bolts (**Figure 162**) and pull out the final drive flange and O-ring.
4. To remove the hub right- and left-hand bearing and distance collar, insert a soft aluminum or brass drift into the right-hand side of the hub. Push the distance collar over to one side and place the drift on the inner race of the left-hand bearing. Tap the bearing out of the hub with a hammer, working around the perimeter of the inner race.
5. Remove the distance collar and tap out the opposite bearing in the same manner.

Inspection

1. Do not clean sealed bearings. If non-sealed bearings are installed, throughly clean them in solvent and dry with compressed air. Do not let the bearing spin while drying.
2. Clean the inside and outside of the hub with solvent. Dry with compressed air.
3. Turn each bearing by hand. Make sure bearings turn smoothly.
4. On non-sealed bearings, check the balls for evidence of wear, pitting or excessive heat

(bluish tint). Replace the bearings if necessary; always replace as a complete set. When replacing the bearings, be sure to take your old bearings along to ensure a perfect matchup.

NOTE
Fully sealed bearings are available from many bearing specialty shops. Fully sealed bearings provide better protection from dirt and moisture that may get into the hub.

5. Inspect the condition of the splines. If any are damaged the final driven flange must be replaced.
6. Check the axle for wear and straightness. Use V-blocks and a dial indicator as shown in **Figure 163**. If the runout is 0.2 mm (0.01 in.) or greater, the axle should be replaced.

Assembly

1. On non-sealed bearings, pack the bearings thoroughly with a good quality bearing grease. Work the grease in between the balls thoroughly; turn the bearing by hand a couple of times to make sure the grease is distributed evenly inside the bearing.
2. Blow any dirt or foreign matter out of the hub prior to installing the bearings.
3. Pack the hub with multipurpose grease.
4. Press the distance collar into the hub from the left-hand side.

CAUTION
Install the standard bearings (they are sealed on one side only) with the sealed side facing out.

5. Tap the bearings squarely into place and tap only on the outer race. Use a socket that matches the outer race diameter. Do not tap on the inner race or the bearing will be damaged. Be sure to tap the bearings in until they seat completely.
6. Install the right-hand bearing into the hub.
7. Install the left-hand bearing into the hub.
8. Apply a light coat of grease (lithium based NLGI No. 2 grease with molybdenum disulfide) to the final driven flange pins.

9. Install the flange into the hub assembly and tighten the bolts to 36-43 ft.-lb. (50-60 N•m).

10. Install the rear wheel as described in Chapter Ten in the main body of this book.

SHOCK ABSORBERS
(CX650C)

Removal/Installation

Removal and installation of the rear shocks is easier if done separately. The remaining unit will support the rear of the bike and maintain the correct relationship between the top and bottom shock mounts.

1. Place the bike on the centerstand and remove the seat.

2. Remove both side covers, the rear grip and the rear fender cover.

3. Adjust both shocks to their softest setting, completely *counterclockwise*.

3. On the left-hand side, remove the lower bolt and the upper special nut, hex nut and washer.

4. On the right-hand side, remove the lower cap nut and washer and the upper special nut, hex nut and washer.

5. Pull the unit straight off the upper bolt and remove it.

6. Install by reversing these removal steps. Tighten the upper hex nuts and lower mounting bolt to 22-29 ft.-lb. (30-40 N•m).

7. Repeat for the other side.

PRO-LINK
SUSPENSION SYSTEM

The single shock absorber and linkage of the Pro-Link rear suspension system are attached to the swing arm just behind the swing arm pivot point and also to the lower rear portion of the frame. All of these items are located forward of the rear wheel. The shock link and shock arm working together with the matched spring rate and damping rates of the shock absorber combine to achieve a "progressive rising rate" rear suspension. This system provides the rider with the best of two worlds—greater rider comfort and better transfer of power to the ground.

As the rear suspension is moved upward by bumps, the shock absorber is compressed by the movement of the shock arm. The shock arm and shock link are attached to the swing arm and to the lower portion of the frame.

As rear suspension travel increases, the portion of the shock arm where the shock absorber is attached rises above the swing arm, thus increasing shock absorber travel (compression). This provides a progressive rise rate in which the shock eventually moves at a faster rate than the wheel. At about halfway through the wheel travel the shock begins to move at a faster rate than it did in the beginning.

SHOCK ABSORBER
(PRO-LINK MODELS)

The single shock absorber used in the Pro-Link suspension system is an air/oil type. The only adjustment for the shock is to vary the air pressure. Less air pressure results in a softer ride for light loads and smooth roadways. Increased air pressure will result in a harder ride and is recommended when carrying heavy loads or when riding on rough terrain.

Removal

NOTE
This procedure is shown with the rear wheel and the air cleaner air box removed. It is not necessary to remove either of these components but additional usable work room is provided if they are removed.

1. Place a milk crate or wood block(s) under the engine to support the bike securely with the rear wheel off of the ground.

2. Remove both side covers and the seat.

3. On Interstate models, remove the saddle bags.

4. Remove the rear wheel as described under *Rear Wheel (Pro-Link Models) Removal/Installation* in this section of the supplement.

5. On the right-hand side, remove the rear footpeg and loosen the clamping band on the right-hand muffler. Slide the muffler out of the collector and remove the muffler.

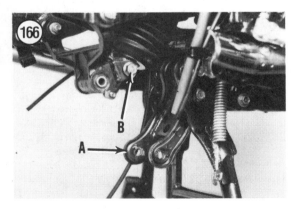

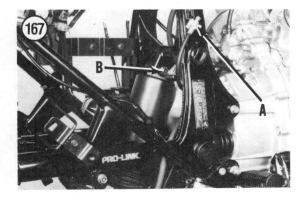

6. Remove the bolts (**Figure 164**) securing the air cleaner air box to the frame. Loosen the clamping bands on the portion going to the carburetors and remove the air box from the frame.

7. Remove the pivot bolt (**Figure 165**) holding the shock arm and shock link together.

8. Swing the shock link down and forward (B, **Figure 166**).

9. Remove the lower mounting bolt (B, **Figure 167**) and nut securing the shock absorber to the shock arm.

10. Unhook the air hose from the clip on the frame (B, **Figure 167**).

11. Hold onto the shock absorber unit and remove the shock absorber upper mounting bolt (B, **Figure 122**). There is no nut as the bolt is screwed into the other side of the shock absorber upper mounting bracket.

12. Remove the shock absorber out through the lower portion of the swing arm (**Figure 168**).

NOTE
Be careful not to damage the air hose during removal.

Inspection

Service by the home mechanic is limited to removal, replacement and installation of the shock unit and its hose. Service is limited to oil seal and guide bushing replacement and should be entrusted to a dealer.

1. Inspect the lower portion of the shock absorber in the area of the rubber boot

(**Figure 169**). If oil is leaking, the oil seal is faulty and should be replaced.

2. If the rubber boot is torn or deteriorated, remove the band securing the rubber boot and replace the rubber boot.

3. Push out the upper mounting bushing (**Figure 170**) and clean with solvent. Thoroughly dry the area and apply molybdenum disulfide grease (**Figure 171**) to the bushing and the receptacle in the shock absorber. Reinstall the bushing into the shock absorber.

4. If an air leak is suspected, remove the air hose from the top of the shock absorber (**Figure 172**). Remove the air valve at the other end of the air hose. Replace the O-ring seal at the fittings at each end of the hose. Rubber O-rings tend to lose their sealing ability with age and when subjected to heat.

NOTE
Always replace the O-rings whenever the air hose or air valve is removed.

5. Apply a light coat of grease to all new O-rings prior to installation.

6. Install the air hose to the shock absorber and the air valve to the air hose and tighten to 3-5 ft.-lb. (4-7 N•m).

Installation

1. Apply a light coat of molybdenum disulfide grease to the upper mounting bracket on the frame.

2. Position the shock absorber assembly in the frame with the hose to the remote reservoir toward the front. This will direct the air hose toward the right-hand side (**Figure 168**).

3. Push the shock absorber up into position and install the upper mounting bolt (**Figure 173**). Tighten the bolt to 33-40 ft.-lb. (45-55 N•m). Fasten the air hose onto the clip on the frame.

4. Apply a coat of molybdenum disulfide grease to the pivot points of the shock arm and shock link (**Figure 174**).

5. Install the shock absorber lower mounting bolt (B, **Figure 166**) from the right-hand side. Install the nut but do not tighten at this time.

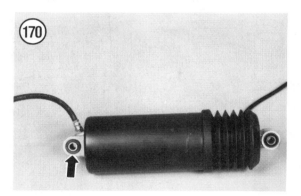

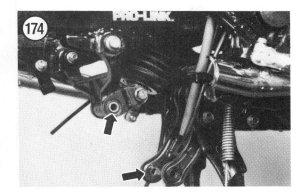

6. Swing up the shock link and align it with the shock arm. Install the pivot bolt from the right-hand side and install the nut. Tighten the bolt and nut to 33-40 ft.-lb. (45-55 N•m).

7. Tighten the shock absorber lower mounting bolt and nut to 33-40 ft.-lb. (45-55 N•m).

WARNING
All bolts and nuts used on the Pro-Link suspension must be replaced with parts of the same type. Do not use a replacement part of lesser quality or substitute design, as this may affect the performance of the system or result in failure of the part which will lead to loss of control of the bike. Torque values listed must be used during installation to assure proper retention of these parts.

8. Remove the milk crate or wood block(s) from under the engine. Push down on the rear of the bike and make sure the rear suspension is operating properly.

9. Rest the bike on the sidestand.

10. Install the air cleaner air box into the frame. Make sure the clamping bands on the portion going to the carburetors are tight.

11. Install the muffler on the right-hand side.

12. Install the rear wheel as described under *Rear Wheel (Pro-Link Models) Removal/ Installation* in this section of the supplement.

13. Install the seat and both side covers.

14. Install the saddle bags on Interstate models.

PIVOT ARM ASSEMBLY (PRO-LINK MODELS)

Removal/Inspection/Installation

Refer to **Figure 175** for this procedure.

1. Remove the shock absorber as described under *Shock Absorber Removal (Pro-Link Models)* in this section of the supplement.

2. From the lower portion of the frame, remove the bolt and nut securing the shock link to the frame (**Figure 176**). Remove the shock link.

3. Remove the bolts (**Figure 177**) and nuts securing the shock arm to the swing arm. Remove the shock arm.

13

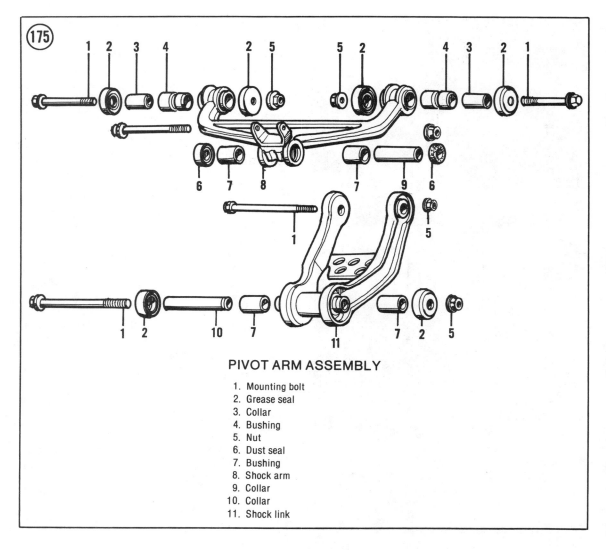

PIVOT ARM ASSEMBLY

1. Mounting bolt
2. Grease seal
3. Collar
4. Bushing
5. Nut
6. Dust seal
7. Bushing
8. Shock arm
9. Collar
10. Collar
11. Shock link

4. Inspect both arms for cracks or damage; replace as necessary.

5. Remove the dust seals at all pivot points and push out the collars.

6. Clean all parts in solvent and thoroughly dry with compressed air.

7. Inspect the collars for scratches, abrasion or abnormal wear; replace as necessary.

8. Inspect the condition of the bushings and the area in both arms where the collars ride. The low-maintenance sintered metal bushings should last for a long time but should be inspected periodically for wear. There are no factory specifications for dimensions for the bushings or the bushing receptacles in the arms.

NOTE
The bushings are pressed into both arms. Do not remove them for inspection as they will be damaged. If removed, they must be replaced.

9. Inspect the condition of the dust seals. Replace all of them as a set if any are worn or starting to deteriorate. If the dust seals are in poor condition they will allow dirt to enter into the pivot areas and cause the bushings to wear.

10. Coat all surfaces of the pivot receptacles, the bushings and the inside of the dust seals with molybdenum disulfide grease. Insert the bushings into the shock link and shock arm and install the dust seals.

NOTE
Make sure the dust seal sealing lips seat correctly. If not seated correctly they will allow dirt and moisture into the bushing areas and cause wear.

11. Install the shock arm onto the swing arm and install the bolts from the outside (**Figure 177**). Install the nuts and tighten to 33-40 ft.-lb. (45-55 N•m).

12. Install the shock link onto the frame and install the pivot bolt (**Figure 176**) from the right-hand side. Install the nut and tighten to 33-40 ft.-lb. (45-55 N•m).

13. Install the shock absorber as described under *Shock Absorber Installation (Pro-Link Models)* in this section of the supplement.

DRIVE SHAFT/ SWING ARM (PRO-LINK MODELS)

In time, the roller bearings will wear and will have to be replaced. The condition of the roller bearings can greatly affect handling performance and if worn parts are not replaced they can produce erratic and dangerous handling. Common symptoms are wheel hop, pulling to one side during acceleration and pulling to the other side during braking.

A special tool is required for loosening and tightening the pivot adjusting bolt and locknut. The tool is the Swing Arm Pivot Locknut Wrench (Honda part No. 07908-4690001). This tool is required for proper and safe installation of the swing arm. If this locknut is not tightened to the correct torque specification it may allow the adjusting bolt to work loose. This could result in the swing arm working loose from the left-hand side of the frame, causing a serious accident.

Removal

1. Place a milk crate or wood block(s) under the engine to support the bike securely with the rear wheel off of the ground.

2. Remove the mufflers as described under *Exhaust System Removal/Installation* in Chapter Six in the main body of this book.

3. Remove the final drive unit as described under *Final Drive Removal/Installation* in Chapter Ten in the main body of this book.

4. Slide back the rubber protective boot and remove the locating bolt (**Figure 178**) on the drive shaft.

5. Disengage the drive shaft from the output shaft on the engine.

6. Remove the shock absorber unit as described under *Shock Absorber Removal (Pro-Link Models)* in this section of the supplement.

7. Grasp the rear end of the swing arm and try to move it from side to side in a horizontal arc. There should be no noticeable side play. If play is evident and the pivot bolt is tightened correctly, the roller bearings are worn and should be replaced.

8. Remove the left-hand pivot cap.

9. Use special tool, Swing Arm Pivot Locknut Wrench (Honda part No. 07908-4690001), and loosen the locknut on the left-hand side (**Figure 179**).

10. Use a 17 mm Allen wrench and remove the left-hand pivot adjusting bolt.

13

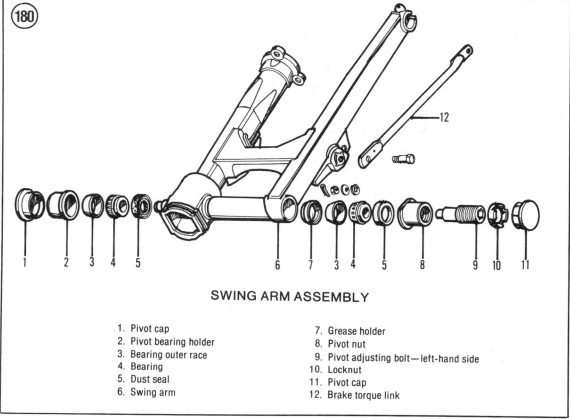

SWING ARM ASSEMBLY

1. Pivot cap
2. Pivot bearing holder
3. Bearing outer race
4. Bearing
5. Dust seal
6. Swing arm
7. Grease holder
8. Pivot nut
9. Pivot adjusting bolt—left-hand side
10. Locknut
11. Pivot cap
12. Brake torque link

11. Remove the rear brake pedal.

12. Pull back on the swing arm, free it from the frame and remove it from the frame.

NOTE
Don't lose the dust seal caps on each side of the pivot points; they will usually fall off when the swing arm is removed.

Disassembly/Inspection/Assembly

Refer to **Figure 180** for this procedure.

1. Remove the cotter pin, nut, washer, lockwasher and bolt and remove the brake torque link from the swing arm.

2. Withdraw the drive shaft out through the front portion of the swing arm.

3. The roller bearings wear very slowly and the wear is difficult to measure. Turn the bearings by hand; make sure they rotate smoothly.

4. If the bearings need replacing, refer to *Rear Swing Arm Bearing Replacement* in this section of the supplement.

5. Apply a coat of molybdenum disulfide grease (NLGI No. 2) to the outer splines of the drive shaft and the inner splines of the drive shaft joint.

6. Install the drive shaft into the swing arm.

7. Install the brake torque link and tighten the bolt and nut securely. Install a new cotter pin and bend the ends over completely.

Installation

1. Position the swing arm into the pivot bearing holder/outer race in the right-hand side of the frame.

2. On the left-hand side, apply a light coat of grease to the inner end of the left-hand pivot adjusting bolt. Install the left-hand pivot adjusting bolt.

3. Make sure the rear swing arm is properly located in the frame and then tighten the left-hand pivot adjusting bolt (A, **Figure 181**) to 7-9 ft.-lb. (9-12 N•m).

4. Move the swing arm up and down several times to make sure all components are properly seated.

5. Retighten the pivot adjusting bolt to 7-9 ft.-lb. (9-12 N•m).

6. Use special tool, Locknut Wrench Adaptor (used during removal) and tighten the locknut (B, **Figure 181**) to 59-78 ft.-lb. (82-108 N•m). Make sure the pivot adjusting bolt does not move while tightening the locknut.

7. Install the shock absorber as described under *Shock Absorber Installation (Pro-Link Models)* in this section of the supplement.

8. Carefully align the drive shaft universal joint splines with the engine output shaft splines.

NOTE
Within the area of the rubber boot, align the universal joint and have a helper push the drive shaft forward from the rear.

9. Install the locating bolt on the drive shaft and tighten to 13-20 ft.-lb. (18-28 N•m). Reposition the rubber protective boot.

10. Install the final drive unit as described under *Final Drive Unit Installation* in Chapter Ten in the main body of this book.

11. Install the mufflers as described under *Exhaust System Removal/Installation* in Chapter Six in the main body of this book.

12. Install the rear brake pedal.

Rear Swing Arm
Bearing Replacement

The swing arm is equipped with a roller bearing at each side. The bearing on the right-hand side is mounted on the outside

surface of the swing arm while the bearing on the left-hand side is mounted within the swing arm end.

The right-hand roller bearing will come right off (no force needed) after the swing arm is removed. The right-hand bearing's outer race is pressed in place in the pivot bearing holder. The pivot bearing holder is mounted in the frame and has to be removed with force. The race will get distorted when removed, so don't remove it unless it is to be replaced.

The left-hand bearing outer race can be removed either with a long drift and hammer or with the use of special tools that are available from a Honda dealer. The special tools are as follows:

a. Bearing race remover (Honda part No. 07936-8890300).

b. Bearing remover handle (Honda part No. 07936-3710100).

c. Bearing remover weight (Honda part No. 07936-3710200).

NOTE
Always replace both bearings as a set even though only one may require replacement.

1. Remove the rear swing arm as described under *Rear Swing Arm (Pro-Link Models) Removal* in this section of the supplement.

2. Secure the swing arm in a vise with soft jaws.

3. Remove the right-hand bearing and dust seal.

4. Carefully remove the dust seal on the left-hand side and remove the left-hand bearing.

5. Carefully tap the bearing outer race out with a soft aluminum or brass drift from the opposite end or use the Honda special tools and pull it out. These special tools, previously described, grab the outer race and then withdraw it from the swing arm with the use of a tool similar to a body shop slide hammer.

6. If the right-hand bearing outer race requires replacement, remove the left-hand pivot cap. Use a piece of pipe or a socket of the appropriate size and from the outside of

13

the frame gently tap the pivot bearing holder and bearing outer race out of the frame.

7. To remove the bearing outer race from the pivot bearing holder, place this assembly in a freezer until it is thoroughly chilled (approximately 1 hour). Heat a pan of water until it is almost boiling. Remove the bearing holder assembly from the freezer. Hold the assembly with a pair of pliers with the *open end up*. Place the assembly, closed end down, into the hot water for approximately 15-30 seconds. Don't submerge it as you don't want the bearing outer race to get hot. Remove from the water and tap the assembly upside down on a piece of soft wood. The bearing outer race should fall out. If not, repeat this step until it does.

8. Thoroughly clean out the inside of the swing arm with solvent and dry with compressed air.

9. Apply a light coat of waterproof grease to all parts prior to installation.

10. If removed, install a new bearing outer race into the pivot bearing holder. Drive the

bearing outer race into the holder until it is completely seated; use a suitable size socket.

11. If removed install the pivot bearing holder assembly onto the frame from the inside of the frame. Tap the assembly into place squarely until the flange is seated against the frame body.

12. On the left-hand side, tap the new roller bearing outer race into place slowly and squarely with a socket that matches the outer diameter of the bearing race. Make sure it is properly seated. Install the bearing and the dust seal.

CAUTION
Never reinstall a bearing outer race that has been removed. During removal it becomes slightly damaged and is no longer true to alignment. If installed, it will damage the roller bearing assembly and create an unsafe riding condition.

13. Install the rear swing arm as described under *Rear Swing Arm (Pro-Link Models) Installation* in this section of the supplement.

CHAPTER ELEVEN

BRAKES

The brake system on 1981-on non-Interstate models consists of a single disc on the front wheel and a drum brake on the rear. Interstate models are equipped with dual front discs and a drum brake on the rear. The disc brake caliper assemblies are either a single- or dual-piston type, depending on model.

The single-piston caliper is covered in Chapter Eleven in the main body of this book and the dual-piston caliper is covered in this section of the supplement. Be sure you follow the correct procedure for your particular model.

FRONT DISC BRAKE

The front disc brake(s) are actuated by hydraulic fluid and are controlled by a hand lever on the master cylinder. As the brake pads wear, the brake fluid level drops in the reservoir and automatically adjusts for wear.

When working on hydraulic brake systems, it is necessary that the work area and all tools be absolutely clean. Any tiny particles of foreign matter and grit in the caliper assembly or the master cylinder can damage the components. Also, sharp tools must not be used inside the caliper or on the piston. If there is any doubt about your ability to

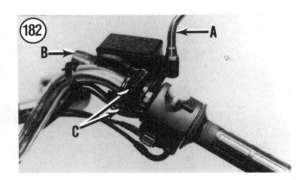

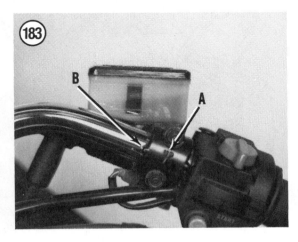

correctly and safely carry out major service on the brake components, take the job to a dealer or brake specialist.

MASTER CYLINDER (ALL MODELS)

Removal/Installation

NOTE
The master cylinder is slightly different among the different models. Removal and installation are basically the same. Where differences occur they are identified.

1. On Interstate models, remove the front fairing as described in the Chapter Twelve section of this supplement.
2. Remove the rear view mirror (A, **Figure 182**) from the master cylinder.

CAUTION
Cover the fuel tank and instrument cluster with a heavy cloth or plastic tarp to protect them from accidental brake

fluid spills. Wash brake fluid off any painted or plated surfaces immediately, as it will destroy the finish. Use soapy water and rinse completely.

3. Pull back the rubber boot (B, **Figure 182**) and remove the union bolt securing the brake hose to the master cylinder. Remove the brake hose. Tie the brake hose up and cover the end to prevent the entry of foreign matter.
4. Remove the clamping bolts (C, **Figure 182**) and clamp securing the master cylinder to the handlebar and remove the master cylinder.
5. Install by reversing these removal steps, noting the following.
6. Install the clamp with the "UP" arrow (A, **Figure 183**) facing up. Align the lug with the punch mark on the handlebar (B, **Figure 183**). Tighten the upper bolt first, then the lower.
7. Install the brake hose onto the master cylinder. Be sure to place a sealing washer on each side of the fitting and install the union bolt. Tighten the union bolt to 18-25 ft.-lb. (25-35 N•m).
8. Bleed the brake as described in Chapter Eleven in the main body of this book.

Disassembly

Refer to **Figure 184** for 1980 CX500, **Figure 185** for CX650C or **Figure 186** for all other models.
1. Remove the master cylinder as described in this section of the supplement.
2. Remove the bolt and nut securing the brake lever and remove the lever.
3. Remove the screws securing the cover and remove the cover and diaphragm; pour out the brake fluid and discard it. *Never reuse brake fluid.*
4. Remove the rubber boot from the area where the hand lever actuates the internal piston.
5. Using circlip pliers, remove the internal circlip from the body.
6. Remove the rubber boot.
7. On CX500 models, remove the stop plate.
8. Remove the piston assembly, primary cup and spring.
9. Remove the brake light switch if necessary.

13

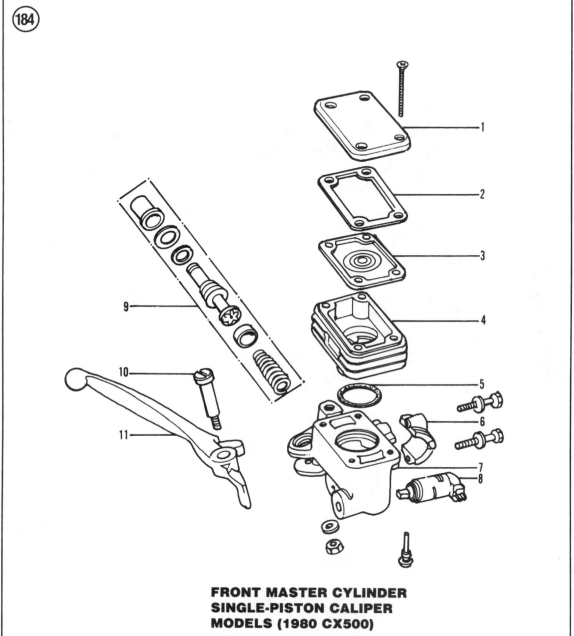

**FRONT MASTER CYLINDER
SINGLE-PISTON CALIPER
MODELS (1980 CX500)**

1. Cover
2. Gasket
3. Diaphragm
4. Reservoir
5. Seal
6. Clamp
7. Master cylinder body
8. Brake light switch
9. Piston assembly
10. Lever bolt
11. Lever

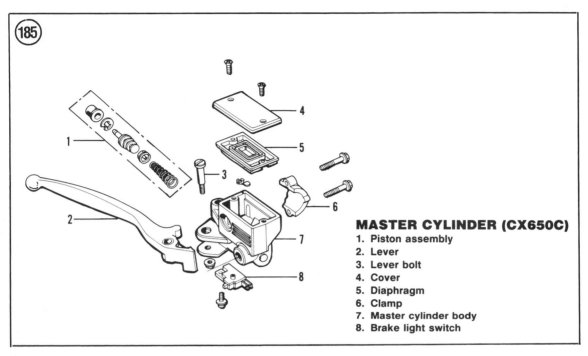

MASTER CYLINDER (CX650C)
1. Piston assembly
2. Lever
3. Lever bolt
4. Cover
5. Diaphragm
6. Clamp
7. Master cylinder body
8. Brake light switch

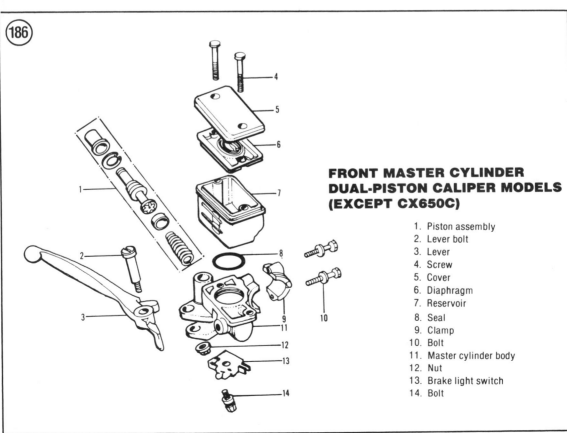

FRONT MASTER CYLINDER DUAL-PISTON CALIPER MODELS (EXCEPT CX650C)

1. Piston assembly
2. Lever bolt
3. Lever
4. Screw
5. Cover
6. Diaphragm
7. Reservoir
8. Seal
9. Clamp
10. Bolt
11. Master cylinder body
12. Nut
13. Brake light switch
14. Bolt

13

Inspection

1. Clean all parts in denatured alcohol or fresh brake fluid. Inspect the cylinder bore and piston contact surfaces for signs of wear and damage. If either part is less than perfect, replace it.
2. Check the end of the piston for wear caused by the hand lever. Replace if worn.
3. Replace the piston if the secondary cup requires replacement.
4. Inspect the pivot hole in the hand lever. If worn or elongated it must be replaced.
5. Make sure the passages in the bottom of the brake fluid reservoir are clear. Check the reservoir cap and diaphragm for damage and deterioration and replace as necessary.
6. Inspect the threads in the bore for the brake line.
7. Check the hand lever pivot lugs on the master cylinder body for cracks.
8. Measure the cylinder bore (**Figure 187**). Replace the master cylinder if the bore exceeds the following dimensions:
   a. CX500, CX650C: 0.5533 in. (14.055 mm).
   b. GL500, GL650: 0.6270 in. (15.925 mm).
   c. Interstate models: 0.5533 in. (14.055 mm).
9. Measure the outside diameter of the piston as shown in **Figure 188** with a micrometer. Replace the piston assembly if it is less than the following dimension at either location:
   a. CX500, CX650C: 0.5490 in. (13.945 mm).
   b. GL500, GL650: 0.6226 in. (15.815 mm).
   c. Interstate models: 0.5490 in. (13.945 mm).

Assembly

1. Soak the new cups in fresh brake fluid for at least 15 minutes to make them pliable. Coat the inside of the cylinder with fresh brake fluid prior to the assembly of parts.

CAUTION
When installing the piston assembly, do not allow the cups to turn inside out as they will be damaged and allow brake fluid leakage within the cylinder bore.

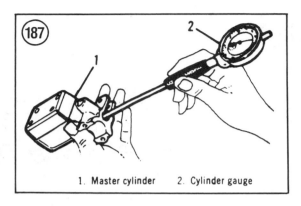

1. Master cylinder   2. Cylinder gauge

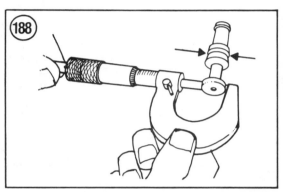

2. Install the spring, primary cup and piston assembly into the cylinder together. Install the spring with the tapered end facing toward the primary cup.

NOTE
Be sure to install the primary cup with the open end in first, toward the spring.

3. On CX500 models, install the stop plates.
4. Install the circlip and slide in the rubber boot.
5. Install the diaphragm and cover. Do not tighten the cover screws at this time as fluid will have to be added later.
6. Install the brake lever onto the master cylinder body.
7. If removed, install the brake light switch.
8. Install the master cylinder as described in this section of the supplement.

DUAL-PISTON CALIPER

Brake Pad Replacement

There is no recommended mileage interval for changing the friction pads in the disc

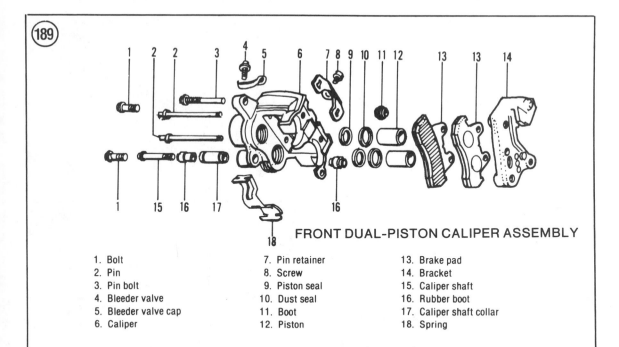

FRONT DUAL-PISTON CALIPER ASSEMBLY

1. Bolt	7. Pin retainer	13. Brake pad
2. Pin	8. Screw	14. Bracket
3. Pin bolt	9. Piston seal	15. Caliper shaft
4. Bleeder valve	10. Dust seal	16. Rubber boot
5. Bleeder valve cap	11. Boot	17. Caliper shaft collar
6. Caliper	12. Piston	18. Spring

brake. Pad wear depends greatly on riding habits and conditions. The pads should be checked for wear every 600 miles (1,000 km) and replaced when worn to the wear indicator. To maintain an even brake pressure on the disc always replace both pads in each caliper at the same time.

CAUTION
Watch the pads more closely when the red line approaches the disc. On some pads the red line is very close to the pad's metal backing plate. If pad wear happens to be uneven for some reason the backing plate may come in contact with the disc and cause damage.

Refer to **Figure 189** for this procedure.
1. Remove the bolts securing the caliper assembly to the caliper bracket (**Figure 190**). Remove the caliper assembly from the disc.
2. Remove the bolt (A, **Figure 191**) securing the pin retainer to the caliper assembly and remove the pin retainer.
3. Remove the 2 pins (**Figure 192**) securing the pads in place.
4. Remove both brake pads.
5. Clean the pad recess and the end of the pistons with a soft brush. Do not use solvent,

13

wire brush or any hard tool which would damage the cylinders or pistons.

6. Carefully remove any rust or corrosion from the disc.

7. Lightly coat the end of the pistons and the backs of the new pads *(not the friction material)* with disc brake lubricant.

> *NOTE*
> *When purchasing new pads, check with your dealer to make sure the friction compound of the new pad is compatible with the disc material. Remove any roughness from the backs of the new pads with a fine cut file; blow them clean with compressed air.*

8. When new pads are installed in the caliper the master cylinder brake fluid level will rise as the caliper pistons are repositioned. Clean the top of the master cylinder of all dirt and foreign matter. Remove the cap and diaphragm from the master cylinder and slowly push the caliper pistons into the caliper. Constantly check the reservoir to make sure brake fluid does not overflow. Remove fluid, if necessary, prior to it overflowing. The pistons should move freely. If they don't and there is evidence of the pistons sticking in the cylinder, the caliper should be removed and serviced as described under *Caliper Rebuilding* in this section of the supplement.

9. Push the caliper pistons in all the way (**Figure 193**) to allow room for the new pads.

10. Install the anti-rattle spring as shown in **Figure 194**.

11. Install the outboard pad (**Figure 195**) and partially install one pin through that pad.

12. Install the inboard pad and push the pin all the way through.

13. Push both pads against the anti-rattle spring, then insert the other pin. Push this pin all the way through.

14. Install the pad pin retainer onto the ends of the pins. Push the pin retainer down and make sure it seats completely on the groove in each pin (B, **Figure 191**).

15. Install the pad pin retaining bolt (A, **Figure 191**).

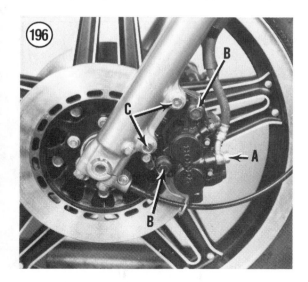

16. Carefully install the caliper assembly onto the disc. Be careful not to damage the leading edge of the pads during installation.

17. Lubricate the caliper upper pivot bolt with silicone grease.

18. Install the caliper upper pivot bolt and tighten to 18-22 ft.-lb. (25-30 N•m). Install the caliper lower mounting bolt and tighten to 14-18 ft.-lb. (20-25 N•m).

19. On models so equipped, repeat for the other caliper assembly.

20. Place wood blocks under the engine or frame so that the front wheel is off the ground. Spin the front wheel and activate the brake lever as many times as it takes to refill the cylinder in the caliper and correctly locate the pads.

21. Refill the master cylinder reservoir, if necessary, to maintain the correct fluid level. Install the diaphragm and top cap.

WARNING
Use brake fluid clearly marked DOT 3 from a sealed container. Other types may vaporize and cause brake failure. Always use the same brand name; do not intermix as many brands are not compatible.

WARNING
Do not ride the motorcycle until you are sure the brake is operating correctly with full hydraulic advantage. If necessary, bleed the brake as described

under **Bleeding the System** in Chapter Eleven in the main body of this book.

22. Bed the pads in gradually for the first 50 miles (80 km) by using only light pressure as much as possible. Immediate hard application will glaze the new friction pads and greatly reduce the effectiveness of the brake.

Dual-piston Caliper Removal/Installation

Refer to **Figure 189** for this procedure.

It is not necessary to remove the front wheel in order to remove either or both caliper assemblies.

CAUTION
Do not spill any brake fluid on the painted portion of the ComStar wheel. Wash off spilled brake fluid immediately, as it will destroy the finish. Use soapy water and rinse completely.

1. Place a container under the brake line at the caliper. Remove the union bolt and sealing washers (A, **Figure 196**) securing the brake line to the caliper assembly. Remove the brake line and let the brake fluid drain out into the container. Dispose of this—never reuse brake fluid. To prevent the entry of moisture and dirt, cap the end of the brake line and tie the loose end up to the forks.

2. Loosen the caliper upper pivot bolt and caliper lower mounting bolt (B, **Figure 196**) gradually in several steps. Push on the caliper while loosening the bolts to push the pistons back into the caliper.

3. Remove the caliper bracket mounting bolts (C, **Figure 196**) and remove the caliper assembly.

4. On models so equipped, repeat Steps 1-3 for the other caliper assembly.

5. Lubricate the caliper upper pivot bolt with silicone grease.

6. Install by reversing these removal steps, noting the following.

7. Carefully install the caliper assembly onto the disc. Be careful not to damage the leading edge of the pads during installation.

13

8. Tighten the caliper mounting bolts to the following torque specifications:

   a. Caliper bracket mounting bolts: 22-33 ft.-lb. (30-45 N•m).

   b. Caliper pivot bolt: 18-22 ft.-lb. (25-30 N•m).

   c. Lower caliper mounting bolt: 14-18 ft.-lb. (20-25 N•m).

9. Install the brake hose, with a sealing washer on each side of the fitting, onto the caliper. Install the union bolt and tighten to 18-25 ft.-lb. (25-30 N•m).

10. Bleed the brake as described under *Bleeding the System* in Chapter Eleven in the main body of this book.

> *WARNING*
> *Do not ride the motorcycle until you are sure that the brakes are operating properly.*

Rebuilding

If the caliper leaks, the caliper should be rebuilt. If the pistons stick in the cylinders, indicating severe wear or galling, the entire unit should be replaced. Rebuilding a leaky caliper requires special tools and experience.

Caliper service should be entrusted to a dealer, motorcycle repair shop or brake specialist. Considerable money can be saved by removing the caliper yourself and taking it in for repair.

BRAKE HOSE REPLACEMENT

There is no factory-recommended replacement interval but it is a good idea to replace all brake hoses every 4 years or when they show signs of cracking or damage.

Refer to **Figure 197** for single-disc models or **Figure 198** for dual-disc models.

> *CAUTION*
> *Cover the front wheel, fender and fuel tank with a heavy cloth or plastic tarp to protect it from accidental spilling of brake fluid. Wash brake fluid off of any painted or plated surface immediately, as it will destroy the finish. Use soapy water and rinse completely.*

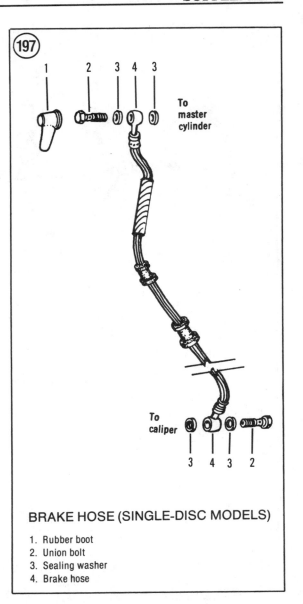

BRAKE HOSE (SINGLE-DISC MODELS)

1. Rubber boot
2. Union bolt
3. Sealing washer
4. Brake hose

1. On Interstate models, remove the front fairing as described in the Chapter Twelve section of this supplement.

2. Place a container under the brake line at the caliper. Remove the union bolt and sealing washer (A, **Figure 199**) securing the brake line to the caliper assembly. Remove brake line from the clip on the fork leg (B, **Figure 199**). Remove the brake line and let the brake fluid drain out into the container. To prevent the entry of moisture and dirt, cap the end of the brake line and tie the loose end up to the forks.

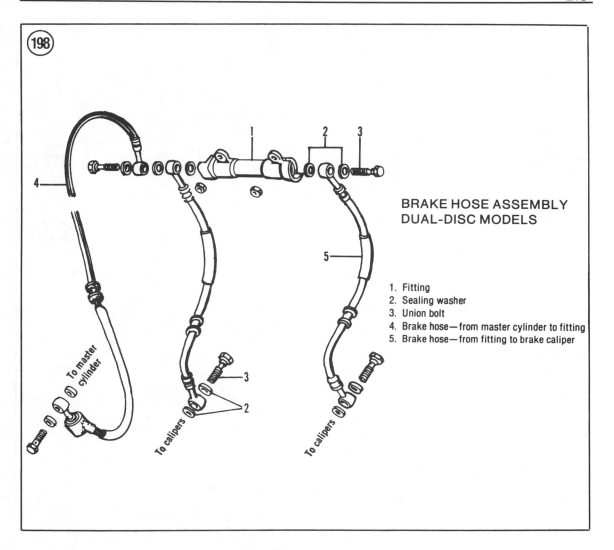

BRAKE HOSE ASSEMBLY
DUAL-DISC MODELS

1. Fitting
2. Sealing washer
3. Union bolt
4. Brake hose—from master cylinder to fitting
5. Brake hose—from fitting to brake caliper

WARNING
Dispose of this brake fluid—never reuse it. Contaminated brake fluid can cause brake failure.

3. On models so equipped, repeat for the other caliper.

4. On Interstate models, remove the fairing air dam (**Figure 200**).

5. Remove the union bolt (A, **Figure 201**) securing the left-hand brake hose to the fitting. Remove the union bolt (B, **Figure 201**) securing the right-hand lower hose and upper hose to the fitting and remove them. Remove the union bolt (**Figure 202**) securing the upper hose to the master cylinder and remove the hose.

13

6. Install new hoses, sealing washers and union bolts in the reverse order of removal. Be sure to install new sealing washers in the correct positions; refer to **Figure 197** or **Figure 198**.

7. Tighten all union bolts to 18-25 ft.-lb. (25-30 N•m).

8. Refill the master cylinder with fresh brake fluid clearly marked DOT 3 only. Bleed the brake as described under *Bleeding the System* in Chapter Eleven in the main body of this book.

> *WARNING*
> *Do not ride the motorcycle until you are sure that the brakes are operating properly.*

9. On Interstate models, install the front fairing air dam and the front fairing as described in the Chapter Twelve section of this supplement.

BRAKE DISC

Removal/Installation

Refer to **Figure 203** for 1980-1982 models or **Figure 204** for 1983 models.

This procedure is shown on an 1982 standard axle fork model. Where differences occur for other models, they are identified.

1. Remove the front wheel as described in the Chapter Nine section of this supplement.

> *NOTE*
> *Place a piece of wood or vinyl tube in the caliper(s) in place of the disc(s). This way, if the brake lever is inadvertently squeezed the pistons will not be forced out of the cylinder. If this does happen, the caliper might have to be disassembled to reseat the pistons and the system will have to be bled. By using the wood, bleeding the system is not necessary when installing the wheel.*

2A. On standard axle fork models, remove the front axle (A, **Figure 205**) and the speedometer housing (B, **Figure 205**).

2B. On leading axle fork models, remove the speedometer housing.

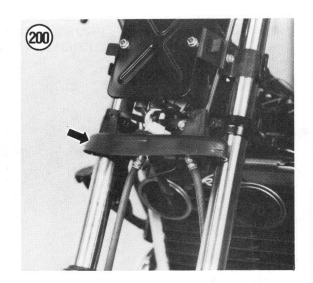
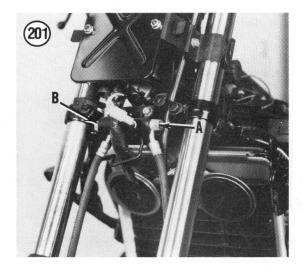
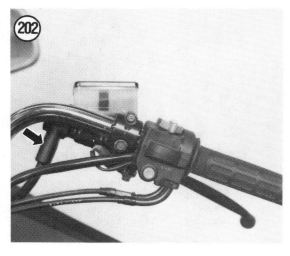

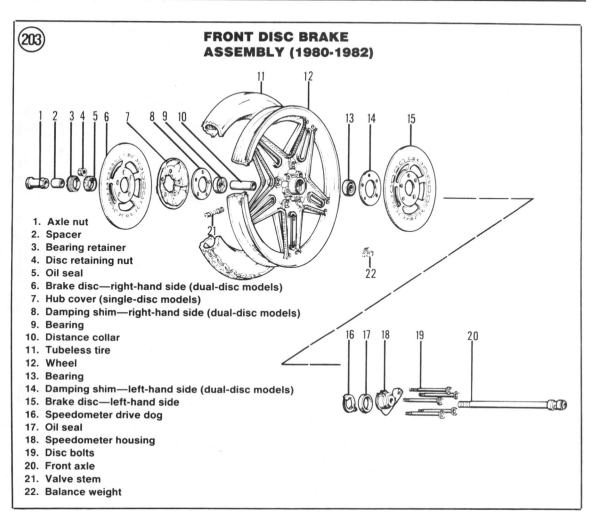

FRONT DISC BRAKE ASSEMBLY (1980-1982)

1. Axle nut
2. Spacer
3. Bearing retainer
4. Disc retaining nut
5. Oil seal
6. Brake disc—right-hand side (dual-disc models)
7. Hub cover (single-disc models)
8. Damping shim—right-hand side (dual-disc models)
9. Bearing
10. Distance collar
11. Tubeless tire
12. Wheel
13. Bearing
14. Damping shim—left-hand side (dual-disc models)
15. Brake disc—left-hand side
16. Speedometer drive dog
17. Oil seal
18. Speedometer housing
19. Disc bolts
20. Front axle
21. Valve stem
22. Balance weight

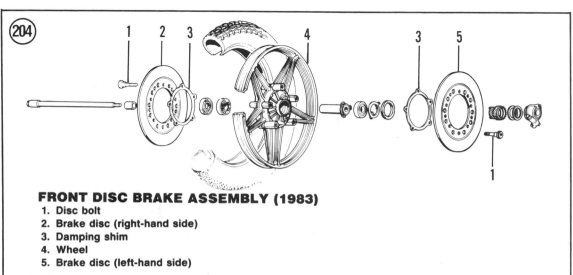

FRONT DISC BRAKE ASSEMBLY (1983)

1. Disc bolt
2. Brake disc (right-hand side)
3. Damping shim
4. Wheel
5. Brake disc (left-hand side)

13

3A. On 1980 CX500 single disc models, remove the bolts securing the brake disc to the hub and remove the disc.

3B. On 1981-on CX500 and GL500 single disc models, remove the bolts and nuts securing the brake disc to the hub. Remove the disc on the left-hand side and the hub cover on the right-hand side.

3C. On GL500 Interstate dual disc models, remove the nuts from the right-hand side and withdraw the bolts from the left-hand side (**Figure 206**). Remove both brake discs and damping shims between each disc and the wheel hub.

3D. On GL560 Interstate dual disc models, remove the Allen bolts that secure each brake disc to the wheel hub. Remove both brake discs and damping shims between each disc and the wheel hub.

4. Install by reversing these removal steps, noting the following.

5. On Interstate models, be sure to install a damping shim between each disc and the wheel hub.

6. On models with bolts and nuts, install the bolts from the left-hand side.

7. Tighten the disc mounting bolts and tighten to the following torque specifications:

   a. CX650C, 1983 GL650 and GL650 Interstate: 22-29 ft.-lb. (35-40 N•m).
   b. All other models: 20-24 ft.-lb. (27-33 N•m).

Inspection

It is not necessary to remove the disc from the wheel to inspect it. Small marks on the disc are not important, but deep radial scratches (deep enough to snag a fingernail) reduce braking effectiveness and increase brake pad wear. If these grooves are found, the disc should be replaced.

1. Measure the thickness of the disc at several locations around the disc with a micrometer or vernier caliper (**Figure 207**). The disc(s) must be replaced if the thickness, in any area, is less than the following:

   a. CX500 (1982-on): 0.16 in. (4.0 mm).
   b. GL500, GL650: 0.24 in. (6.0 mm).

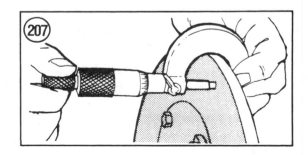

c. CX650C and Interstate: 0.16 in. (4.0 mm).

2. Make sure the disc bolts are tight prior to running this check. Check the disc runout with a dial indicator as shown in **Figure 208**. Slowly rotate the wheel and watch the dial indicator. On all models, if the runout exceeds 0.012 in. (0.30 mm), the disc(s) must be replaced.

3. Clean the disc of any rust or corrosion and wipe clean with lacquer thinner. Never use an oil based solvent that may leave an oil residue on the disc.

CHAPTER TWELVE

FRAME AND REPAINTING

INTERSTATE EQUIPMENT

Front Fairing
Removal/Installation

1. Rest the bike on the centerstand.
2. Remove the upper and lower screws and collars (**Figure 209**) on the lower fairing panel. Remove the lower fairing panel. Repeat for the other side.

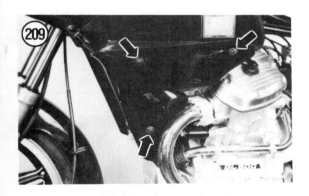

3. Disconnect the 9-pin electrical connector. On models since 1982, separate the green ground wire going from the fairing to the main harness. These are located on the inside left-hand side of the fairing (**Figure 210**).
4. Remove the headlight as described under *Headlight Replacement (Interstate Models)* in the Chapter Seven section of this supplement.

> *NOTE*
> *To avoid damage to the fairing the following step requires the use of a helper. The fairing is not heavy but is difficult to hold in place while removing the bolts.*

5. Remove the bolts located on each side (**Figure 211**) and carefully pull the fairing forward and off of the mounting bracket.
6. Install by reversing these removal steps.

Fairing Bracket
Removal/Installation

Refer to **Figure 212** for this procedure.
1. Remove the front fairing as described in this section of the supplement.
2. Disconnect the electrical wires to both horns. Remove the bolts and remove both horns (**Figure 213**).
3. Remove the bolts securing the right- and left-hand cowl brackets and remove both brackets.
4. Remove the lower 10 mm nuts and washers (A, **Figure 214**) on each side.

13

5. Remove the upper 8 mm bolt and nut (B, **Figure 214**).

6. Carefully slide the main bracket down and out of the frame.

7. Install by reversing these removal steps. Tighten all bolts securely.

Windshield Replacement

This procedure is best done with the aid of a helper, especially when installing the new windshield, to prevent it from getting scratched.

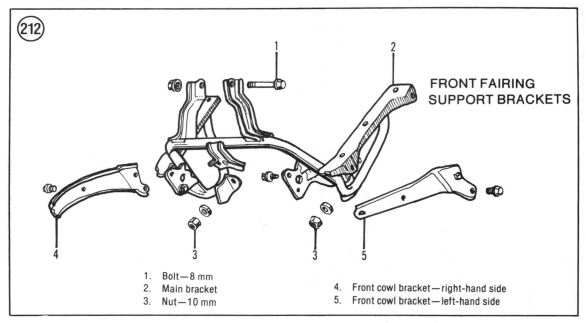

FRONT FAIRING SUPPORT BRACKETS

1. Bolt—8 mm
2. Main bracket
3. Nut—10 mm

4. Front cowl bracket—right-hand side
5. Front cowl bracket—left-hand side

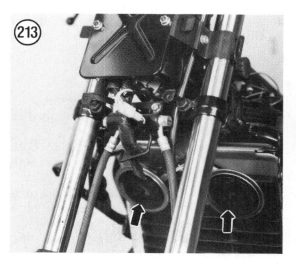

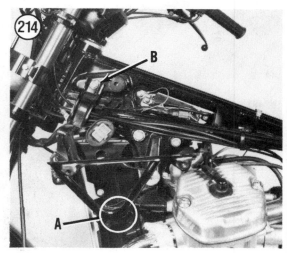

1. Remove the screws, special nuts and collars (**Figure 215**) securing each rear view mirror. Remove both mirrors.

2. Remove the center screws, special nuts and collars (**Figure 216**).

3. Remove the trim panel, windshield and windshield cushion panel.

4. Install by reversing these removal steps, noting the following.

5. Be sure to install the cushion panel between the fairing surface and the windshield.

6. Make sure that the metal collars are used on each hole with each bolt.

> *CAUTION*
> *Do not install or tighten the bolts without these metal collars in place as the windshield will be damaged in the area around the mounting hole. These metal collars act as stops for the bolts and eliminate most of the bolt pressure on the windshield.*

7. Make sure to position the special nuts with the flat portion facing downward as shown in **Figure 217**.

Windshield Adjustment

The windshield can be adjusted one inch in either direction from the standard location.

To adjust, loosen the windshield mounting screws and rear view mirror mounting screws in the sequence shown in **Figure 218**.

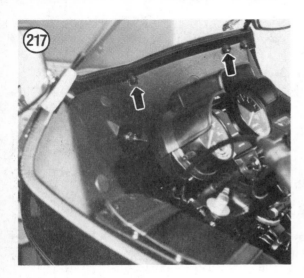

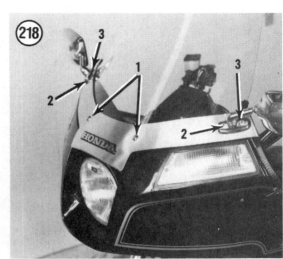

13

Carefully move the windshield into the desired position and retighten the screws in the reverse order.

Windshield Cleaning

The windshield is made of a scratch resistant polycarbonate plastic. This material is fairly resistant to damage and scratching but care must still be taken when cleaning it.

Do not use a cleaner with an abrasive or a combination cleaner and wax. Never use gasoline or cleaning solvent. These products will either scratch or totally destroy the surface of the windshield.

To remove oil, grease or road tar use isopropyl alcohol, naptha or kerosene. Then wash the windshield with a solution of mild soap and water. Dry gently with a soft cloth or chamois—do not press hard.

INDEX

14

14

1978 CX500

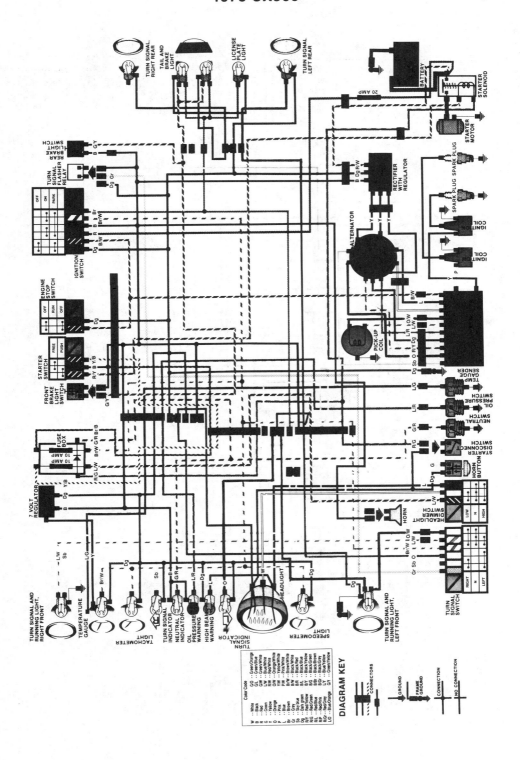

WIRING DIAGRAMS

1979-1981 CX500 Custom & Deluxe

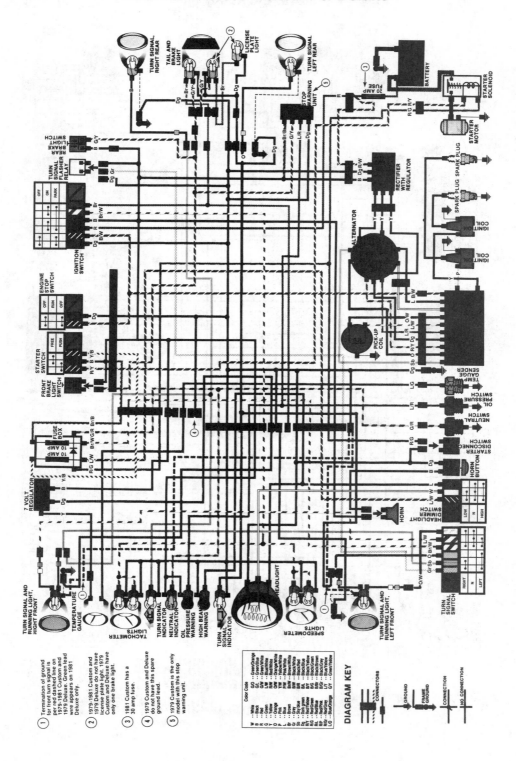

1981 GL500 Interstate

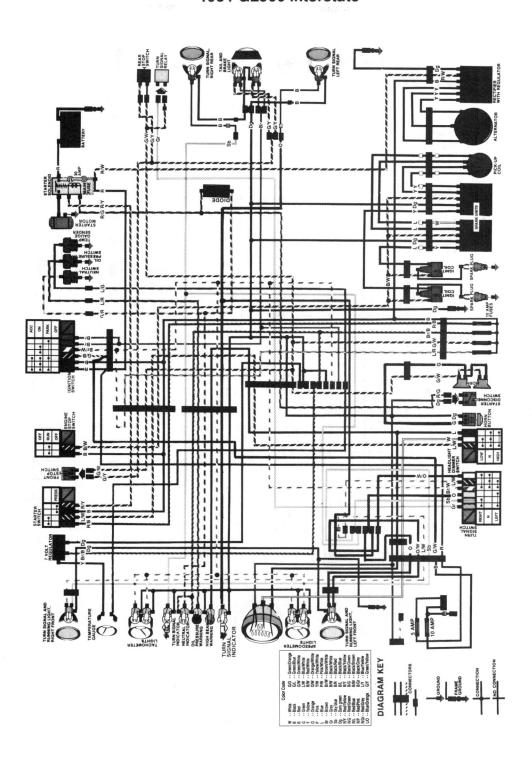

1982 CX500 Custom &
1981-1982 GL500

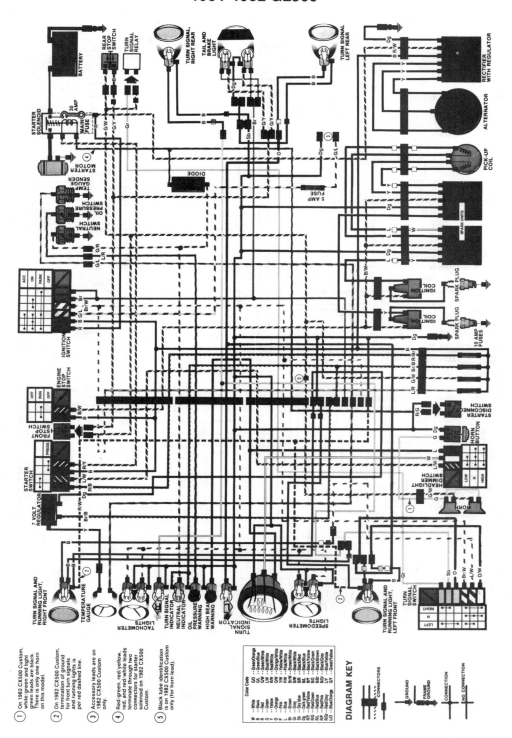

1982 GL500 Interstate

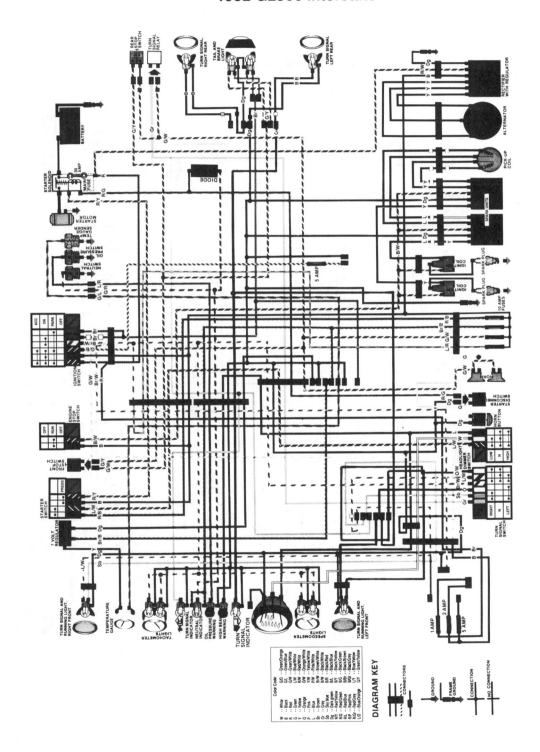

1983 CX650C

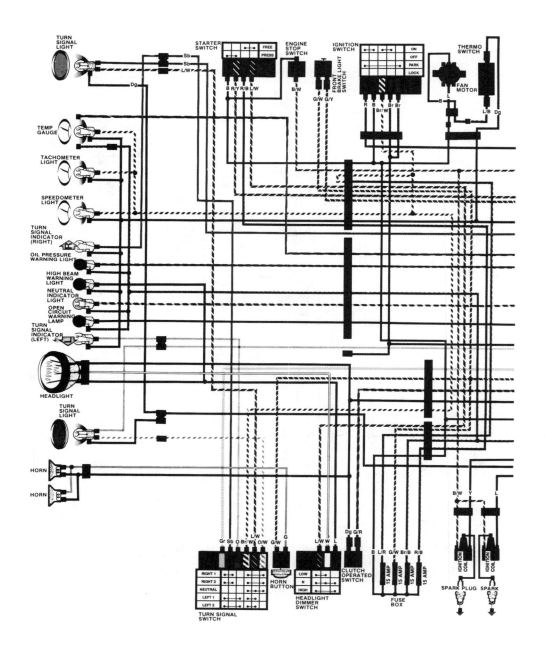

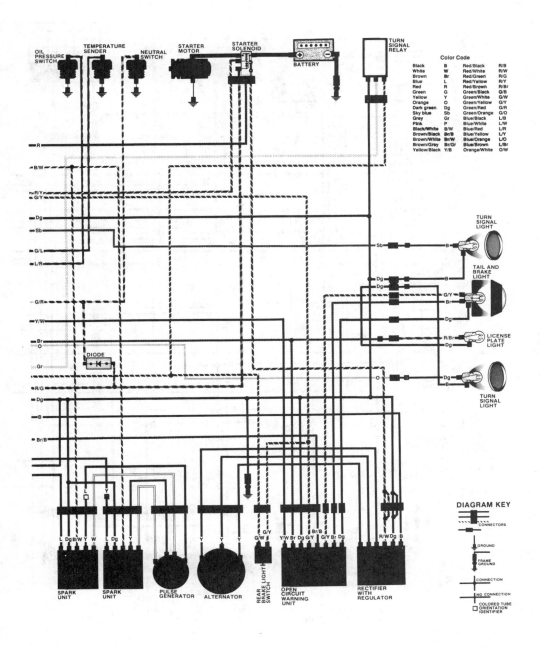

1983 GL650 Interstate

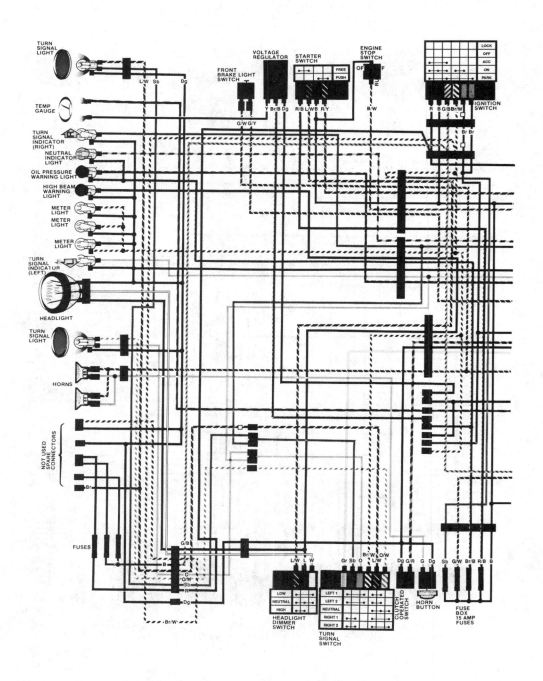

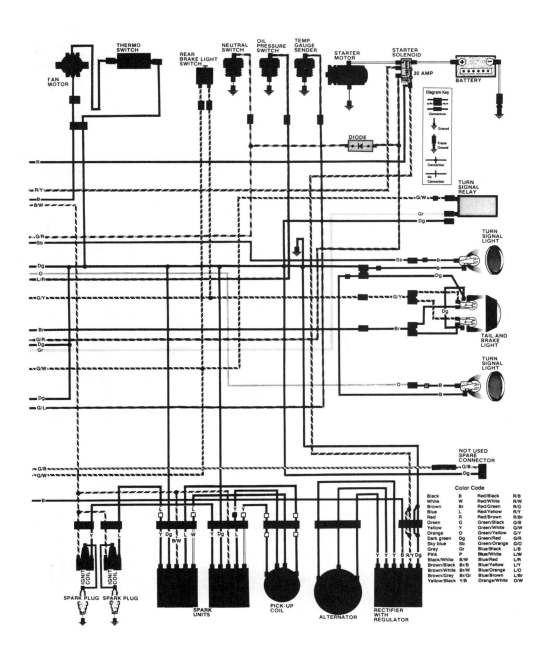

THERMO SWITCH

FAN MOTOR

REAR BRAKE LIGHT SWITCH

NEUTRAL SWITCH

OIL PRESSURE SWITCH

TEMP GAUGE SENDER

STARTER MOTOR

STARTER SOLENOID

30 AMP

BATTERY

DIODE

Diagram Key

Connectors

Ground

Frame Ground

Connection

No Connection

TURN SIGNAL RELAY

G/W

Gr

Dg

TURN SIGNAL LIGHT

Sb

B

Dg

G/Y

Dg

Br

TAIL AND BRAKE LIGHT

TURN SIGNAL LIGHT

O

B

B

NOT USED SPARE CONNECTOR

G/B

Dg

IGNITION COIL

IGNITION COIL

SPARK PLUG

SPARK PLUG

SPARK UNITS

PICK-UP COIL

ALTERNATOR

RECTIFIER WITH REGULATOR

Color Code			
Black	B	Red/Black	R/B
White	W	Red/White	R/W
Brown	Br	Red/Green	R/G
Blue	L	Red/Yellow	R/Y
Red	R	Red/Brown	R/Br
Green	G	Green/Black	G/B
Yellow	Y	Green/White	G/W
Orange	O	Green/Yellow	G/Y
Dark green	Dg	Green/Red	G/R
Sky blue	Sb	Green/Orange	G/O
Grey	Gr	Blue/Black	L/B
Pink	P	Blue/White	L/W
Black/White	B/W	Blue/Red	L/R
Brown/Black	Br/B	Blue/Yellow	L/Y
Brown/White	Br/W	Blue/Orange	L/O
Brown/Grey	Br/Gr	Blue/Brown	L/Br
Yellow/Black	Y/B	Orange/White	O/W

1983 GL650

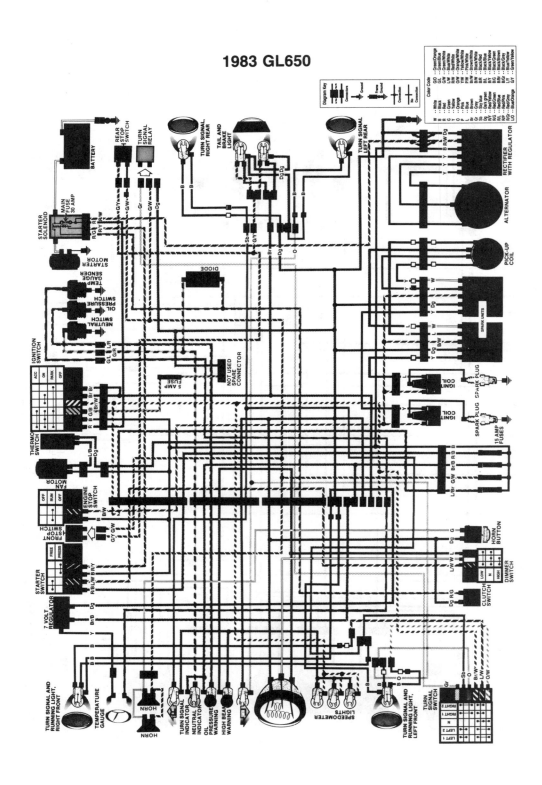

NOTES

NOTES

NOTES

NOTES

NOTES

MAINTENANCE LOG

Service Performed **Mileage Reading**

Oil change (example)	2,836	5,782	8,601		